# An Annotated Critical
# Bibliography of Modernism

# Harvester Annotated Critical Bibliographies

Advisory Editor: Frank Gloversmith, University of Sussex

This major new series provides extensive guides to literary movements and to major figures in English literature. Each volume is edited by a scholar of international repute, and writings by authors and the location of manuscript collections are presented in detail together with information on the secondary writings of each author.

**An Annotated Critical Bibliography of Modernism**
Editor: Alistair Davies

**Forthcoming:**

**An Annotated Critical Bibliography of George Eliot**
Editor: George Levine

**An Annotated Critical Bibliography of Virginia Woolf**
Editor: Andrew McNeillie

**An Annotated Critical Bibliography of James Joyce**
Editor: Matthew Hodgart

**An Annotated Critical Bibliography of Jane Austen**
Editor: Brian Southam

# An Annotated Critical Bibliography of Modernism

## Alistair Davies
*Lecturer in English, University of Sussex*

THE HARVESTER PRESS · SUSSEX

BARNES & NOBLE BOOKS · NEW JERSEY

First published in Great Britain in 1982 by
THE HARVESTER PRESS LIMITED
*Publisher: John Spiers*
16 Ship Street, Brighton, Sussex

and in the USA by
BARNES & NOBLE BOOKS
81 Adams Drive, Totowa, New Jersey 07512

*British Library Cataloguing in Publication Data*

Davies, Alistair
  A critical annotated bibliography of modernism.
(Harvester annotated critical bibliographies; 1)
  1. Modernism (Literature) — Bibliography
  I. Title
  016.820'9      Z6514.M/

ISBN 0-7108-0031-2

**Library of Congress Cataloging in Publication Data**

  Main entry under title:
  An Annotated critical bibliography of modernism
    (Harvester/Barnes & Noble annotated *critical*
  bibliographies; no. 1)
    Bibliography: p.
    1. English literature — 20th century — History and criticism
  — Bibliography.
    2. English literature — 20th century — History and criticism.
    3. Modernism (Literature) — Bibliography.
    4. Modernism (Literature)
  I. Davies, Alistair. II. Series.
  Z2014.M6A56 1982 [PR478.M6] 016.82'09'0091 82-13864

ISBN 0-389-20303-3

Typeset in 10/11 point Times by
C. Leggett & Son Ltd., Mitcham, Surrey and
printed in Great Britain by Mansell Limited, Witham, Essex

And yet what is Modernism? It is undefined. Henry James stopped before a certain piece of sculpture to apostrophize "the beautiful modern spirit"; but he did not attempt a definition where a more incompetent man would surely have done it.

John Crowe Ransom

# Contents

## V: THOMAS STEARNS ELIOT 1888-1965

# Advice to the Reader

The purpose of this bibliography is twofold. Firstly, it provides an annotated bibliography of the major books and articles which discuss the concept of literary Modernism, account for its origins, describe its literary context and techniques, analyse its influence on fiction, poetry and drama, assess its importance, examine its philosophical, political and social ideas, and consider its relationship with the other arts. Secondly, it provides separate bibliographies of the major books and articles on the life, works, and social, political and critical ideas of W.B. Yeats, Wyndham Lewis, D.H. Lawrence and T.S. Eliot. My principal aim has been to describe briefly the contents of each book and article listed, and, where relevant, to indicate its place within a particular critical debate. The quotations given in a citation are in all cases taken from the book or article cited. I have given particular attention to anthologies of articles, which have, during the past twenty years, made the most important articles on the above writers readily available.

I have arranged books and articles on Modernism and on the work of W.B. Yeats, Wyndham Lewis, D.H. Lawrence and T.S. Eliot under the headings given in the contents pages. Entries are arranged *chronologically* within the sections indicated by these headings, so that the reader might follow more easily the development of a critical discussion or idea.

When citing a book, I have given name of author, full title, and the first place and date of English and/or American publication. I enclose in brackets the last republication date of a book still in print. When I have cited part of a book, I have given inclusive pagination. If the same edition has two places and dates of publication, the pages refer to the edition given first in the citation. When citing articles, I have given name of author, title of journal, volume and number, date and inclusive pagination. I have given the titles of journals in full, with the exception of the *Publications of the Modern Language Association of America*, which is given in its usual abbreviated form as *PMLA*.

The bibliography is divided into five major sections: Modernism, William Butler Yeats 1865-1939, Percy Wyndham Lewis 1882-1957, David Herbert Lawrence 1885-1930, and Thomas Stearns Eliot 1888-1965. Each entry within these sections has been individually numbered, using the following abbreviations: MOD, WBY, WL, DHL and TSE. There are two separate indexes, an index of the authors of books and articles cited in the bibliography and a subject index. These indexes have also been divided into the five major sections given above.

# Acknowledgements

I could not have prepared this bibliography without the help of the staff of the University of Sussex Library. I am grateful to past and present librarians who have established the Library's comprehensive collection of books and journals on literature; to the staff of the Inter-Library Loans Office, who acquired promptly and efficiently those books and articles I could not consult at Sussex; to Jenny Marshman and the staff of the Reader's Advisory Service, who quickly solved the problems I encountered in my research; to Shirley Kirby-Turner, who undertook a computer search for titles of books and articles on Modernism and for the titles of books on W.B. Yeats, Wyndham Lewis, D.H. Lawrence and T.S. Eliot. I wish to thank Sue Roe, of Harvester Press, and Frank Gloversmith, of the University of Sussex, for their help. Above all, I wish to thank Kate Wilcox, without whose advice, assistance and encouragement, this bibliography would not have been completed.

Alistair Davies
*Brighton*
*October 1981*

# Part I
# MODERNISM

# The Theory of Modernism

## Modernism and Romanticism

MOD 1:    Wilson, Edmund
AXEL'S CASTLE: A STUDY IN THE
IMAGINATIVE LITERATURE OF 1870-1930 (New
York and London: Charles Scribner's Sons, 1931)

The first major study of Modernism, now a classic, which treated W.B. Yeats, T.S. Eliot, Gertrude Stein, James Joyce, along with Marcel Proust, Paul Valéry, Villiers de l'Isle Adam and Arthur Rimbaud, as the heirs of Symbolism. Modernism was a second wave of Symbolism, which, in turn, was a second wave of Romanticism. The French Symbolists had rejected science and the common life to pursue, as did de l'Isle Adam, aestheticism, or as did Rimbaud, the primitive, the irrational, the life-of-action. Wilson declared himself suspicious of the withdrawal from life, the denial of reason, the reactionary rejection of belief in progress and in history, of the Symbolist tradition. He found similar tendencies in the literature of Modernism. Still an important and profoundly influential thesis.

MOD 2:    Spender, Stephen
THE DESTRUCTIVE ELEMENT: A STUDY OF
MODERN WRITERS AND BELIEFS (London:
Jonathan Cape, 1935; New York: Houghton Mifflin,
1936) (1970)

Not only a stimulating discussion of Modernism, but also an historically important one, for it outlines the critical response of a principal figure of the generation of the thirties to its modernist predecessors. "All these writers [Henry James, W.B. Yeats, T.S. Eliot, Wyndham Lewis and D.H. Lawrence] seem to me faced by the destructive element; that is, by the experience of an all-pervading Present, which is a world without belief." By confronting

1

the chaos of the present, they "are all approaching in different ways, and with varying success, the same political subject." However, they do so in an individualist rather than collective fashion, disdaining belief in science, progress and collective action.

MOD 3:     Heath-Stubbs, John
THE DARKLING PLAIN: A STUDY OF THE LATER FORTUNES OF ROMANTICISM FROM GEORGE DARLEY TO W.B. YEATS (London: Eyre and Spotttiswoode, 1950; Folcroft, Pa.: Folcroft, 1950)

Traces the evolution of Romanticism through the Catholic Decadents to W.B. Yeats.

MOD 4:     Spender, Stephen
THE CREATIVE ELEMENT: A STUDY OF VISION, DESPAIR AND ORTHODOXY AMONG SOME MODERN WRITERS (London: Hamish Hamilton, 1953)

A revision of Spender's *The Destructive Element* (MOD 2). In a series of wide-ranging essays (on Arthur Rimbaud, W.B. Yeats, R.M. Rilke, T.S. Eliot, D.H. Lawrence, E.M. Forster, James Joyce, Virginia Woolf, W.H. Auden and Evelyn Waugh) Spender argues approvingly that the great moderns, unlike their successors of the thirties, have in common "the idea that the individual in his own solitude, accepting the modern environment as the 'destructive element' in which he is immersed, can create out of that solitude an 'answer'."

MOD 5:     Blackmur, Richard Palmer
ANNI MIRABILES 1921-1925: REASON IN THE MADNESS OF LETTERS (Washington: Library of Congress, 1956) (1974)

Four wide-ranging lectures on English, American and continental writers. Modernist literature finds techniques for controlling man's irrational powers.

MOD 6:     Bayley, John
THE ROMANTIC SURVIVAL: A STUDY IN

POETIC EVOLUTION (London: Constable, 1957; Fair Lawn, N.J.: Essential Books, 1957)

A major statement of the Romantic tenets and the Romantic dilemmas of modernist poetry – in W.B. Yeats, W.H. Auden and Dylan Thomas.

MOD 7:  Kermode, (John) Frank
ROMANTIC IMAGE (London: Routledge & Kegan Paul, 1957; New York: Macmillan, 1958)

One of the richest and most subtle studies of modernist poetics and of modernist theory. Kermode argues for a continuity between Romantic, Symbolist and modernist poets in "these two beliefs – in the Image as a radiant truth out of space and time, and in the necessary isolation or estrangement of men who can perceive it," both of which he sees as "thoroughly Romantic" but "true for critics and poets who are militantly anti-Romantic." In "the Image," he argues, modern poets seek to reconcile opposites such as action and contemplation, and take for their most frequent emblem "the beauty of a woman, and particularly of a woman in movement." Contains a brilliant analysis of W.B. Yeats's poem "An Irish Airman Foresees His Death" and an important re-evaluation of T.S. Eliot's critical principles.

MOD 8:  Fraser, George Sutherland
VISION AND RHETORIC: STUDIES IN MODERN POETRY (London: Faber and Faber, 1959; New York: Barnes & Noble, 1960)

A series of separate critical essays on modern Romantic and anti-Romantic views of poetry, and the work of modern English and American poets: W.B. Yeats, Ezra Pound, T.S. Eliot, E.E. Cummings, Wallace Stevens, Robert Graves, W.H. Auden and Louis MacNeice. The first chapter, "The Romantic Tradition and Modern Poetry," pp. 15-38, ably discusses those English critics — Herbert Read, John Bayley and Frank Kermode — who argue that modern poetry "can be considered, in fact, as continuing and perhaps completing" the Romantic tradition. The final chapter, "Contemporary Poetry and the Anti-Romantic Idea," pp. 254-73, discusses the anti-Romantic theory of Yvor Winters and the anti-Romantic practice of the Movement poets.

MOD 9:     Murdoch, Iris
"Against Dryness," *Encounter*, 16:1 (January 1961),
16-20

Seminal essay on the ethics of fiction, which discusses
shortcomings in the presentation of character in modernist
and contemporary fiction. Perhaps the single, most
influential essay on the development of a liberal critique of
Modernism in recent English criticism.

MOD 10:     Barzun, Jacques
"The Modern Ego," CLASSIC, ROMANTIC AND
MODERN (Boston and Toronto: Little, Brown and Co.,
1961), pp. 115-31 (1975)

Discusses the "intellectual vices, [the] perverse critical
deficiencies" of a Modernism which has lost the
Romantic faith in man.

MOD 11:     Levin, Harry
"What Was Modernism?" VARIETIES OF
LITERARY EXPERIENCE, ed. Stanley Burnshaw
(New York: New York University Press, 1962),
pp. 307-29. Reprinted in Harry Levin, REFRACTIONS
(New York: Oxford University Press, 1966), pp. 271-95

A broad, retrospective survey of the great modernist
writers; of their creative, "metamorphic" response to
their times; of their humane achievements (which have not
been equalled by the post-modernists); and of their
demanding intelligence. "In so far as we are still moderns,
I would argue, we are the children of Humanism and the
Enlightenment."

MOD 12:     Spender, Stephen
THE STRUGGLE OF THE MODERN (London:
Hamish Hamilton, 1963; Berkeley: University of
California Press, 1963)

A collection of essays which discusses the debt of Modernism to the Romantic theory of the imagination; outlines the purposes of Modernism: "the confrontation of the past with the present . . . seems to me the fundamental aim of Modernism"; contrasts "the moderns" (James Joyce, Virginia Woolf, D.H. Lawrence, T.S. Eliot, Wyndham Lewis and Ezra Pound), "who deliberately set out to invent a new literature as a result of their feeling that our age is in many ways unprecedented, and outside all the conventions of past literature and art" with "the contemporaries" (H.G. Wells and Arnold Bennett), who recognise that there is a modern situation, but "refuse to regard it as a problem special to art"; assesses the dangers of the modernists' nostalgia for the past and their hatred of the present; traces the influence of these views on neo-traditionalist criticism, particularly that of F.R. Leavis; and concludes with a discussion of the relevance of modernist ideas to the contemporary situation. A first-rate discussion of Modernism and of its literary context.

MOD 13:    Ellmann, Richard and Feidelson, Charles (eds.)
THE MODERN TRADITION: BACKGROUNDS
OF MODERN LITERATURE (New York and
London: Oxford University Press, 1965)

A comprehensive anthology from the writings of philosophers, theologians, psychologists, writers and political thinkers. Modernism is a distinctive mode of imagination which derives from the Enlightenment — a mode which "strongly implies some sort of historical discontinuity, either a liberation from inherited patterns, or, at another extreme, deprivation and disinheritance." At the same time, modernists have striven to overcome this sense of loss: "modernists have been as much imbued with a feeling for their historical role, their relation to the past, as with a feeling of historical discontinuity." An indispensable guide to the intellectual sources and impulses of Modernism.

MOD 14:    Trilling, Lionel
"On the Teaching of Modern Literature," BEYOND
CULTURE: ESSAYS ON LITERATURE AND
LEARNING (New York: Viking Press, 1965; London:
Secker & Warburg, 1966), pp. 3-30 (1980)

An important essay which discusses and is troubled by "a particular theme of modern literature . . . the disenchantment of our culture with culture itself."

MOD 15:    Frye, Northrop
THE MODERN CENTURY (New York and Toronto: Oxford University Press, 1967; London: Oxford University Press, 1968)

Relates the developments and crises of Canadian life to those of the Western world. Modernist literature has best exemplified and comprehended them.

MOD 16:    Kampf, Louis
ON MODERNISM: THE PROSPECTS FOR LITERATURE AND FREEDOM (Cambridge, Mass. and London: Massachusetts Institute of Technology Press, 1967)

A wide-ranging exploration of the roots and the dangers of the *critical* spirit of Modernism, with its scepticism, its sense of impermanence, its "condition of permanent revolution."

MOD 17:    Kermode, (John) Frank
THE SENSE OF AN ENDING: STUDIES IN THE THEORY OF FICTION (London and New York: Oxford University Press, 1967)

A literary-philosophical inquiry into the nature of (and need for) fictions, distinguishing between *open* fictions, which posit their own provisionality, and *closed* fictions, which, unable to cope with the provisional and the contingent, interpret the world through all-inclusive explanatory systems. The usual mode of the closed fiction is mythic, while its political perspective is illiberal. Kermode explores the propensity of most modernists for closed forms, contrasting the open fiction of James Joyce with the closed fictions of D.H. Lawrence, Wyndham Lewis and T.S. Eliot. One of the richest and most important recent studies of Modernism.

MOD 18: Kermode, (John) Frank
CONTINUITIES (London: Routledge & Kegan Paul, 1968; New York: Random House, 1968)

An outstanding collection of essays on Modernism and modernist writers. The first section, "The Modern," contains important and influential essays: "Discrimination of Modernisms," pp. 1-10, on the various attempts to define Modernism; "Objects, Jokes and Art," pp. 10-27, on the relation between Modernism and post-Modernism; "Definitions and Variations," pp. 27-32, on the relations between the "Modern" and the "avant-garde". The volume also contains Kermode's brilliant essays on T.S. Eliot's *The Waste Land*, "A Babylonish Dialect," pp. 67-77; on D.H. Lawrence, "D.H. Lawrence and the Apocalyptic Types," pp. 122-51; and on Edmund Wilson as critic of Modernism, "Inside and Painentralia," pp. 100-13.

MOD 19: Bergonzi, Bernard
"The Advent of Modernism 1900-1920," HISTORY OF LITERATURE IN THE ENGLISH LANGUAGE: Vol.7 THE TWENTIETH CENTURY, ed. Bernard Bergonzi (London: Barrie and Jenkins, 1970), pp. 17-48

Following Stephen Spender (MOD 12), Bergonzi provides a brief survey of "contemporary" and "modernist" fiction and poetry in the first two decades of the century.

MOD 20: Josipovici, Gabriel D.
"The Birth of the Modern: 1885-1914," FRENCH LITERATURE AND ITS BACKGROUND: Vol.6 THE TWENTIETH CENTURY, ed. John Cruickshank (London, Oxford and New York: Oxford University Press, 1970), pp. 1-20

Brilliant historico-cultural discussion of Modernism as an European phenomenon, "a question of redefining Romanticism" which "affected the cultural life of France more than any other country."

MOD 21: Langbaum, Robert
THE MODERN SPIRIT: ESSAYS ON THE

CONTINUITY OF NINETEENTH AND
TWENTIETH-CENTURY LITERATURE (New
York: Oxford University Press, 1970; London: Chatto
and Windus, 1970)

A series of essays on "the post-Enlightenment tradition
that connects the nineteenth and twentieth centuries."
Contains many references to the English modernists and
their relation to Romanticism.

MOD 22:    Spears, Monroe K.
DIONYSUS AND THE CITY: MODERNISM IN
TWENTIETH-CENTURY POETRY (New York:
Oxford University Press, 1970)

Gives an exhaustive survey of "the sense of the modern"
in twentieth-century English and American literature
(with some references to painting); discusses those
American and English scholars (Edmund Wilson, Frank
Kermode, Northrop Frye) who have attempted both to
define Modernism and to account for its underlying sense
of crisis in the face of the discontinuity of the present
century; and concludes that the modernists turned to myth
to provide themselves with "a central means of continuity
with the past". Perhaps more useful for its discussion of
the recent critics of Modernism than for its own
elucidation of the subject.

MOD 23:    Howe, Irving
"The Culture of Modernism," THE DECLINE OF
THE NEW (New York: Harcourt Brace, 1971; London:
V. Gollancz, 1971), pp. 3-33

A wide-ranging essay on English, American and continental modernists: "Into the vacuum of belief left by the
collapse of Romanticism there race a number of compet-
ing world views, and these are beyond reconciling or even
aligning . . . .. Literary modernism is a battle of internal
conflicts more than a coherent set of theories or values."

MOD 24:    Josipovici, Gabriel D.
THE WORLD AND THE BOOK: A STUDY OF
MODERN FICTION (London: Macmillan, 1971;

# Modernism 9

Stanford: Stanford University Press, 1971) (1979)

"... the influence of [Ezra] Pound and [T.S.] Eliot in England has always led to the unexpressed assumption that modernism is primarily an affair of the *diction* of poetry. But of course it is prose fiction and painting which raise the real questions about the nature of modernism, because it is here that the Renaissance norms of verisimilitude, against which the moderns were reacting, play the largest role."

A brilliant and subtle study, ranging from Geoffrey Chaucer to Marcel Proust, Saul Bellow to William Golding, by one of the foremost theorists of European and American Modernism. Chapter 7, "Modernism and Romanticism," presents an important historico-philosophical account of Modernism as an European reaction to Romanticism: "Kierkegaard's problems, and some of his solutions, are the problems and solutions of modernism."

MOD 25:  Szabolcsi, Miklos
"Avant-garde, New-avant-garde, Modernism: Questions and Suggestions," *New Literary History*, 3:1 (Autumn 1971), 49-70

The avant-garde movement is Romantic and Symbolist in origin and is anti-realist in practice. Discusses the way in which the modernist artist dislocates his art in an attempt to reform art and society.

MOD 26:  Trilling, Lionel
SINCERITY AND AUTHENTICITY (London and New York: Oxford University Press, 1971)

Wide-ranging essay which, in its later stages, discusses the modern tendency to equate authenticity with extreme states of being, particularly madness.

MOD 27:  Currie, Robert
GENIUS: AN IDEOLOGY IN LITERATURE (London: Chatto and Windus, 1974; New York: Schocken, 1974)

Presents an important philosophico-cultural critique of
the degeneration of Romanticism into modernist pessimism in Sören Kierkegaard, Wyndham Lewis, Franz Kafka
and Samuel Beckett.

MOD 28:    Johnsen, William A.
"Toward a Redefinition of Modernism," *Boundary 2*, 2:3
(Spring 1974), 539-56

The modernists sought to escape the techniques of binary
opposition which characterise the totalitarian mind,
offering a third alternative to the opposition of order and
chaos: coincidence. Concentrates on James Joyce's
*Portrait of the Artist as a Young Man* and *Ulysses*.

MOD 29:    Bornstein, George Jay
TRANSFORMATIONS OF ROMANTICISM IN
YEATS, ELIOT AND STEVENS (Chicago and
London: University of Chicago Press, 1976)

A convincing and valuable study of the links between
Romanticism and Modernism, which explores "the
obsessive relation to British romanticism of three major
poets of our century" — W.B. Yeats, T.S. Eliot and
Wallace Stevens. The book "systematically argues that
the growing critical recognition of romanticism's importance to modernism should apply to overtly anti-romantic
Eliot as to pro-romantic Yeats and Stevens. The best way
to see such importance seems to me to alter our way of
analysing poems to emphasise their mental action. By that
I mean paying more attention to the acts of mind of the
speaker as he utters the poem than to the content of his
statements . . . . Poets of this era began writing under the
sway of debased, turn-of-the-century romanticism, freed
themselves by an anti-romantic reaction, and then later
reconciled themselves with their predecessors." The
introduction, "The Poem of the Act of the Mind,"
pp. 1-26, presents an excellent review of the various
Romantic and anti-Romantic interpretations of Modernism.

MOD 30:    Josipovici, Gabriel D.
THE LESSONS OF MODERNISM: AND OTHER

ESSAYS (London and New York: Macmillan, 1977;
New York: Rowman, 1977)

"The present volume falls into three interrelated sections:
essays on writers [Franz Kafka, Fernando Pessoa, Saul
Bellow and Walter Benjamin]; essays on culture and
education; and essays on the limits of expression, the
relation of words to music, and the entire problem of the
viability of opera and music-theatre today." Contains two
key chapters, 6 and 7: "The Lessons of Modernism,"
pp. 109-23, which suggests that "the two lessons of
modern art are those of silence and of game," and
"Linearity and Fragmentation," pp. 124-39, which
argues that "the fragmented or spiralling work denies us
the comfort of finding a centre, a single meaning, a
speakable truth, either in works of art or in the world. In
its stead it gives us back a sense of the potential of each
moment, each word, each gesture and each event, and
acknowledges the centrality of the processes of creation
and expression in all our lives." Subtle and important
essays on the forms and purposes of modernist fiction,
poetry and music-drama.

MOD 31:    Abrams, M.H.
"Coleridge, Baudelaire, and Modernist Poetics," NEW
PERSPECTIVES IN GERMAN LITERARY
CRITICISM, ed. Richard E. Amacher and Victor Lange
(Princeton, N.J.: Princeton University Press, 1979),
pp. 150-82

Qualifies the views of Edmund Wilson (MOD 1) and of
Frank Kermode (MOD 7). "To a striking degree the
various forms of modernist poetics were formulated with
persistent reference to Romantic precedents. . . . But
when we judge them . . . by the premises and general
directions of their thinking, we see that the various
founders of Modernism who thought of themselves as
anti-Romantic were not mistaken."

MOD 32:    Garvin, Harry R. (ed.)
ROMANTICISM, MODERNISM,
POSTMODERNISM (Lewisburg: Bucknell University
Press, 1980: London and Toronto: Associated University
Press, 1980)

A series of separate essays brought together (somewhat misleadingly) under the portentous title above. The second section, "Romanticism and Modernism," contains: Florence K. Riddle, "Form and Meaning in Hopkins's Mortal Beauty Sonnet," pp. 69-87; L.J. Swingle, "Virginia Woolf and Romantic Prometheanism," pp. 88-106 (on the Romantic view of creativity in *Between the Acts*); and Donald R. Riccomini, "Defamiliarization, Reflexive Reference, and Modernism," pp. 107-13 (Shklovsky's theory of fiction is unable to account for modernist fiction). See also Wallace Martin, "Ultima Thule or Seim Anew?", pp. 142-54 (on the theorists of Modernism and of Postmodernism).

MOD 33:   Kiely, Robert
BEYOND EGOTISM: THE FICTION OF JAMES JOYCE, VIRGINIA WOOLF AND
D.H. LAWRENCE (Cambridge, Mass. and London: Harvard University Press, 1980)

On the similarities between these three: "Nothing preoccupied the great writers of the Modern period more than the need to do what God had either ceased doing or might never have done in the first place. They felt radically obliged to put things together. And they saw this aspect of their work less as imitation than as invention and restoration." An illuminating study.

MOD 34:   Wilde, Alan
HORIZONS OF ASSENT: MODERNISM, POSTMODERNISM AND THE IRONIC
IMAGINATION (Baltimore and London: Johns Hopkins University Press, 1981)

Distinguishes between *mediate* (pre-modernist), *disjunctive* (modernist) and *suspensive* (post-modernist) irony in the work of E.M. Forster, Christopher Isherwood, Ivy Compton-Burnett and Donald Barthelme. An over-schematic study, which is often more anxious to establish its position in relation to traditional and contemporary criticism than to illuminate Modernism.

*The Intellectual Context of Modernism*

MOD 35:    Hoffman, Frederick John
           FREUDIANISM AND THE LITERARY MIND
           (Ann Arbor, Michigan: Louisiana State University Press,
           1945) (1977)

           Discusses the influence of Sigmund Freud on modern
           writing (particularly on Franz Kafka and Thomas Mann);
           and the response of some modern writers to Freud
           (principally D.H. Lawrence).

MOD 36:    Benziger, James
           "Modern Instances: Yeats, Stevens, Eliot," IMAGES
           OF ETERNITY: STUDIES IN THE POETRY OF
           RELIGIOUS VISION FROM WORDSWORTH TO
           T.S. ELIOT (Carbondale: Southern Illinois University
           Press, 1962), pp. 226-49

           Argues that W.B. Yeats, Wallace Stevens and T.S. Eliot
           share the "transcendentalising imagination" of the
           Romantics. Useful comparison of *Four Quartets* and *The
           Prelude*.

MOD 37:    Cornwell, Ethel F.
           THE STILL POINT: THEMES AND VARIATIONS
           IN THE WRITINGS OF T.S. ELIOT, COLERIDGE,
           YEATS, HENRY JAMES, VIRGINIA WOOLF
           AND D.H. LAWRENCE (New Brunswick, N.J.:
           Rutgers University Press, 1962)

           Compares the treatment of the themes of the "ecstatic
           moment," the "moment of reality," and "the still point of
           the turning world" in these writers.

MOD 38:    Brooks, Cleanth
           THE HIDDEN GOD: STUDIES IN HEMINGWAY,
           FAULKNER, YEATS, ELIOT AND WARREN (New
           Haven and London: Yale University Press, 1963) (1970)

           On the spiritual achievements of, and the spiritual plights
           revealed in, modern writing. Discusses the work of Ernest
           Hemingway, William Faulkner, W.B. Yeats, T.S. Eliot
           and Robert Penn Warren.

MOD 39:    Montgomery, Marion
THE REFLECTIVE JOURNEY TOWARDS
ORDER: ESSAYS ON DANTE, WORDSWORTH,
ELIOT AND OTHERS (Athens: University of Georgia
Press, 1963)

A subtle exploration of "the quest for certitude, for a point
of rest which reflects an order and harmony of mind" in
Dante, William Wordsworth and T.S. Eliot. "One might
go so far as to call the whole of this period, from Dante to
the present . . . the romantic age."

MOD 40:    Hoffman, Frederick John
THE MORTAL NO: DEATH AND THE MODERN
IMAGINATION (Princeton, N.J.: Princeton
University Press, 1964)

Discusses how the changing views of death (and of
immortality) in the present century affect the choice of
image and metaphor by which the significance of human
life is expressed in a wide range of American, English, and
continental writers: Henry James, D.H. Lawrence,
James Joyce, E.M. Forster, Virginia Woolf, Franz
Kafka, Ernest Hemingway, André Malraux, Jean-Paul
Sartre and Albert Camus.

MOD 41:    Miller, Joseph Hillis
POETS OF REALITY: SIX
TWENTIETH-CENTURY WRITERS (Cambridge,
Mass.: Belknap Press of Harvard University Press, 1965)

Important philosophico-critical essays on Joseph Conrad,
W.B. Yeats, T.S. Eliot, Dylan Thomas, Wallace Stevens
and William Carlos Williams, which discuss the way in
which the modern writer faces and overcomes the nihilism
of pure subjectivism "which is one of the possible
consequences of romanticism." One of the most significant (and demanding) studies on modernist fiction and
poetry.

MOD 42:    Hoffman, Daniel
BARBAROUS KNOWLEDGE: MYTH IN THE
POETRY OF YEATS, GRAVES AND MUIR (New

York and London: Oxford University Press, 1967) (1970)

Shows how W.B. Yeats, Robert Graves and Edwin Muir use the Romantic strategy of countering scientific materialism by myth.

MOD 43: Thatcher, David S.
NIETZSCHE IN ENGLAND 1890-1914: THE GROWTH OF A REPUTATION (Toronto: University of Toronto Press, 1970)

A thorough and convincing account of Friedrich Nietzsche's influence on the thinkers and writers of the period, covering John Davidson, Havelock Ellis, W.B. Yeats, G.B. Shaw and A.R. Orage.

MOD 44: Feder, Lillian
ANCIENT MYTH IN MODERN POETRY
(Princeton, N.J.: Princeton University Press, 1971)

Defines the nature of myth "as a continuous and evolving mode of expression" and analyses the adaptation and use of ancient Greek and Roman myth "as a creative instrument" in W.B. Yeats, T.S. Eliot, Ezra Pound and W.H. Auden. Particularly interesting in its discussion of the links between myth and history in Giambattista Vico, Oswald Spengler and the poets mentioned.

MOD 45: Bridgwater, Patrick
NIETZSCHE IN ANGLO-SAXONY: A STUDY OF NIETZSCHE'S IMPACT ON ENGLISH AND AMERICAN LITERATURE (Leicester, England: Leicester University Press, 1972)

Discusses the influence of Friedrich Nietzsche on Walter Pater and Arthur Symons; George Moore; John Davidson; H.G. Wells and Bernard Shaw; W.B. Yeats; Herbert Read and Edwin Muir; D.H. Lawrence and J.C. Powys; "Nietzsche in Georgian England"; "The 'men of 1914' and Nietzsche" (Wyndham Lewis, T.E. Hulme, T.S. Eliot, James Joyce, Ezra Pound and A.R. Orage); "Nietzsche and American Literature"; Jack London and Theodore Dreiser; John Gould

Fletcher; Eugene O'Neill; Wallace Stevens. Contains a full bibliography.

MOD 46:    Vickery, John B.
THE LITERARY IMPACT OF *THE GOLDEN BOUGH* (Princeton, N.J.: Princeton University Press, 1973)

A brilliant and rewarding study of the impact of Sir James Frazer's ideas and methods, embodying "the many strands of the modern spirit," on the thinkers and writers of the period, with separate chapters on W.B. Yeats, T.S. Eliot, D.H. Lawrence and James Joyce. One of the most important intellectual and cultural histories of the period.

MOD 47:    Fussell, Paul
THE GREAT WAR AND MODERN MEMORY (New York and London: Oxford University Press, 1975)

A startling and original account of the literary means by which the British experience on the Western Front "has been remembered, conventionalized, and mythologized." Contains references throughout to T.S. Eliot, D.H. Lawrence, Ezra Pound, Virginia Woolf and Wyndham Lewis.

## *Modernism and the Problem of Language*

MOD 48:    Steiner, George
LANGUAGE AND SILENCE: ESSAYS ON LANGUAGE, LITERATURE AND THE INHUMAN 1958-1966 (London: Faber and Faber, 1967; New York: Atheneum, 1970)

A brilliant and moving collection of essays on the modern crisis of language; on the failure of belief in humanism and of humanist hope; on the problems for writing, education and criticism in the light of that failure; on the contribution and the limitations of Marxist criticism.

MOD 49: Kenner, Hugh
THE POUND ERA (Berkeley: University of California
Press, 1971; London: Faber and Faber, 1972)

A scintillating survey of the age of Ezra Pound and of
T.S. Eliot, James Joyce and Wyndham Lewis, who all
followed Pound in exploring and revitalising the associa-
tions contained within European languages. The modernist writer set free the latent energies of language, creating
the future by renewing the inherited modes of feeling and
of thought of past European civilisation. The study,
however, is elegaic: the world the 'men of 1914' hoped to
create is no longer possible. One of the key books on
Modernism.

MOD 50: Steiner, George
EXTRA-TERRITORIAL: PAPERS ON
LITERATURE AND THE LANGUAGE
REVOLUTION (New York: Atheneum, 1971; London:
Faber and Faber, 1972)

Essays on language, on the relations of language to mind,
and on the language revolution which coincides "in time
and sensibility with that crisis of morals and of formal
values which immediately precedes and follows on the
First World War."

MOD 51: Ackroyd, Peter
NOTES FOR A NEW CULTURE: AN ESSAY ON
MODERNISM (London: Vision Press, 1976; New
York: Barnes & Noble, 1976)

Philisophico-critical essay on Modernism: "that movement in which created form began to interrogate itself, and
to move toward an impossible union with itself in
self-identity." This "is the life which first appeared in the
writings of Mallarmé and Nietzsche, and it finds its
specific reference in the novel idea of literature. Language
is seen to constitute meaning only within itself, and to
excise the external references of subjectivity and its
corollary. Language thus moves beyond the instrumental
language of positivism at the same time as it denies the
force of humanism." Suggests that a proper recognition of
the achievements of Modernism would provide a solution
to the present crisis in English studies.

MOD 52:     Korg, Jacob
            LANGUAGE IN MODERN LITERATURE:
            INNOVATION AND EXPERIMENT (New York:
            Barnes & Noble, 1979; Brighton, Sussex: Harvester
            Press, 1979)

            A detailed examination of the linguistic innovation and
            experiment of T.S. Eliot, Gertrude Stein, Ezra Pound,
            T.E. Hulme, E.E. Cummings, and William Carlos Wil-
            liams. Special attention is given to James Joyce's
            *Finnegans Wake*.

## The Politics of Modernism

MOD 53:     Bowra, Cecil Maurice
            POETRY AND POLITICS 1900-1960 (Cambridge and
            New York: Cambridge University Press, 1966)

            Lectures on the political and the private vision in modern
            Russian, French, German and English poets, with
            suggestive references to W.B. Yeats and T.S. Eliot.

MOD 54:     Harrison, John Raymond
            THE REACTIONARIES: A STUDY OF THE
            ANTI-DEMOCRATIC INTELLIGENTSIA
            (London: V. Gollancz, 1966; New York: Schocken, 1966)

            A pioneering and still controversial study, in which
            W.B. Yeats, Wyndham Lewis, Ezra Pound, T.S. Eliot
            and D.H. Lawrence are chosen as the literary and
            intellectual exemplars of "the anti-democratic
            intelligentsia" in the twentieth century. "What Yeats,
            Pound, Lewis and Eliot wanted in literature was bareness,
            a hard intellectual approach ruled by the authority of strict
            literary principles. They rejected the humanist tradition in
            literature, and in society, the democratic, humanitarian
            tradition. The same principles governed their social
            criticism as their literary criticism, and led them to support
            the fascist cause, either directly, as did Pound and Lewis,
            or indirectly, as Yeats and Eliot did."

MOD 55:    Spender, Stephen
"Writers and Politics," *Partisan Review*, 34:3 (Summer
1967), 359-81

A comprehensive discussion of the political commitments
of English writers between the wars. The political
elements in W.B. Yeats, Ezra Pound, Wyndham Lewis,
T.S. Eliot and D.H. Lawrence are rhetorical, "secondary effects of their thoughts about the tragedy of culture
in modern industrial society."

MOD 56:    Alter, Robert
"Eliot, Lawrence and the Jews," *Commentary*, 50:4
(Oct. 1970), 81-6

D.H. Lawrence's *Kangaroo* uses anti-Semitism to criti-
cise the hypertrophy of Western culture, while
T.S. Eliot's anti-Semitism in his early poems suggests his
aloofness from European culture.

MOD 57:    Hamilton, Alastair
"England," THE APPEAL OF FASCISM: A STUDY
OF INTELLECTUALS AND FASCISM 1919-1945
(London: A. Blond, 1971; New York: Macmillan, 1971)
pp. 257-90

Perhaps the best general discussion of the links between
the modernists (Ezra Pound, T.S. Eliot, Wyndham
Lewis, D.H. Lawrence and W.B. Yeats) and the politics
of the Right.

MOD 58:    Howe, Irving
"Beliefs of the Masters," THE DECLINE OF THE
NEW (New York: Harcourt Brace, 1971; London: V.
Gollancz, 1971), pp. 34-42

"For middle-aged readers," Harrison's *The Reactionaries* (MOD 54) comes "as a sharp reminder of
unfinished business." What can be charged against
W.B. Yeats, Ezra Pound, T.S. Eliot, Wyndham Lewis
and D.H. Lawrence is "intellectual . . . arrogance and
irresponsibility." In revolting against bourgeois Europe,
they failed to make the essential distinction between

transient bourgeois institutions and abiding values of liberal freedom.

MOD 59:    Panichas, George Andrew (ed.)
THE POLITICS OF TWENTIETH-CENTURY
NOVELISTS (New York: Hawthorn Books, 1971)

Contains separate essays on British, continental and American writers. See the following: George A. Panichas: "The Writer and Society: Some Reflections," pp. XXIII-LIV; Vivian de Sola Pinto, "D.H. Lawrence (1885-1930)," pp. 30-49 (DHL 150); Geoffrey Wagner, "Wyndham Lewis (1886-1957)," pp. 51-64 (WL 38).

MOD 60:    Steiner, George
IN BLUEBEARD'S CASTLE: SOME NOTES
TOWARDS THE REDEFINITION OF CULTURE
(London: Faber and Faber, 1971; New Haven: Yale
University Press, 1971)

A series of lectures speculating on the links between modernist high culture and political atrocity. Brilliant and provocative.

MOD 61:    Watson, George
"The Myth of Catastrophe," *Yale Review*, 65:3 (Spring 1976), 357-69

Between the two World Wars, many writers and thinkers — including D.H. Lawrence, W.B. Yeats, James Joyce, T.S. Eliot, Scott Fitzgerald, Bertrand Russell, Arnold Toynbee, and W.H. Auden — adhered to a simplistic, melodramatic view of complex events.

MOD 62:    Morris, J.A.
"Flirtations with Authoritarianism," WRITERS AND
POLITICS IN MODERN BRITAIN (London and
Toronto: Hodder and Stoughton, 1977), pp. 43-65

Contains brief discussions of W.B. Yeats, T.S. Eliot, D.H. Lawrence and Wyndham Lewis.

MOD 63: Jameson, Fredric
FABLES OF AGGRESSION: WYNDHAM LEWIS,
THE MODERNIST AS FASCIST (Berkeley, Los
Angeles and London: University of California Press,
1979)

Scintillating Marxist-structuralist and neo-Freudian
analysis of the transformations in Lewis's work, from the
democratic prose of the early short stories to the static,
death-filled figuration of his later fiction. Jameson seeks to
describe and explain the social, political and literary
choices by which early modernists became, after the First
World War, supporters of fascism. (See WL 41).

## Modernism and Tradition

MOD 64: Cronin, Anthony
A QUESTION OF MODERNITY (London: Secker &
Warburg, 1966)

"There is a sense in which the (modernist) revolution
was . . . a return to principles which had been largely
forgotten or ignored." The work of Ezra Pound,
T.S. Eliot, 'late' W.B. Yeats, James Joyce and Samuel
Beckett achieved the highest level of psychological
truthfulness and saw the minutiae of life steadily and
whole.

MOD 65: Sisson, Charles Hubert
ENGLISH POETRY 1900-1950: AN ASSESSMENT
(London: R. Hart-Davis, 1971)

A lively and stimulating account which contains separate
essays on Imagism, Ezra Pound, T.S. Eliot, W.B. Yeats
and which discusses *inter alia* the verse and prose of
James Joyce, the prose of D.H. Lawrence and the poetry
of Wyndham Lewis. Sisson emphasises the key influence
of the prose of Ford Madox Ford on the development of
modernist poetics, and stresses the anti-Romanticism of
English Modernism.
    The essays on W.B. Yeats, Ezra Pound and T.S. Eliot
are reprinted in C.H. Sisson (MOD 67).

MOD 66:    Chiari, Joseph
           THE AESTHETICS OF MODERNISM (London:
           Vision Press, 1970; New York: Humanities Press, 1970)

           Philosophical discussion of the origins of Modernism in a
           culture "split between Christianity and anti-Socratic
           rationalism." The great modernists attempt, through the
           powers of the imagination, to heal the breach. Contains an
           appendix on "T.S. Eliot as a European Writer,"
           pp. 190-210.


MOD 67:    Sisson, Charles Hubert
           THE AVOIDANCE OF LITERATURE:
           COLLECTED ESSAYS, ed. Michael Schmidt
           (Manchester: Carcanet Press, 1978; New York: Persea
           Books, 1979)

           A collection of the political and literary essays of an
           English critic — Anglican, monarchist and classicist —
           who places himself within what he terms the "anti-
           Romantic tradition" of T.S. Eliot, Wyndham Lewis,
           Ezra Pound and Ford Madox Ford. Reprints separate
           essays on: "The Politics of Wyndham Lewis," pp. 243-9;
           "Wyndham Lewis's Study of Himself," pp. 250-4;
           "W.B. Yeats," pp. 255-70; "Yeats and Swift,"
           pp. 271-4; "T.S. Eliot," pp. 275-94; "Ezra Pound,"
           pp. 295-316; "Ford Madox Ford: Saltavit et Placuit,"
           pp. 324-34; "Wyndham Lewis as Critic," pp. 472-80.
             Sisson not only provides stimulating criticism of the
           work of W.B. Yeats, Ezra Pound, T.S. Eliot and
           Wyndham Lewis, but also gives, through his historical,
           political and cultural essays, one of the clearest and most
           sympathetic analyses from the Right of the political and
           cultural intentions of English Modernism.

# Modernism and its Literary Context

## The Antecedents of Modernism

MOD 68:    Langbaum, Robert
THE POETRY OF EXPERIENCE: THE
DRAMATIC MONOLOGUE IN MODERN
LITERARY TRADITION (New York: Random
House, 1957; London: Chatto and Windus, 1957) (1963)

Still the best account of the continuity between Romantic
and modernist poetry. Gives particular attention to
Robert Browning.

MOD 69:    Lester, John A.
JOURNEY THROUGH DESPAIR 1880-1914:
TRANSFORMATIONS IN BRITISH LITERARY
CULTURE (Princeton, N.J.: Princeton University
Press, 1968)

"What gives (the period) its distinctive character is the
clear emergence in English literary consciousness of a
conviction that the known bearings of literary culture,
whether humanist, romantic, or Victorian, have been
forever lost. . . . More and more, writers of this time had
to find ways to dispense with fixity and absolutes, and to
embrace uncertainty. It was they who began to learn the
lesson of our time, how to live with uncertainty, how
indeed to draw strength and life from it. They left us few
classics; but their reorientation, the beginnings of which
are recorded in their literature, exerts a greater shaping
force on our own imaginative life, I believe, than any we
have known since the Renaissance." The period was not
an end nor a period of transition: "it was a beginning."
Places the early W.B. Yeats in his pre-modernist context.

MOD 70:   Bolsterli, Margaret
          "Aesthetic Revaluation: The Recognition of Modern
          Consciousness," *Centennial Review*, 18:4 (Fall 1974),
          307-18

          The Aesthetic Movement, by embodying the "immediate
          moment," prepared the way for Modernism.


MOD 71:   Flowers, Betty S.
          BROWNING AND THE MODERN TRADITION
          (London: Macmillan, 1976)

          Argues convincingly the case for Robert Browning "as a
          major influence on modern poetry" and discusses clearly
          what is specifically "modern" about the modern tradition.


MOD 72:   Rowe, John Carlos
          HENRY ADAMS AND HENRY JAMES: THE
          EMERGENCE OF A MODERN CONSCIOUSNESS
          (Ithaca and London: Cornell University Press, 1976)

          An outstanding study of Henry Adams and of Henry
          James, which argues that "they illuminate the unfolding,
          self-conscious position that has characterized modern
          literature since the turn of the century."


MOD 73:   Nettels, Elsa
          JAMES AND CONRAD (Athens: The University of
          Georgia Press, 1977)

          Analyses the relationship between the two writers and
          their work and the distinctive contributions made by each
          writer to the development of the modern novel. More
          convincing on Joseph Conrad than on Henry James.


MOD 74:   Perosa, Sergio
          HENRY JAMES AND THE EXPERIMENTAL
          NOVEL (Charlottesville: University Press of Virginia,
          1978)

          Subtle and helpful study which argues that James's
          technical innovations "marked him out as a significant
          novelist and a father of Modernism."

# Modernism and the Movements of the Avant-Garde

MOD 75:   Hughes, Glenn
IMAGISM AND THE IMAGISTS: A STUDY OF
MODERN POETRY (Stanford: Stanford University
Press, 1931) (1973)

Discusses the origins of Imagism and Imagism as a
movement, with separate chapers on Richard Aldington,
H.D., John Gould Fletcher, F.S. Flint, D.H. Lawrence,
Amy Lowell and Ezra Pound.

MOD 76:   Poggioli, Renato
THE THEORY OF THE AVANT-GARDE, trans.
Gerald Fitzgerald (Cambridge, Mass.: Belknap Press of
Harvard University Press, 1968)

Important comparative sociological study of avant-garde
art in England, America and continental Europe "as a
historical concept, a center of tendencies and ideas."
Considers the relations between avant-garde art and
radical politics.

MOD 77:   Ray, Paul C.
THE SURREALIST MOVEMENT IN ENGLAND
(Ithaca and London: Cornell University Press, 1971)

Contains short accounts of the response of Wyndham
Lewis and of T.S. Eliot to the surrealist movement.

MOD 78:   Wees, William C.
VORTICISM AND THE ENGLISH
AVANT-GARDE (Toronto: University of Toronto
Press, 1972; Manchester: Manchester University Press,
1972)

First-rate contextual study, describing Vorticism as a
movement, and analysing the social forces which shaped
it.

MOD 79: Weightman, John
THE CONCEPT OF THE AVANT-GARDE:
EXPLORATIONS IN MODERNISM (London:
Alcove Press, 1973; La Salle, Ill.: Open Court, 1973)

Occasional (and often slight) essays on the theory and the
history of the avant-garde, with particular reference to
French literature.

MOD 80: Ford, Hugh
PUBLISHED IN PARIS: AMERICAN AND
BRITISH WRITERS, PRINTERS AND
PUBLISHERS IN PARIS 1920-1939 (London:
Garnstone Press, 1975; New York: Macmillan, 1975)
(1980)

Discusses T.S. Eliot, James Joyce, D.H. Lawrence,
Ezra Pound and Wyndham Lewis, usefully placing them
in the wider context of the post-war European movement
of letters.

MOD 81: Harmer, J.B.
VICTORY IN LIMBO: IMAGISM 1908-1917 (London:
Secker & Warburg, 1975; New York: St. Martin's, 1975)

A detailed account of the Imagists: of their repudiation of
Symbolism; of Vorticism; of their legacy.

MOD 82: Cork, Richard
VORTICISM AND ABSTRACT ART IN THE
FIRST MACHINE AGE (2 Vols.) (London: Gordon
Fraser, 1976; Berkeley and Los Angeles: University of
California Press, Vol.1, 1976; Vol.2, 1977)

Monumental study of English Vorticism, showing the
breadth and variety of the movement.

MOD 83: Homberger, Eric
"Modernists and Edwardians," EZRA POUND: THE
LONDON YEARS 1908-1920, ed. Philip Grover (New
York: AMS Press, 1977), pp. 1-14

Challenges the view of Modernism as a struggle against a reactionary age: "It was the discovery of modernity *within* Edwardian culture itself which seems such a remarkable phenomenon: Pound and Eliot were distinctly part of that culture, they were themselves Edwardians." An important and rewarding article.

MOD 84:  Materer, Timothy
VORTEX: POUND, ELIOT AND LEWIS (Ithaca and London: Cornell University Press, 1979)

The Vortex was a collective symbol for Ezra Pound, T.S. Eliot and Wyndham Lewis of hope, of energy, of creative practice. "James Joyce was potentially a force within the Vortex. The principles that eventually took Joyce out of Pound's orbit help to define through contrast those that held the Vortex together." Contains an interesting discussion of the politics of the Vortex.

## *Modernism and the Revolution of Style*

MOD 85:  Bowra, Cecil Maurice
THE CREATIVE EXPERIMENT (London: Macmillan, 1949)

The modern movement in poetry, as exemplified by Guillaume Apollinaire, Vladimir Mayakovsky, Boris Pasternak, T.S. Eliot, Frederico Garcia Lorca and Rafael Alberti, was "a reaction [in favour of psychological and emotional realism] against what preceded it," involving a profound enquiry into the nature of poetry itself, into its themes and content. "In the self modern poetry has a subject which demands the highest standards of truth as they have never been demanded before, and to do its duty by this it must possess a suitable technique." Contains a fine reading of *The Waste Land*.

MOD 86:  Isaacs, Jacob
AN ASSESSMENT OF TWENTIETH-CENTURY LITERATURE (London: Secker & Warburg, 1951; New York: E.P. Dutton, 1952) (1968)

Six suggestive lectures on the nature of twentieth-century literature in an age, like the seventeenth century, "of psychology and criticism, of science and politics and tough poetry." "What is so remarkable about the twentieth century . . . is the intense awareness it has of its own processes, and its innumerable attempts to describe what is happening, while it is still happening." English Modernism placed in an European context.

MOD 87:    Tindall, William York
THE LITERARY SYMBOL (Columbia: Columbia University Press, 1955)

A clear and comprehensive exposition of the use of "symbolist elements" in modernist literature. Considers in detail W.B. Yeats, T.S. Eliot, D.H. Lawrence, James Joyce, Thomas Mann, Paul Valéry, Joseph Conrad, Virginia Woolf, Wallace Stevens and William Faulkner.

MOD 88:    Melchiori, Giorgio
THE TIGHTROPE WALKERS: STUDIES OF MANNERISM IN MODERN ENGLISH LITERATURE (London: Routledge & Kegan Paul, 1956; New York: Macmillan, 1956)

The literature of the period of crisis in the first half of the century "will be classed with those dominated by the taste for asymmetry and instability, with Mannerism, or Rococco, or early Romanticism." Somewhat derivative essays on Henry James and Gerard Manley Hopkins; on "Joyce and the Tradition of the Novel"; "Echoes in 'The Waste Land' "; the imagery of *Four Quartets*; "Eliot and the Theatre"; Christopher Fry; "The Moment as a Time Unit in Fiction" (on Virginia Woolf and James Joyce); "The Abstract Art of Henry Green"; the poetry and drama of Dylan Thomas.

MOD 89:    Frank, Joseph
"Spatial Form in Modern Literature," THE WIDENING GYRE: CRISIS AND MASTERY IN MODERN LITERATURE (New Brunswick, N.J.: Rutgers University Press, 1963) (1968)

Describes the emphasis in modern literature upon non-naturalist techniques; considers their spatialising and detemporalising effects; suggests that these involve "the transformation of the historical imagination into myth — an imagination for which historical time does not exist."

MOD 90:  Barthes, Roland
WRITING DEGREE ZERO, trans. Annette Lavers and Colin Smith (London: Jonathan Cape, 1967; New York: Hill and Wang, 1968)

A seminal essay, which argues that the prose stylisation of modernist writing seeks to release the reader from automatic response. Thereby the reader recovers the privacy and independence lost in the world of controlled consumption.

MOD 91:  Alvarez, Alfred
BEYOND ALL THIS FIDDLE (London: Allen Lane, 1968; New York: Random House, 1969)

In the first section, entitled "Modernism," Alvarez argues (against the Movement) that the techniques of Modernism alone are adequate to describe the sense of contemporary reality.

MOD 92:  Schorer, Mark
THE WORLD WE IMAGINE (New York: Farrar, Straus and Giroux, 1968)

A wide-ranging collection of essays on English and American writers (including George Eliot, Emily Bronte, D.H. Lawrence, Ford Madox Ford, Sinclair Lewis, Hamlin Garland, Gertrude Stein, Sherwood Anderson, Scott Fitzgerald and Ernest Hemingway) which discusses the nature of fictional technique; identifies the transformations from nineteenth-century to twentieth-century fiction; outlines the differences of technique within modern writing. Contains an important essay on *Women in Love*, pp. 107-21.

MOD 93:  Beebe, Maurice
"Joyce and the Meanings of Modernism," LETTERS

FROM ALOFT: PAPERS DELIVERED AT THE
SECOND CANADIAN JAMES JOYCE SEMINAR,
ed. Richard M. Kain (Oklahoma: University of Tulsa
Monograph Series, No.13, 1971), pp. 15-25

Brief but exemplary definitions of Modernism, of its ironic
perspectives, its use of mythic structures, its view of the
autonomy of art, with a fine account of Joyce's centrality
to the modernist movement.

MOD 94:  Kartiganer, Donald
"Process and Product: A Study of Modern Literary
Form," *Massachusetts Review*, 12:2 (Spring 1971),
297-328

Modernist writers were conscious "of two distinct kinds
of illusion possible in literary form: the sense of rigorous
control and that of comparative looseness and fragmentation." A brilliant discussion of the forms of modernist
poetry and fiction, with particular emphasis on William
Carlos Williams's *Paterson* and T.S. Eliot's *Four Quartets*.

MOD 95:  Friedrich, Hugo
THE STRUCTURE OF MODERN POETRY, trans.
Joachim Neugroschel (Evanston: Northwestern
University Press, 1974)

Discusses the particular techniques of modern European
poetry (particularly Charles Baudelaire, Arthur Rimbaud,
Stéphane Mallarmé) with brief references to T.S. Eliot,
Ezra Pound and W.B. Yeats.

MOD 96:  Martin, Graham and Furbank, P.N. (eds.)
TWENTIETH-CENTURY POETRY: CRITICAL
ESSAYS AND DOCUMENTS (Milton Keynes: Open
University Press, 1975; New York: Humanities Press,
1975)

A useful and well-balanced compilation of essays and
reviews presenting the various approaches to and issues in
twentieth-century poetry. A separate section is entitled
"Modernism," pp. 196-254. Particularly good on the
styles and the social context of modern poetry.

MOD 97: Partridge, Astley Cooper
THE LANGUAGE OF MODERN POETRY:
YEATS, ELIOT, AUDEN (London: A. Deutsch, 1976;
Boulder, Col.: Westview Press, 1977)

An account of the development and impact of free verse
on modern English poetry; of its forebears — Robert
Browning and Walt Whitman; of its effect upon form and
rhythm; of its practice in the poetry of W.B. Yeats,
T.S. Eliot and W.H. Auden. "The plan is to treat poems
empirically, and to discover the modernity of poets in their
technique, in the range of their experiments rather than
the theories they have followed less successfully."
Among the "obstinate questionings of this study, one will
be to establish free verse, like any other kind, as a
vigorous discipline for the genuine poet; but also to
suggest that . . . such poets do not commit themselves to
this style, except for special kinds of thematic invention."
Contains excellent close textual analysis.

MOD 98: Faulkner, Peter
MODERNISM (London and New York: Methuen, 1977)

A short but immensely helpful account which discusses
the relation of Modernism to Victorian culture (particularly in Henry James and W.B. Yeats); analyses "the era
of Modernism, 1910-1930," concentrating on the criticism
of T.S. Eliot and Virginia Woolf, James Joyce's *Ulysses*,
Ezra Pound's *Hugh Selwyn Mauberley*; investigates
D.H. Lawrence's complex relation to Modernism; and
concludes with a short bibilographical essay on the critical
reception of Modernism since 1930. Provides an excellent
bibliography.

MOD 99: Lodge, David
MODERNISM, ANTIMODERNISM AND
POSTMODERNISM (Birmingham: University of
Birmingham, 1977)

Suggests "not only that . . . two kinds of writing,
modernist and antimodernist, persist throughout the
modern period, but that we can map out alternating phases
of dominance of one kind or another"; defines the nature
of modernist and antimodernist fiction; and assesses the

state of contemporary English and American fiction. Reprinted, in a revised version, in David Lodge, WORKING WITH STRUCTURALISM: ESSAYS AND REVIEWS ON NINETEENTH AND TWENTIETH CENTURY LITERATURE (Boston and London: Routledge & Kegan Paul, 1981), pp. 3-16.

MOD 100: Lodge, David
THE MODES OF MODERN WRITING:
METAPHOR, METONYMY AND THE
TYPOLOGY OF MODERN LITERATURE (London:
Edward Arnold, 1977; Ithaca: Cornell University Press,
1977)

An outstanding and stimulating book which, applying structuralist techniques, establishes a polarity between metaphoric (analogous, symbolist, lyric) and metonymic (contiguous, realistic, epic) techniques of expression to explore modernist and contemporary writing.

MOD 101: Sultan, Stanley
*ULYSSES, THE WASTE LAND* AND
MODERNISM: A JUBILEE STUDY (Port
Washington, N.Y. and London: Kennikat Press, 1977)

Attempts to define Modernism by examining the distinctive features, the similarities and the dissimilarities, of its two most important works.

MOD 102: Adams, Robert Martin
"What Was Modernism?" *Hudson Review*, 31:1 (Spring 1978), 19-33

An excellent account of the difficulties of defining Modernism, formally and historically, which, at the end, attempts to give a definition of Modernism: "When it is understood to refer to distinct structural features that some artistic works of this period have in common, it has real meaning."

MOD 103: Poirier, Richard
"The Difficulties of Modernism and the Modernism of

Difficulty," IMAGES AND IDEAS IN AMERICAN
CULTURE: THE FUNCTIONS OF CRITICISM, ed.
Arthur Edelstein (Waltham: Brandeis University Press,
1979), pp. 124-40

Explores the "volatile nature of reading and writing" of
Modernism, which "happened when reading got to be
grim." "Modernism . . . enters history as a mode of
experience, a way of reading, a way of being with great
difficulty conscious of structures, techniques, codes and
stylization."

MOD 104:   White, Allon
THE USES OF OBSCURITY: THE FICTION OF
EARLY MODERNISM (London and Boston:
Routledge & Kegan Paul, 1981)

A suggestive exploration of the reasons for the difficulty
and opacity of modernist writing in George Meredith,
Henry James and Joseph Conrad.

## Modernism and the Little Magazines

MOD 105:   Hoffman, Frederick John
THE LITTLE MAGAZINE: A HISTORY AND A
BIBLIOGRAPHY (Princeton, N.J.: Princeton
University Press, 1947; London: Oxford University
Press, 1947)

Still the most detailed and intelligent account of the little
magazines and of their function in promoting Modernism.

MOD 106:   Joost, Nicholas
YEARS OF TRANSITION: *THE DIAL* 1912-1920
(Barre, Mass.: Barre Publishers, 1967)

Excellent account of the transformations of the Chicago
*Dial*, from its liberal-idealist origins, to its championship
of the modernists, publishing W.B. Yeats, Ezra Pound,
Wyndham Lewis, D.H. Lawrence and T.S. Eliot. Joost
gives an important insight into the American context of,

and the American contribution to, the history of Modernism.

MOD 107:   Korg, Jacob
"Language Change and Experimental Magazines, 1910-1930," *Contemporary Literature*, 13:2 (Spring 1972), 144-61

*The Criterion*, *transition*, *Adelphi* and *Blast* not only provided a focus for various modernist movements; they also brought a revolution in language and language use.

MOD 108:   McMillan, Dougald
*TRANSITION*: THE HISTORY OF A LITERARY ERA 1927-1938 (London: Calder and Boyars, 1975; New York: Braziller, 1976)

Excellent account of *transition*, which first published parts of Hart Crane's *The Bridge*, James Joyce's *Work in Progress* and Samuel Beckett's early prose. Outlines Wyndham Lewis's opposition to the magazine.

MOD 109:   Hamilton, Ian
THE LITTLE MAGAZINES: A STUDY OF SIX EDITORS (London: Weidenfeld and Nicolson, 1976)

Discusses *The Little Review; Poetry; The Criterion; New Verse; Partisan Review; Horizon*.

MOD 110:   Bradbury, Malcolm
"The Shock Troops of Modernism," *Times Literary Supplement*, October 15, 1976, 1297-8

On the importance of the little magazines in promoting Modernism.

## *Memoirs of the Modernists*

MOD 111:   Carswell, John
LIVES AND LETTERS 1906-1957 (London: Faber and

Faber, 1978; New York: New Directions, 1978)

Illuminating memoirs of some of the major figures of English Modernism: A.R. Orage, D.H. Lawrence, Katherine Mansfield, John Middleton Murry, S.S. Koteliansky and Ford Madox Ford.

MOD 112:  Levin, Harry
MEMORIES OF THE MODERNS (New York: New Directions, 1980)

Reprints Levin's essays on and reminiscences of the Moderns — T.S. Eliot, James Joyce, Ernest Hemingway, John Dos Passos, William Carlos Williams, W.H. Auden — including "Ezra Pound, T.S. Eliot and the European Horizon," pp. 13-31 (MOD 147).

# Modernism and Poetry

## *Origins and Techniques*

MOD 113: Riding, Laura and Graves, Robert
A SURVEY OF MODERNIST POETRY (London:
W. Heinemann, 1927)

Historically important: the first detailed exposition (and
defence) of modernist poetry, concentrating upon the
difficulties modernist poetry presents for "the plain
reader."

MOD 114: Leavis, Frank Raymond
NEW BEARINGS IN ENGLISH POETRY: A
STUDY OF THE CONTEMPORARY SITUATION
(London: Chatto and Windus, 1932; revised 2nd edn.,
London: Chatto and Windus, 1950; Ann Arbor:
University of Michigan Press, 1960) (1972)

The pioneering study of modernist poetry in English
criticism, which, profoundly influenced by the poetry and
criticism of T.S. Eliot, established the case for considering T.S. Eliot and Ezra Pound to be the poets who, aware
of "the poetic tradition," were most alive to the
complexities and needs of the age. Leavis briefly
examined the poetry of the late Victorians, the Georgians
and the War Poets, but found their work severely limited.
W.B. Yeats alone, on account of his Irish background and
situation, escaped the "debilitated nineteenth-century
tradition," but, even so, his "career, magnificent as the
triumph was that he compelled out of defeat," was a
testament to the disadvantage of writing in ignorance of
the tradition. Leavis's expositions of *The Waste Land* and
*Hugh Selwyn Mauberley* are still to be considered
amongst the liveliest and most convincing in the critical
literature. The volume also contains an essay on the
originality of the hitherto neglected Gerard Manley

Hopkins, "the only influential poet of the Victorian age, and he seems to me the greatest." The second edition and subsequent reprints contain Leavis's "Retrospect 1950": on the academic institutionalisation of Eliot; on the failure of a poetic renaissance to realise itself in England; on the disintegration of an educated public; on his current estimation of Hopkins, Pound and Eliot.

MOD 115: Bullough, Geoffrey
THE TREND OF MODERN POETRY (London and Edinburgh: Oliver and Boyd, 1934)

A short history of modern English poetry, which is particularly good on defining the different trends of modern poetry and on showing their links with earlier schools of English poetry. Discusses W.B. Yeats; Georgian Poetry; the Imagists; the War Poets; the Sitwell Group; Herbert Read, D.H. Lawrence and T.S. Eliot; and W.H. Auden.

MOD 116: Brooks, Cleanth
MODERN POETRY AND THE TRADITION
(Chapel Hill: University of North Carolina Press, 1939)
(1970)

A series of essays, including Brooks's classic essays on T.S. Eliot's *The Waste Land* and on W.B. Yeats as myth-maker, which represented the first major assimilation into American academic criticism of the tenets of T.S. Eliot. In considering the history of English poetry, "the thesis frankly maintained . . . is that we are witnessing . . . a critical revolution of the order of the Romantic Revolt." The position advanced, however, is firmly anti-Romantic. Particularly suggestive on the impact of Modernism on American poetics.

MOD 117: Daiches, David
POETRY AND THE MODERN WORLD: A STUDY OF POETRY IN ENGLAND BETWEEN 1900 AND 1939 (Chicago: University of Chicago Press, 1940) (1978)

An elegant and well-argued "series of suggestive studies." "If we were asked to say what general shift in attitudes took place when the Victorian era gave way to the modern, we might answer that, in very general terms, the shift was from an attitude which, in various ways . . . recognised the responsibility of the poet to the world in which he found himself, to an attitude which rejected that responsibility...''. ''The modern poet — using the term to denote the poets of the first forty years of the present century — tends to be concerned with gestures of rejection and can on the whole be opposed to the poet of the Victorian tradition, whose gestures were mainly of acceptance.''

MOD 118:   Savage, Derek Stanley
THE PERSONAL PRINCIPLE: STUDIES IN MODERN POETRY (London: Routledge & Kegan Paul, 1944; Port Washington, N.Y.: Kennikat Press, 1969)

A spirited defence of modernist poetry, and of its sense of ''joyous, personal creation,'' against the criticism of Edmund Wilson (MOD 1) and others. Discusses W.B. Yeats, T.S. Eliot, Hart Crane, Harold Monro, D.H. Lawrence and W.H. Auden.

MOD 119:   Pinto, Vivian de Sola
CRISIS IN ENGLISH POETRY 1880-1940 (London: Hutchinson, 1951; New York: Longmans, 1951) (1968)

''The crisis in English poetry which began about thirty years before the outbreak of the First World War is a part of the moral, intellectual, social and economic crisis of England and of Western Europe in which we are still living today.'' The crisis, brought about by mass industralisation and urbanisation, by standardisation and uniformity, by the weakening of the alliance between poetry and the governing class, meant that there could be no successor to Alfred, Lord Tennyson. ''A new kind of poetry was needed to express that 'schism in the soul' which is the most significant fact in the modern world, and, at the same time, to attempt the . . . task of overcoming it and creating a new spiritual integration.'' Discusses Thomas Hardy, A.E. Housman, Gerard Manley Hopkins, Robert Bridges, W.B. Yeats, J.M. Synge, the Georgians, the War poets, the Imagists and D.H. Lawrence, T.S. Eliot and the poetry of the thirties. Particularly good on placing the crisis of literature in its historical context.

MOD 120: Quinn, Sister M. Bernetta
THE METAMORPHIC TRADITION IN MODERN POETRY (New Brunswick, N.J.: Rutgers University Press, 1955)

An inelegantly written but rewarding study of the metamorphic theme in the poetry of Ezra Pound, Wallace Stevens, William Carlos Williams, T.S. Eliot, Hart Crane, Randall Jarrell and W.B. Yeats.

MOD 121: Alvarez, Alfred
THE SHAPING SPIRIT: STUDIES IN MODERN ENGLISH AND AMERICAN POETS (London: Chatto and Windus, 1958). Published in America as STEWARDS OF EXCELLENCE: STUDIES IN MODERN ENGLISH AND AMERICAN POETRY (New York: Charles Scribner's Sons, 1958) (1967)

Historically important and still rewarding study, which distinguished the modernist from the contemporary and the traditional poetry of the period; stressed the American origins and nature of poetic Modernism; analysed the failure of English Modernism. Discusses W.B. Yeats, T.S. Eliot, Ezra Pound, William Empson, W.H. Auden, Hart Crane, Wallace Stevens, D.H. Lawrence.

MOD 122: Kermode, (John) Frank
THE ROMANTIC IMAGE (London: Routledge & Kegan Paul, 1957; New York: Macmillan, 1958)

See MOD 7.

MOD 123: Press, John
THE CHEQUER'D SHADE: REFLECTIONS ON OBSCURITY IN POETRY (London and New York: Oxford University Press, 1958) (1963)

On the difficulty of traditional and modernist poetry, which must be the case since "most great verse hints at the existence of a realm where supernatural values are supreme.'' Excellent analysis of the religious inspiration of much modernist verse.

MOD 124:   Cohen, John Michael
POETRY OF THIS AGE: 1908 TO 1958 (London: Hutchinson, 1960; Philadelphia: Dufour Editions, 1962)

W.B. Yeats and T.S. Eliot seen in the context of poetic and metaphysical changes common to twentieth-century French, German, Italian, Spanish, Russian and American poetry.

MOD 125:   Starkie, Enid
FROM GAUTIER TO ELIOT: THE INFLUENCE OF FRANCE ON ENGLISH LITERATURE 1851-1939 (London: Hutchinson, 1960; New York: Humanities Press, 1960) (1971)

An excellent general survey, particularly helpful in showing the influences of French poetry on the development of English Modernism. ''English literature did obtain from France, in the period under review, more than from any other country.''

MOD 126:   Wright, George Thaddeus
THE POET IN THE POEM: THE PERSONAE OF ELIOT, YEATS AND POUND (Berkeley, Los Angeles and London: University of California Press, 1960) (1974)

Still the best study of personae and the mask in modernist poetry: ''the divergence between the point of view of the personae and the point of view of the poets is what gives much modern poetry its impersonal quality, its ambiguity, its ironic, oblique manner of statement.''

MOD 127:   Stead, Christian Karlson
THE NEW POETIC: YEATS TO ELIOT (London: Hutchinson, 1964) (1979)

An important history (challenging Frank Kermode's

*Romantic Image*) (MOD 7) of the origins and the development of modernist verse. Stead argues that the doctine of the Image was a direct response, on the one hand, to aestheticism, and, on the other hand, to "the forces of mediocrity" represented by the patriotic verse of Rudyard Kipling and Sir Henry Newbolt, which is discussed in detail. W.B. Yeats and T.S. Eliot employed quite different techniques to overcome the dissociation of sensibility exemplified by such contemporary poetry, seeking "to avoid the isolation of 'aesthetic' and 'moral' qualities in poetry, to achieve a fusion of these into a new wholeness." As Yeats and Eliot became assured of the emergence of a new audience willing "to take modern poetry on its own terms," they began to shift from the symbolist to the discursive in their poetry. The study contains a detailed analysis of the structure of *Four Quartets*.

MOD 128: Hamburger, Michael
THE TRUTH OF POETRY: TENSIONS IN MODERN POETRY FROM BAUDELAIRE TO THE 1960s (London: Weidenfeld and Nicolson, 1969; New York: Harcourt Brace, 1969)

A wide-ranging series of essays on English, American and continental poetry, discussing the French origins of modern poetry; the modernist techniques, styles and politics of W.B. Yeats, T.S. Eliot and Ezra Pound; and the nature of post-modernist poetry. Consistently interesting in its presentation and analysis of the function, assumptions and diversity of modernist poetry.

MOD 129: Press, John
A MAP OF MODERN ENGLISH VERSE (London and New York: Oxford University Press, 1969)

"I am convinced that the major poetic achievement of the century is the work of the modernist poets, of whom the three major representatives are Yeats, Pound and Eliot. . . . Nevertheless, I have tried to give a fair hearing to what one might call the alternative discussion." Contains a brief discussion of the later poetry of W.B. Yeats; Imagism; Ezra Pound, 1909-1919; T.S. Eliot; D.H. Lawrence; the Georgians; the War poets; *Wheels* and

Edith Sitwell; Edwin Muir and Robert Graves; W.H. Auden; poets of the 1930s; Dylan Thomas; poets of the Second War and 1940s; the Movement and the poets of the 1950s. An exemplary survey, useful in particular for its ample quotation from the manifestoes and critical essays of modern poets themselves.

MOD 130:    Donoghue, Denis
"The Holy Language of Modernism," LITERARY ENGLISH SINCE SHAKESPEARE, ed. George Watson (London, Oxford and New York: Oxford University Press, 1970), pp. 386-407

Discusses "the two ways of modern writing." In the first, "words are deemed to be instrumental"; in the second – Symbolist–way, "they are constituted as the only 'certain good'." Contrasts the poetry of D.H. Lawrence and T.S. Eliot.

MOD 131:    Pondrom, Cyrena
THE ROAD FROM PARIS: THE FRENCH INFLUENCE ON ENGLISH POETRY 1900-1920 (Cambridge: Cambridge University Press, 1974)

Presents key documents and letters, with a useful introduction. Includes essays by F.S. Flint, Richard Aldington, John Middleton Murry and Ezra Pound which show the profound engagement of modernists, writing in English, with the techniques and principles of French poetry, 1900-1920. Essential reading.

MOD 132:    Perkins, David
A HISTORY OF MODERN POETRY FROM THE 1890s TO THE HIGH MODERNIST MODE (Cambridge, Mass. and London: Belknap Press of Harvard University Press, 1976)

The first volume of a wide-ranging history of modern English and American poetry (covering 130 poets) which "may seem to fit in with the contemporary reaction both in England and America, against the long hegemony of high Modernist poetry and criticism." It is particularly good at tracing different assumptions about poetry in the period and in detailing the links (in publishing and distribution) between poetry and its audience. Importantly, it presents "the poetry of the British Isles and the United States . . . in interplay rather than separately." It was, Perkins argues, American poets who led the reaction against the genteel tradition in poetry. "The main single influence on both sides of the Atlantic over the last fifty years has, in each case, been the writing of the other country." Contains separate and discriminating accounts of Ezra Pound, T.S. Eliot and W.B. Yeats. An important, helpful and well-presented account.

MOD 133: Rosenthal, Macha Louis
SAILING INTO THE UNKNOWN: YEATS, POUND AND ELIOT (New York and London: Oxford University Press, 1978)

"These three men helped to make a new world of poetry. They came to realize they were sailing into the unknown, in an apocalyptic era, on seas only partially charted by earlier masters and a few revolutionary thinkers. All three brought into the foreground of their practice the implicitly presentative and improvisatory character of poetry."

MOD 134: Hobsbaum, Philip
"The Growth of English Modernism," TRADITION AND EXPERIMENT IN ENGLISH POETRY (London: Macmillan, 1979; New York: Rowman, 1979), pp. 289-307

Distinguishes between the "chief heroes of English modernism," (Edward Thomas, Wilfred Owen and Isaac Rosenberg), the American modernists (T.S. Eliot and Ezra Pound), "who broke down form," and the traditionalists, the Georgians.

MOD 135: Houston, John Porter
FRENCH SYMBOLISM AND THE MODERNIST MOVEMENT: A STUDY OF POETIC STRUCTURES (Baton Rouge and London: Louisiana State University Press, 1980)

An excellent elucidation of "the structural and stylistic

differences that distinguish what is usually called modern poetry from that which preceded it.'' Houston re-examines the nature of French Symbolism and the debt to it of modernist French, German, Italian and English poetry (W.B. Yeats, T.S. Eliot, and Ezra Pound) suggesting that Symbolism had at first "a psychological value around which more ambiguous theories and configurations [concerning Christian revelation and prophecy] arise.'' Illuminating on the style and purposes of modernist poetry.

MOD 136:   Pritchard, William Harrison
LIVES OF THE MODERN POETS (London: Faber and Faber, 1980; New York: Oxford University Press, 1980)

The crucial time, when Anglo-American poetry became "certifiably modern," was " 'somewhere around' 1914." Pritchard explores (while disclaiming any wish to establish a particular canon or hierarchy of modern poets) the differing forms of modern poetry. He discusses the work of Thomas Hardy, W.B. Yeats, E.A. Robinson, Robert Frost, Ezra Pound, T.S. Eliot, Wallace Stevens, Hart Crane and William Carlos Williams. A perceptive and well-written account, which provides a helpful introduction to twentieth-century English and American poetry.

## The American Origins of Modernism

MOD 137:   Gregory, Horace and Zaturenska, Marya
A HISTORY OF AMERICAN POETRY 1900-1940 (New York: Harcourt Brace, 1946)

Historically important and still useful account of American poetry, which sets Ezra Pound and T.S. Eliot within the context of the much larger renaissance of American poetry in the twentieth century.

MOD 138:   Bolgan, Louise
ACHIEVEMENT IN AMERICAN POETRY (Chicago: Regnery, 1951)

A sociological history of American poetry in the last fifty years — discussing the various publics for poetry — which argues that its major aim was to seek connection with European thought and feeling.

MOD 139: Wilson, Edmund
THE SHORES OF LIGHT: A LITERARY CHRONICLE OF THE TWENTIES AND THIRTIES (New York: Farrar, Straus and Young, 1952)

A collection of essays written in the twenties and thirties, many of which discuss the possibility of an exclusively American Modernism. See "Imaginary Dialogues," pp. 125-55, in which the figures of American Modernism define its nature and possibilities.

MOD 140: Hoffman, Frederick John
THE TWENTIES: AMERICAN WRITING IN THE POSTWAR DECADE (New York: Viking Press, 1955; revised 2nd edn., New York: Free Press, 1965)

An excellent expository guide to American writing of the inter-war period, with close analyses of the major texts. Includes discussion of Ezra Pound, Ernest Hemingway, Scott Fitzgerald, T.S. Eliot and Hart Crane.

MOD 141: Pearce, Roy Harvey
THE CONTINUITY OF AMERICAN POETRY (Princeton, N.J.: Princeton University Press, 1961)

An important revisionary account of American poetry, which sees Ezra Pound and T.S. Eliot as unacceptable exceptions to the mainstream of American Romantic poetry from Edgar Allan Poe, Ralph Waldo Emerson and Walt Whitman to William Carlos Williams and Wallace Stevens. Still one of the most stimulating works on the history of American poetry.

MOD 142: Dembo, Laurence S.
CONCEPTIONS OF REALITY IN MODERN AMERICAN POETRY (Berkeley and Los Angeles: University of California Press, 1966)

Philisophico-literary discussion of the "objectivist" metaphysics of Imagism and of the idealisation of language — which "is a direct manifestation of objectivist logic" — in William Carlos Williams, Wallace Stevens, Marianne Moore, E.E. Cummings, Hart Crane, Ezra Pound, T.S. Eliot, Charles Olson and Robert Duncan.

MOD 143:  Levin, Harry
"The American Voice in English Poetry,"
REFRACTIONS: ESSAYS IN COMPARATIVE LITERATURE (New York: Oxford University Press, 1966), pp. 171-91

Considers "the unity and the diversity of English as a literary medium" in nineteenth- and twentieth-century American poetry.

MOD 144:  Fussell, Edwin
LUCIFER IN HARNESS: AMERICAN METER, METAPHOR, AND DICTION (Princeton, N.J.: Princeton University Press, 1973)

"Lucifer is the frustrated and rebellious American poet in harness to the English language and English literary tradition." Presents Ezra Pound, and his disciple T.S. Eliot, as the most important successors to Walt Whitman's radical tradition in American poetry. Discusses also William Carlos Williams, Hart Crane and Wallace Stevens. A suggestive and stimulating study.

MOD 145:  Spender, Stephen
LOVE-HATE RELATIONS: A STUDY OF ANGLO-AMERICAN SENSIBILITIES (London: Hamish Hamilton, 1974; New York: Random House, 1974)

Contains throughout fascinating observations on T.S. Eliot and Ezra Pound. Their fierce commitment to the civilising powers of poetry was peculiarly American.

MOD 146:  Kenner, Hugh
A HOMEMADE WORLD: THE AMERICAN

MODERNIST WRITERS (New York: Alfred A.
Knopf, 1975)

Brilliant, idiosyncratic account of the nature of American
Modernism. "Joyce and Pound, say, were engaged on a
common enterprise. We cannot say the same of Williams
and Scott Fitzgerald, or of Stevens and Hemingway. The
novelists were courting readers, and homeland readers at
that. . . . The poets were courting no one, and were hardly
read." The home-made world of American Modernism
terminates not in climactic masterworks but in "an age of
transition — we live in it — where the very question gets
raised, what the written word may be good for." Such a
questioning, of language and of literature itself, is the key
characteristic of American Modernism.

MOD 147: Levin, Harry
EZRA POUND, T.S. ELIOT AND THE
EUROPEAN HORIZON (Oxford: Clarendon Press,
1975)

The Taylorian lecture for 1974, in which Levin compares,
contrasts and evaluates the careers and achievement of
Ezra Pound and T.S. Eliot, with particular emphasis upon
their senses of "tradition." (See MOD 112).

MOD 148: Hobsbaum, Philip
"The Growth of English Modernism," TRADITION
AND EXPERIMENT IN ENGLISH POETRY
(London: Macmillan, 1979; New York: Rowman, 1979),
pp. 255-88

Discusses T.S. Eliot, Ezra Pound, Wallace Stevens and
Robert Lowell: "Most frequently the qualities that critics
find in their work are described as modernism. If this
chapter has done its work, henceforth we shall recognise
that quality as Americanness."

MOD 149: Hoffman, Daniel (ed.)
HARVARD GUIDE TO CONTEMPORARY
AMERICAN WRITING (Cambridge, Mass. and
London: Belknap Press of Harvard University Press,
1979)

Contains two essays detailing the central contribution of T.S. Eliot and Ezra Pound to American literary criticism and poetics. See A. Walton Litz: "Literary Criticism," pp. 51-83 and Daniel Hoffman: "Poetry: After Modernism," pp. 439-95.

# Modernism and Fiction

## *Origins and Techniques*

MOD 150: Beach, Joseph Warren
THE TWENTIETH CENTURY NOVEL: STUDIES
IN TECHNIQUE (New York: Appleton, 1932)

Old-fashioned but still valuable study which discusses
"certain outstanding features of form in the twentieth-
century novel in English." For Beach, the techniques of
twentieth-century fiction are reflections of the relativist,
post-Freudian sensibility of the modern period. Joseph
Conrad and D.H. Lawrence are placed under Impres-
sionism; James Joyce under Post-Impressionism; Virginia Woolf under Expressionism.

MOD 151: Kettle, Arnold
AN INTRODUCTION TO THE ENGLISH NOVEL:
Vol.2 FROM HENRY JAMES TO 1950 (London and
New York: Hutchinson, 1953) (1974)

Well-written essays which rehearse traditional Marxist
objections to modern and modernist fiction: they fail to
achieve "a standpoint from which vital experience can be
defined, organised and controlled."
Part 2, "The Twentieth Century — The First Quarter,"
presents separate accounts of the following: Joseph
Conrad: *Nostromo*; Arnold Bennett: *The Old Wives'
Tale*; H.G. Wells: *Tono-Bungay*; John Galsworthy: *The
Man of Property*; Virginia Woolf: *To the Lighthouse*;
D.H. Lawrence: *The Rainbow*; James Joyce: *Ulysses*;
and E.M. Forster: *A Passage to India*. Excellent on
explicating the grounds of the Virginia Woolf-Arnold
Bennett dispute.

MOD 152: Edel, Leon
THE PSYCHOLOGICAL NOVEL (New York:

49

J.B. Lippincott, 1955; revised 2nd edn., Gloucester, Mass.: Peter Smith, 1972)

Exemplary discussion of the new ways of reading demanded by the stream-of-consciousness novel, concentrating on James Joyce, William Faulkner, Dorothy Richardson and Virginia Woolf. The revised edition considers C.P. Snow's criticism of "subjective fiction" and the development of the *nouveau roman* by Alain Robbe-Grillet.

MOD 153:    Edel, Leon and Ray, Gordon N.
HENRY JAMES AND H.G. WELLS: A RECORD OF THEIR FRIENDSHIP, THEIR DEBATE ON THE ART OF FICTION AND THEIR QUARREL (Urbana: University of Illinois Press, 1958)

Presents the key documents, with an outstanding introduction.

MOD 154:    Noon, William T.
"Modern Literature and the Sense of Time," *Thought*, 33 (1958), 571-603

An impressive and wide-ranging essay by a Catholic critic on the topics of time, history and eternity in T.S. Eliot, W.B. Yeats, James Joyce, Marcel Proust and Samuel Beckett. Reprinted in Philip Stevick (ed.), THE THEORY OF THE NOVEL (New York: Free Press, 1967; London: Collier-Macmillan, 1967), pp. 280-313.

MOD 155:    Daiches, David
THE NOVEL AND THE MODERN WORLD (Cambridge: Cambridge University Press, 1960; Chicago: University of Chicago Press, 1960) (1965)

A collection of illuminating essays on the themes and techniques of Joseph Conrad, James Joyce, D.H. Lawrence and Virginia Woolf. ". . . the breakdown of public agreement about what is significant in experience and therefore about what the novelist ought to select, the new view of time, and the new view of the nature of consciousness — co-operate to encourage the novelist to concentrate on aspects of the human situation which were not the major concern of earlier novelists . . . and to discover new techniques for achieving their aims.'' In the modern novel, ''loneliness is the great reality, love the great necessity: how can the two be brought together?''

MOD 156: Kumar, Shiv K.
BERGSON AND THE STREAM OF CONSCIOUSNESS NOVEL (New York: New York University Press, 1963) (1979)

Discusses Henri Bergson's theory of consciousness and its impact upon modernist fiction, with specific chapters on the fiction of Dorothy Richardson, Virginia Woolf and James Joyce.

MOD 157: Friedman, Alan
THE TURN OF THE NOVEL: THE TRANSITION TO MODERN FICTION (New York and London: Oxford University Press, 1966)

Still the most interesting and most important discussion of the nature of modernist fiction and of its relation to earlier fiction.

MOD 158: Raleigh, John Henry
TIME, PLACE AND IDEA: ESSAYS ON THE NOVEL (Carbondale and Edwardsville: Southern Illinois University Press, 1968)

Contains two important essays, ''The English Novel and the Three Kinds of Time,'' pp. 43-55 and ''Victorian Morals and the Modern Novel,'' pp. 137-63, which examine the changes from Victorian to modernist fiction.

MOD 159: Beja, Morris
EPIPHANY IN THE MODERN NOVEL (London: Peter Owen, 1971; Seattle: University of Washington Press, 1971)

First-rate discussion of the notion of epiphany in modernist literature, with separate chapers on James

Joyce, Virginia Woolf, Thomas Wolfe and William Faulkner.

MOD 160:    Speirs, John
POETRY TOWARDS NOVEL (London: Faber and Faber, 1971; New York: New York University Press, 1971)

Victorian and modernist novelists — Henry James, Joseph Conrad and D.H. Lawrence — are "at least as much successors of the English poets as of the 18th-century novelists."

MOD 161:    Kermode, (John) Frank
NOVEL AND NARRATIVE (Glasgow: University of Glasgow, 1972)

The twenty-fourth W.P. Ker memorial lecture, in which Kermode discusses the pluralist nature of narrative, revealed by Roland Barthes and "long ago exploited" by modernist writers — Henry James and Joseph Conrad — who knew that "their medium was inherently pluralistic." (See MOD 162).

MOD 162:    Halperin, John (ed.)
THE THEORY OF THE NOVEL: NEW ESSAYS (New York, London and Toronto: Oxford University Press, 1974)

A series of essays on the theory of the novel which accept — in the wake of Modernism — "the modern view" which "emphasises the structure of the work and the symbiosis of its component elements rather than the fiction itself as representative or non-representative of moral or mimetic 'reality'." See in particular Irving H. Buchen, "The Aesthetics of the Supra-Novel," pp. 91-108; A. Walton Litz, "The Genre of Ulysses'," pp. 109-20; Alan Warren Friedman, "The Modern Multivalent Novel," pp. 121-40; Frank Kermode, "Novel and Narrative," pp. 155-74, which applies Roland Barthes' notions to Joseph Conrad (see MOD 161); John Halperin, "Twentieth-Century Trends in Continental Novel-Theory," pp. 375-92, an excellent bibliographical essay which ends with a descriptive bibliography.

MOD 163: Alter, Robert
"The Modernist Revival of Self-Conscious Fiction,"
PARTIAL MAGIC: THE NOVEL AS A SELF
CONSCIOUS GENRE (Berkeley, Los Angeles and
London: University of California Press, 1975), pp.
138-79

Discusses the way in which the European modernists
(with particular reference to James Joyce, Virginia Woolf
and D.H. Lawrence) destroyed nineteenth-century fictional form.

MOD 164: Bradbury, Malcolm (ed.)
THE NOVEL TODAY (Manchester: Manchester
University Press, 1977; New York: Rowan, 1977)

A series of essays which consider the current state of the
modern novel, and the impact upon it of Modernism. With
an introductory essay by the editor, the volume contains
essays by, or excerpts from the writing of, Iris Murdoch,
Philip Roth, Michel Butor, Saul Bellow, John Barth,
David Lodge, Frank Kermode (in interview with Iris
Murdoch), John Fowles, B.S. Johnson, Doris Lessing,
Philip Stevick and Gerald Graff.

MOD 165: Steinberg, Erwin R.
THE STREAM-OF-CONSCIOUSNESS
TECHNIQUE IN THE MODERN NOVEL (Port
Washington, N.Y. and London: Kennikat Press, 1979)

Brings together the psychological writings of Henri
Bergson, Sigmund Freud and William James; the literary
writings of Virginia Woolf, Marcel Proust and Dorothy
Richardson; and the academic writings of assorted critics
on the stream-of-consciousness. "The stream-of-
consciousness technique appeared as an identifiable form
and flowered at the high point of what we have come to call
the Age of Modernism."

# Modernism and Drama

## *Origins and Techniques*

MOD 166: Williams, Raymond
DRAMA FROM IBSEN TO ELIOT (London: Chatto
and Windus, 1952; New York: Oxford University Press,
1953) A revised and extended 2nd edn. is published under
the title DRAMA FROM IBSEN TO BRECHT
(London: Chatto and Windus, 1969; New York: Oxford
University Press, 1969)

The fullest and most intelligent discussion yet of the
drama of English Modernism, setting the drama of
W.B. Yeats, James Joyce, T.S. Eliot and D.H. Lawrence in the context of European drama.

MOD 167: Krutch, Joseph Wood
"MODERNISM" IN MODERN DRAMA: A
DEFINITION AND AN ESTIMATE (Ithaca: Cornell
University Press, 1953)

Covers Henrik Ibsen, August Strindberg, G.B. Shaw,
Luigi Pirandello and J.M. Synge, with a concluding
chapter on twentieth-century American drama.

MOD 168: Worth, Katharine
"Towards Modernism: A New Theatrical Syntax," THE
IRISH DRAMA OF EUROPE FROM YEATS TO
BECKETT (London: Athlone Press, 1978; Atlantic
Highlands, N.J.: Humanities Press, 1978), pp. 1-47

Discusses the influence of Symbolism on Modernist
drama, "wherein actor becomes transformed into dancer,
dancer into musician, musician into lyric poet."

# The Critique of Modernism

## *The Limits of Modernism*

MOD 169: Winters, Yvor
PRIMITIVISM AND DECADENCE: A STUDY OF
AMERICAN EXPERIMENTAL POETRY (New
York: Arrow Editions, 1937) (1974)

Arguing that poetry should be capable of complete prose
paraphrase, Winters finds most twentieth-century American modernist poetry deficient. Historically, the most
important (and perhaps the best argued) objection to
modernist poetics.

MOD 170: Auerbach, Erich
"The Brown Stocking," MIMESIS: THE
REPRESENTATION OF REALITY IN WESTERN
LITERATURE, trans. Willard R. Trask (Princeton,
N.J.: Princeton University Press, 1953), pp. 525-53 (1974)

Masterly analysis of the modernist fiction of Virginia
Woolf, Marcel Proust and James Joyce, placing it in its
historical and cultural context. ". . . the method is not
only a symptom of the confusion and helplessness . . . of
our world. There is . . . a good deal to be said for such a
view."

MOD 171: Davie, Donald
"What Is Modern Poetry?" ARTICULATE ENERGY:
AN INQUIRY INTO THE SYNTAX OF ENGLISH
POETRY (London: Routledge & Kegan Paul, 1955; New
York: Harcourt Brace, 1958), pp. 147-60 (1971)

Modernist poetry owes its origins (and its shortcomings)
to the Symbolist rejection of normal syntax.

MOD 172:   Hough, Graham
REFLECTIONS ON A LITERARY REVOLUTION
(Washington, D.C.: Catholic University of America
Press, 1960)

A succinct and stimulating critique of Modernism. "The
years between 1910 and the second world war saw a
revolution in the literature of the English language as
momentous as the Romantic one a century ago. It is an
Anglo-American development that is itself part of a whole
European affair." Hough examines in Ezra Pound,
W.B. Yeats, James Joyce and T.S. Eliot, the Imagist
rather than Symbolist ideas which, for him, "are the
centre of the characteristic poetic procedures of our
time"; discusses the neo-classicist literary theory of
T.E. Hulme and of T.S. Eliot; considers the significant
(and still unexamined) re-alignment in Anglo-American
literary relations brought about by Pound and Eliot;
concludes with severe reservations about the modernist
revolution: "What gives Romantic poetry . . . its strong,
deep and steady movement is not only that it was part of a
more inclusive movement in thought, politics and society;
it is also that the most living questions of the age were
actually worked out in poetry." The poetic revolution of
the twentieth century is not of the same order. Bringing
merely a change in poetic technique, it was not, as was
Romanticism, "a spiritual revolution." Accordingly,
Hough concludes that the modernists will not leave any
lasting legacy to contemporary writers.

Reprinted in Graham Hough (MOD 173).


MOD 173:   Hough, Graham
IMAGE AND EXPERIENCE: STUDIES IN A
LITERARY REVOLUTION (London: Duckworth,
1960; Westport, Conn.: Greenwood, 1978) (1978)

A collection of essays, (including MOD 172), which
consider: free verse; psychoanalysis and literary interpretation; Lord Byron and D.H. Lawrence as representatives of nineteenth-century and twentieth-century
Romanticism; the aesthetics of John Ruskin and Roger
Fry; the fiction of George Moore; and Joseph Conrad's
*Chance*.

MOD 174: Holloway, John
THE COLOURS OF CLARITY: ESSAYS ON
CONTEMPORARY LITERATURE AND
EDUCATION (London: Routledge & Kegan Paul, 1964;
Hamden, Conn.: Archon, 1964)

A series of essays on various topics which suggest that the
modernist movement has left little of enduring value for
future generations of poets and critics.

MOD 175: Miller, James E. Jnr. and Herring, Paul D. (eds.)
THE ARTS AND THE PUBLIC (Chicago and London:
University of Chicago Press, 1967)

A series of lectures and discussions from a conference on
"The Arts and the Public," held in 1966 at the University
of Chicago, which was concerned with the breakdown in
the relationship between the modern (and modernist)
writer and the modern public. Includes contributions from
Saul Bellow, Granville Hicks and Wright Morris.

MOD 176: Poirier, Richard
"A Literature of Law and Order," *Partisan Review*, 36:2
(Spring 1969), 189-204

Criticises the submersion of human beings amidst a
mutliplicity of patterns, myths and techniques in modernist and post-modernist writing.

MOD 177: Rochberg, George
"The Avant-Garde and the Aesthetics of Survival," *New
Literary History*, 3:1 (Autumn 1971), 71-92

On the dangers, which beset avant-garde art, of losing
human contact.

MOD 178: Davie, Donald
THOMAS HARDY AND BRITISH POETRY
(London: Routledge & Kegan Paul, 1972; New York:
Oxford University Press, 1972)

An important, revisionary contribution to the history of

twentieth-century English poetry. The key influence in the period has not been the modernists, W.B. Yeats, T.S. Eliot, Ezra Pound or D.H. Lawrence, but Thomas Hardy.

MOD 179:   Nuttall, Anthony D.
A COMMON SKY: PHILOSOPHY AND THE LITERARY IMAGINATION (London: Chatto and Windus for Sussex University Press, 1974; Berkeley: University of California Press, 1974)

Contains a subtle discussion and critique of "solipsistic fear" in modern literature, in Jean-Paul Sartre and T.S. Eliot.

## The Marxist Critique of Modernism

MOD 180:   West, Alick
CRISIS AND CRITICISM (London: Lawrence and Wishart, 1937; revised 2nd edn., London: Lawrence and Wishart, 1975)

A Marxist critique of the writing and criticism of the modernists. The need to transcend bourgeois individualism leads not to a sense of collective unity but to a mystification of authority to which the individual must submit. The revised edition contains an hitherto unpublished essay on D.H. Lawrence.

MOD 181:   Lukacs, Georg
THE MEANING OF CONTEMPORARY REALISM, trans. John and Necke Mander (London: Merlin Press, 1963)

One of the most important Marxist critiques of literary Modernism, from Franz Kafka, James Joyce and Robert Musil to Samuel Beckett and William Faulkner. Lukacs criticises Modernism for its subjectivism, its 'static' view of the human condition, its dissolution of 'character,' its obsession with pathological and extreme states, and above all, its lack of a sense of and belief in History. See particularly, "The Ideology of Modernism," pp. 17-46.

MOD 182: Eagleton, Terence (Terry)
EXILES AND EMIGRES: STUDIES IN MODERN
LITERATURE (London: Chatto and Windus, 1970;
New York: Schocken 1970)

Owing to the "inability of indigenous English writing,
caught within its partial and one-sided attachments, to
'totalise' the significant movements of its own culture" at
the moment of the first crisis of imperialism, it was the
emigré writers — Henry James, Joseph Conrad and
T.S. Eliot — who found the means to do so. Explores the
techniques by which they did this, and the socio-cultural
reasons for the failure of English writers to do the same —
D.H. Lawrence, W.H. Auden, Evelyn Waugh, George
Orwell and Graham Greene. Perhaps Eagleton's best
study to date.

MOD 183: Williams, Raymond
THE ENGLISH NOVEL FROM DICKENS TO
LAWRENCE (London: Chatto and Windus, 1970; New
York: Oxford University Press, 1970)

In the concluding four chapters, the works of Joseph
Conrad, James Joyce, H.G. Wells, George Gissing and
D.H. Lawrence are placed in socio-cultural context.
Presents an important and influential thesis about the
failures of modern and modernist English novelists to
cope with the contradictions of the imperialist period.

MOD 184: Robinson, Lillian S. and Vogel, Lise
"Modernism and History," *New Literary History*, 3:1
(Autumn 1971), 177-99

By denying the shaping forces of race, class and sex on the
creation of modernist art, as modernist artists and their
critical apologists do, we accept the values of the white
male ruling class.

MOD 185: Leroy, Gaylord C. and Beitz, Ursula (eds.)
PRESERVE AND CREATE: ESSAYS ON
MARXIST LITERARY CRITICISM (New York:
Humanities Press, 1973)

Part Two is devoted to the Marxist theory of Modernism. See Werner Mittenzwei, "Contemporary Drama in the West," pp. 105-37 (on Samuel Beckett, Eugène Ionesco, Tennessee Williams and Thornton Wilder) and B.G. Zhantieva: "Joyce's *Ulysses*," pp. 138-72. The collection also contains an essay by Werner Mittenzwei on "The Brecht-Lukacs Debate," pp. 199-230.

MOD 186:   Craig, David
"Loneliness and Anarchy: Aspects of Modernism," THE REAL FOUNDATION: LITERATURE AND SOCIAL CHANGE (London: Chatto and Windus, 1973; New York: Oxford University Press, 1974), pp. 171-94

Presents a history and a critique of English Modernism, emphasising its cultural and political context. The best essay of its kind. The volume also reprints the following: "Shakespeare, Lawrence, and Sexual Freedom," pp. 17-38; "Lawrence and Democracy," pp. 143-67; "The Defeatism of *The Waste Land*," pp. 195-212.

MOD 187:   Swingewood, Alan
"Realism, Modernism and Revolution," THE NOVEL AND REVOLUTION (London: Macmillan, 1975; New York: Barnes & Noble, 1975), pp. 45-67

Argues, from a Marxist viewpoint, against Georg Lukacs's view of Modernism (MOD 181).

MOD 188:   Zeraffa, Michel
FICTIONS: THE NOVEL AND SOCIAL REALITY, trans. Caroline Burns and Tom Burns (Harmondsworth, Middlesex and New York: Penguin, 1976)

A subtle contribution to the sociology of the novel, which argues *contra* Georg Lukacs (MOD 181) that the modernist novel authentically expresses the contradictions of contemporary reality. Particularly good on American modernist fiction.

# Modernism: The Problem of Critical Reception

MOD 189:  Krieger, Murray
NEW APOLOGISTS FOR POETRY (Minneapolis:
University of Minnesota Press, 1956) (1977)

Important study which was one of the first to suggest the
Romantic basis of New Criticism in T.S. Eliot,
T.E. Hulme and I.A. Richards.


MOD 190:  Bradbury, John M.
THE FUGITIVES: A CRITICAL ACCOUNT
(Chapel Hill: University of North Carolina Press,
1958)

Detailed analysis of the critical ideas of John Crowe
Ransom, Alan Tate, Robert Penn Warren and Cleanth
Brooks.


MOD 191:  Cowan, Louise
THE FUGITIVE GROUP: A LITERARY HISTORY
(Baton Rouge: Louisiana State University Press, 1959)

A comprehensive (strongly biographical) history of the
Fugitives.


MOD 192:  Karanikas, Alexander
TILLERS OF A MYTH: SOUTHERN AGRARIANS
AS SOCIAL AND LITERARY CRITICS (Madison,
Milwaukee and London: University of Wisconsin
Press, 1966) (1970)

Considers Donald Davidson, John Crowe Ransom and
Alan Tate and the influence of T.S. Eliot upon them.

MOD 193:  De Man, Paul
"Literary History and Literary Modernity,"
BLINDNESS AND INSIGHT (London and New
York: Oxford University Press, 1971), pp.
142-65

On the "generative" and revolutionary power of Modernism as a concept in literary history.


MOD 194:  Fraser, John
"Leavis, Winters and 'Tradition'," *Southern Review*, 7:4
(Fall 1971), 963-85

Explicates and defends F.R. Leavis and Yvor Winters in
their censure of much modernist literature.


MOD 195:  Jameson, Fredric
MARXISM AND FORM: TWENTIETH-CENTURY
DIALECTICAL THEORIES OF LITERATURE
(Princeton, N.J.: Princeton University Press, 1971)
(1974)

Important analyses of the criticism of T.W. Adorno,
Walter Benjamin, Herbert Marcuse, Ernst Bloch, Georg
Lukacs and J.-P. Sartre, with particular reference to their
discussions of Modernism.


MOD 196:  Thurley, Geoffrey
THE IRONIC HARVEST: ENGLISH POETRY IN
THE TWENTIETH CENTURY (London: Edward
Arnold, 1974; New York: St. Martin's, 1974)

Presents a spirited critique of the "intellectualist" and
"ironic" tradition in English poetry and criticism
(originating with T.S. Eliot) and suggests alternative
traditions (the Surrealists, W.H. Auden, Dylan Thomas
and Ted Hughes.)


MOD 197:  Gillespie, Gerald
"New Apocalypse for Old: Kermode's Theory of
Modernism," *Boundary 2*, 3:2 (Winter 1975), 307-23

Kermode's conservative criticism is based upon the
notion of cultural continuity.

MOD 198: Eagleton, Terence (Terry)
CRITICISM AND IDEOLOGY: A STUDY IN
MARXIST LITERARY THEORY (London: New Left
Books, 1976; Atlantic Highlands, N.J.: Humanities
Press, 1976)

Important essay in Marxist aesthetics, which presents a
critique of the traditional reception of English Modernism
within the English (specifically Leavisite) critical tradition.

MOD 199: Fekete, John
THE CRITICAL TWILIGHT: EXPLORATIONS IN
THE IDEOLOGY OF ANGLO-AMERICAN
LITERARY THEORY FROM ELIOT TO
McLUHAN (London and Boston: Routledge & Kegan
Paul, 1978)

Historical critique from a Marxist viewpoint of the
tradition of Anglo-American criticism founded by
T.E. Hulme, I.A. Richards and T.S. Eliot and
developed by John Crowe Ransom, Northrop Frye and
Marshall McLuhan.

MOD 200: Goodheart, Eugene
"Modernism and the Critical Spirit," THE FAILURE
OF CRITICISM (Cambridge, Mass. and London:
Harvard University Press, 1978), pp. 8-27 (1980)

On the problems posed by Modernism for the humanist
tradition of criticism.

# Anthologies of the Key Documents of Modernism

MOD 201: Hoffman, Frederick John (ed.)
PERSPECTIVES ON MODERN LITERATURE
(Evanston, Ill. and Elmsford, N.Y.: Row, Peterson and
Co., 1962)

A well-chosen survey from T.E. Hulme, Ezra Pound,
D.H. Lawrence, T.S. Eliot and Hart Crane; from the
first academic critics of Modernism and from subsequent
critics of Modernism in the thirties, forties and fifties.

MOD 202: Shapiro, Karl (ed.)
PROSE KEY TO MODERN POETRY (New York,
Evanston and London: Harper & Row, 1962)

Shapiro "brings together most of the chief prose
documents upon which modern poetry is based and
without which the poetry is all but meaningless. . . . The
essays divide naturally into those of the 'Classical' school
and those of the 'Romantic'." An excellent collection,
including selections from Charles Baudelaire, Arthur
Rimbaud, Edgar Allan Poe, T.E. Hulme, Ernest Fenol-
losa, Ezra Pound, W.B. Yeats, T.S. Eliot, D.H. Lawrence, Wallace Stevens, William Carlos Williams and
W.H. Auden.

# Guides to Modern Writing and to Modernism

MOD 203:  Tindall, William York,
FORCES IN MODERN BRITISH LITERATURE
1885-1946 (New York: Alfred A. Knopf, 1947; revised
2nd edn., New York: Vintage Books, 1956)

A stimulating and thorough cultural and literary history
of the period, including W.B. Yeats, D.H. Lawrence,
Ezra Pound, Wyndham Lewis and T.S. Eliot. "1885 . . .
seemed a good beginning because at that time naturalism
and symbolism began to shape British literature; around
that time Yeats, Shaw, and Moore commenced their work
and Hopkins was in full career; and shortly before that
time Joyce and Virginia Woolf were born." Yeats,
Lawrence, Pound, Lewis and Eliot are placed firmly with
the forces of the Right.


MOD 204:  Fraser, George Sutherland
THE MODERN WRITER AND HIS WORLD
(London: D. Verschoyle, 1953; revised 2nd edn.,
London: A. Deutsch, 1964; Westport, Conn.:
Greenwood, 1965)

"This whole book is an extensive but summary . . .
consideration of the set of tendencies which we call the
'modern movement' in English literature." A comprehensive and highly intelligent survey, containing useful
definitions of the 'modern' in literature, which is
conscious throughout of the various and opposed traditions at work in twentieth-century English fiction, drama
and poetry.


MOD 205:  Stewart, John Innes MacIntosh
EIGHT MODERN WRITERS: THE OXFORD

65

HISTORY OF ENGLISH LITERATURE Vol.12
(Oxford: Clarendon Press, 1963; New York: Oxford
University Press, 1963)

Elegant and illuminating essays on Thomas Hardy, Henry
James, G.B. Shaw, Joseph Conrad, Rudyard Kipling,
W.B. Yeats, James Joyce and D.H. Lawrence. Contains
a comprehensive bibliography.

MOD 206:  Bergonzi, Bernard (ed.)
HISTORY OF LITERATURE IN THE ENGLISH
LANGUAGE: Vol.7 THE TWENTIETH CENTURY
(London: Barrie and Jenkins, 1970)

A series of first-rate essays — particularly on W.B. Yeats,
James Joyce and D.H. Lawrence — which discuss
twentieth-century English fiction, poetry and drama.
Bernard Bergonzi, "The Advent of Modernism
1900-1920," pp. 17-48 (See MOD 19); Thomas Parkinson,
"W.B. Yeats," pp. 49-74 (See WBY 38); Arnold Goldman,
"James Joyce," pp. 75-105; John Goode, "D.H. Law-
rence," pp. 106-52 (See DHL 16); John Fuller, "T.S.
Eliot," pp. 153-79; Malcolm Bradbury, "The Novel in
the 1920s," pp. 180-221; Stephen Wall, "Aspects of the
Novel 1930-1960," pp. 222-76; G.S. Fraser, "English
Poetry 1930-1960," pp. 277-309; G.K. Hunter, "English
Drama 1900-1960," pp. 310-35; Andrew Bear, "Popular
Reading: The New 'Sensation Novel'," pp. 336-61;
David Lodge, "Literary Criticism in England in the
Twentieth Century," pp. 362-403.

MOD 207:  Chapple, J.A.V.
DOCUMENTARY AND IMAGINATIVE
LITERATURE 1880-1920 (London: Blandford Press,
1970; New York: Barnes & Noble, 1970)

Succinct and helpful account of the literary and cultural
developments of the period, which places Modernism in
context.

MOD 208:  Robson, William Wallace
MODERN ENGLISH LITERATURE (London,
Oxford and New York: Oxford University Press, 1970)

A straightforward, well-written guide to twentieth-century English fiction, poetry and drama, with a strong sense of historical context. Discusses the age of G.B. Shaw and H.G. Wells; the Edwardian realists; the poetry of the early twentieth century; James Joyce and D.H. Lawrence; the Bloomsbury Group; T.S. Eliot, Ezra Pound and Gerard Manley Hopkins; from W.H. Auden to George Orwell; literature since 1950.

MOD 209: Bradbury, Malcolm
THE SOCIAL CONTEXT OF MODERN ENGLISH LITERATURE (Oxford: Basil Blackwell, 1971; New York: Schocken, 1971)

An important sociological and cultural study, which discusses how "modernisation" has changed our world, thought and consciousness; examines the impact of these changes on the arts, giving rise to Modernism; and considers the effect social changes have had on the position of the writer and of his profession. Contains an excellent short bibliography.

MOD 210: Gillie, Christopher
MOVEMENTS IN ENGLISH LITERATURE 1900-1940 (Cambridge and New York: Cambridge University Press, 1975)

Clearly written presentation of the major movements in fiction, poetry and drama, covering the Henry James-H.G. Wells debate; Joseph Conrad and D.H. Lawrence; "the recovery of poetry, 1900-1920" by the traditionalists (A.E. Housman, Thomas Hardy and Edward Thomas) and by the modernists (W.B. Yeats, T.S. Eliot); the diversification of the modern novel (James Joyce, Virginia Woolf, Ivy Compton-Burnett and E.M. Forster); the differences between W.H. Auden and George Orwell; late W.B. Yeats and T.S. Eliot; the drama of the period (G.B. Shaw, W.B. Yeats and T.S. Eliot). Contains a useful bibliography.

MOD 211: Bradbury, Malcolm and McFarlane, James Walter
MODERNISM 1890-1930 (Harmondsworth, Middlesex: Penguin, 1976; published in hardback, Hassocks, Sussex:

Harvester Press, 1978; Atlantic Highlands, N.J.:
Humanities Press, 1978)

A collection of essays on Modernism as an international
movement; modernist poetry; modernist fiction; modernist drama. Contains an extensive bibliography.

MOD 212:  Pritchard, William Harrison
SEEING THROUGH EVERYTHING: ENGLISH
WRITERS 1918-1940 (London: Faber and Faber, 1977;
New York: Oxford University Press, 1977)

Discusses the post-war fiction of Aldous Huxley,
G.B. Shaw, Arnold Bennett and Wyndham Lewis;
T.S. Eliot, 1918-1922; D.H. Lawrence, 1920-1930; Ford
Madox Ford, E.M. Forster, Virginia Woolf; Robert
Graves and D.H. Lawrence as poets; T.S. Eliot, Wynd-
ham Lewis, Edgell Rickword and F.R. Leavis as critics;
W.H. Auden, Stephen Spender and Louis MacNeice; the
satirists of the thirties: Evelyn Waugh; Anthony Powell;
George Orwell and Wyndham Lewis; T.S. Eliot's *Four
Quartets*. A spirited revision of current literary history, in
which the objectivity and insight of Wyndham Lewis (and
of T.S. Eliot) are counterposed to the subjectivism
and self-deception of the others.

MOD 213:  Bell, Michael (ed.)
THE CONTEXT OF ENGLISH LITERATURE
1900-1930 (London: Methuen, 1980; New York: Holmes
and Meier, 1980)

Six survey essays on modern themes. Contains: Michael
Bell, "Introduction: modern movements in literature,"
pp. 1-93 (a wide-ranging assessment of the 'modern' and
the 'modernist' in the English literature of the period);
Fred Reid, "The disintegration of Liberalism, 1895-
1931," pp. 94-125; David Holdcroft, "From the one to
the many: philosophy 1900-1930," pp. 126-59 (an excellent account of the philosophical developments of the
period and of their influence upon the modernists);
Christopher Nash, "Myth and modern literature,"
pp. 160-85; R.A. Gekoski, "Freud and English literature
1900-1930," pp. 186-217; Cyril Barrett, "Revolutions in
the visual arts," pp. 218-40 (discusses developments in
painting and cinema). Contains useful short bibliographies.

# Literary Modernism and the Other Arts

MOD 214: Sypher, Wylie
"The Cubist Perspective," ROCOCO TO CUBISM IN ART AND LITERATURE (New York: Random House, 1960), pp. 255-330

Discusses the links between Cubism and literary Modernism.

MOD 215: Praz, Mario
MNEMOSYNE: THE PARALLEL BETWEEN LITERATURE AND THE VISUAL ARTS (Princeton, N.J.: Princeton University Press, 1970)

Contains references to the influence of modern art on literary Modernism.

MOD 216: Smith, John
THE ARTS BETRAYED (London: Herbert Press, 1978; New York: Universe, 1978)

"The intention of this book is to show how, through their various media, certain artists, because of an innate temperamental affinity or the deliberate pursuit of a particular philosophy of art, develop in an extraordinarily similar manner." Links W.B. Yeats with Béla Bartók; T.S. Eliot with Igor Stravinsky and Pablo Picasso; Samuel Beckett with Alberto Giacometti and Francis Bacon.

# Part II
# WILLIAM BUTLER YEATS
# 1865-1939

# Bibliographical Information

For the standard bibliography of Yeats's writings, see the revised edition of Allan Wade's A BIBLIOGRAPHY OF THE WRITINGS OF W.B. YEATS, revised and edited by Russell K. Alspach (London: Rupert Hart-Davis, 1968).

For the most recent and fullest annotated bibliography of criticism of W.B. Yeats, see K.P.S. Jochum's monumental W.B. YEATS: A CLASSIFIED BIBLIOGRAPHY OF CRITICISM (Chicago and London: University of Illinois Press, 1978; Folkestone: Dawson, 1978). This not only includes additions to Allan Wade's *Bibliography of the Writings of W.B. Yeats*, but also provides a comprehensive account of criticism dealing with the Irish and Dramatic Revival. It supersedes all other bibliographies of criticism of Yeats.

For the best bibliographical essay on criticism of Yeats, see Richard J. Finneran, "W.B. Yeats," ANGLO-IRISH LITERATURE: A REVIEW OF RESEARCH, edited by Richard J. Finneran (New York: The Modern Language Association of America, 1976), pp. 216-314. This comprehensive and spirited essay covers, with wit and erudition, the various editions of Yeats's writings and letters, biographies and background materials, specialist studies on Yeats and articles in journals. Well-organised according to theme, astringent in its judgements, it is a model of its kind.

# Memoirs and Biographies

WBY 1:     Gwynn, Stephen L. (ed.)
           SCATTERING BRANCHES: TRIBUTE TO THE
           MEMORY OF W.B. YEATS (London and New York:
           Macmillan, 1940). Reprinted under the title WILLIAM
           BUTLER YEATS: ESSAYS IN TRIBUTE (Port
           Washington, N.Y.: Kennikat Press, 1965)

           The most important collection of contemporary memoirs,

with contributions by Stephen Gwynn, "Scattering Branches," pp. 1-14; Maud Gonne, "Yeats and Ireland," pp. 15-33 (a tribute to Yeats's nationalist activities); Sir William Rothenstein, "Yeats as a Painter saw Him," pp. 35-54; Lennox Robinson, "The Man and the Dramatist," pp. 55-114; W.G. Fay, "The Poet and the Actor," pp. 115-34; Edmund Dulac, "Without the Twilight," pp. 135-44; F.R. Higgins, "Yeats as Irish Poet," pp. 145-55 (on his debt to the Gaelic); C. Day Lewis, "A Note on W.B. Yeats and the Aristocratic Tradition," pp. 157-82; L.A.G. Strong, "William Butler Yeats," pp. 183-229 (on his occult interests).

WBY 2:     Hone, Joseph
W.B. YEATS 1865-1939 (London: Macmillan, 1942)

The 'official' biography, authorised by Yeats's widow. The account is reticent and uncritical, lacking judgement on Yeats's achievements and failures as a writer.

WBY 3:     Ellmann, Richard
YEATS: THE MAN AND THE MASKS (London and New York: Macmillan, 1948; New York: E.P. Dutton, 1958) (1978)

A critical biography which details Yeats's constant search for unity. The work concentrates upon Yeats's difficult relations with his father, and was a pioneer in giving prominence to Yeats's debts to Theosophy and the Order of the Golden Dawn.

WBY 4:     Jeffares, Alexander Norman
W.B. YEATS: MAN AND POET (London: Routledge & Kegan Paul, 1949; New Haven: Yale University Press, 1949)

A biographical-critical study, which provides valuable information about Yeats's family and circle. The reading of Yeats's poetry in the light of his biography is less successful.

WBY 5:     Ellmann, Richard
           THE IDENTITY OF YEATS (London: Macmillan,
           1954; New York: Oxford University Press, 1954)

           One of the key studies on Yeats, tracing the development
           of his style and thought throughout his career. Discusses
           Yeats's roles as seer, victim and assessor; the importance
           of "moods" rather than "belief" in his poetry; the nature
           and use of iconography; the ideas of *A Vision* and their
           influence on his poetry; his style and rhetoric; his attitudes
           to Asia and Europe. A seminal and exemplary study.

WBY 6:     Moore, Virginia
           THE UNICORN: WILLIAM BUTLER YEATS'
           SEARCH FOR REALITY (New York: Macmillan,
           1954)

           A somewhat chaotic intellectual biography, which sets
           out to provide an account of Yeats's life and ideas. It
           discusses Yeats's relationship with Maud Gonne, and
           considers the debt of his philosophy to esoteric and
           Eastern sources; its links with Christianity; the synthesis
           of these in *A Vision*. Contains much interesting
           information, badly presented.

WBY 7:     Jeffares, Alexander Norman
           THE CIRCUS ANIMALS: ESSAYS ON
           W.B. YEATS (London: Macmillan, 1970; Stanford:
           Stanford University Press, 1970)

           A collection of background essays, by one of the foremost
           authorities on Yeats: "Yeats's Mask," pp. 3-14 (on the
           theory of the mask); "Yeats, Public Man," pp. 15-28 (on
           Yeats's political career); "Poet's Tower," pp. 29-46 (on
           the tower symbol and Yeats's debts to Milton and
           Shelley); "Yeats, Critic," pp. 47-77; "Women in Yeats's
           Poetry," pp. 78-102 (the treatment of women changes as
           Yeats matures and marries); "Gyres in Yeats's Poetry,"
           pp. 103-14 (succinct account of *A Vision*); "John Butler
           Yeats, Anglo-Irishman," pp. 117-46 (on the relations
           between Yeats and his father); "Oliver St. John Gogarty,
           Irishman," pp. 147-74 (on their friendship and possible
           collaboration).

WBY 8:   Webster, Brenda Ann Schwabacher
YEATS: A PSYCHOANALYTIC STUDY (Stanford:
Stanford University Press, 1973; London: Macmillan,
1974)

Traces the links between Yeats's traumatic childhood
experiences, particularly the "non-existent" relationship
with his mother, and his later life and work; his sexual
anxieties, his dependence upon Lady Gregory; the escape
motifs; the father-son theme; the relationship with Maud
Gonne; the concept of the mask which allowed him to
explore and control his psychic anxieties. In old age,
"Yeats's earlier fears of castration and loss of integrity
were reawakened by declining potency and approaching
death. The heroic mask no longer sufficed." Yeats turned
to the use of "talismanic objects." Contains a wide-
ranging discussion of the poetry and plays.

WBY 9:   Lynch, David
YEATS: THE POETICS OF THE SELF (Chicago and
London: University of Chicago Press, 1979)

Discusses the "narcissistic origins of the poet's creativity." The Oedipal account is inadequate. Yeats needed
not only to overcome but to create the powerful Oedipal
antagonist against which he "forms and malforms"
himself: "The poet's need to 'create' his precursors is an
expression of his even more fundamental need to create
himself." An important contribution to the biographical
studies of Yeats.

# Guides, Commentaries and Concordances

WBY 10:   Saul, George Brandon
PROLEGOMENA TO THE STUDY OF YEATS'S
POEMS (Philadelphia: University of Pennsylvania
Press, 1957; London: Oxford University Press, 1958)
(1970)

WBY 11:   Saul, George Brandon
PROLEGOMENA TO THE STUDY OF YEATS'S

PLAYS (Philadelphia: University of Pennsylvania Press, 1958) (1970)

Each book provides basic information about dates of composition and of publication, with cross-references to other works and useful annotations. Superseded by Jeffares (WBY 13 and WBY 14).

WBY 12:  Unterecker, John
A READER'S GUIDE TO WILLIAM BUTLER YEATS (New York: Noonday Press, 1959; London: Thames and Hudson, 1959)

Provides basic information the reader "will need in order to come to an intelligent evaluation of these poems."

WBY 13:  Jeffares, Alexander Norman
A COMMENTARY ON THE COLLECTED POEMS OF W.B. YEATS (London: Macmillan, 1968; Stanford: Stanford University Press, 1968)

Provides not only information about dates of composition and of publication, but also annotates and explicates. An indispensable guide to the *Collected Poems*.

WBY 14:  Jeffares, Alexander Norman and Knowland, A.S.
A COMMENTARY ON THE COLLECTED PLAYS OF W.B. YEATS (London and New York: Macmillan, 1975; Stanford: Stanford University Press, 1975)

A commentary on the plays published in the *Collected Plays*. Indispensable scholarly commentary by a leading Yeats scholar.

# Introductory Studies

WBY 15:  Rajan, Balachandra
W.B. YEATS: A CRITICAL INTRODUCTION (London: Hutchinson, 1965; 2nd edn., with revised bibliography, 1969)

The best introductory study. Yeats is placed in the mainstream of English poetry and his major poems and plays are summarised and convincingly explicated: "The driving force in Yeats's poetry is the assertion of man's creative power against the strength of circumstance. . . . It is also a deep sense of man as the continuing battleground and of tension and combat as the springs of his being."

WBY 16:     Donoghue, Denis
YEATS (London: Fontana/Collins, 1971; New York: Viking Press, 1971, under the title *W.B. YEATS*)

An exploration of Yeats's "sensibility," which, influenced by Nietzsche, is seen to be preoccupied with "power," "conflict" and the creative urgency of the imagination. Somewhat disappointing as an introductory study of the poet.

WBY 17:     Malins, Edward
A PREFACE TO YEATS (London: Longman, 1974; New York: Charles Scribner's Sons, 1975) (1977)

A straightforward and useful introductory guide to Yeats's background, his view of Irish history, his reading, his friends and acquaintances, with a discussion of some of his early, middle and late poetry.

# Full-length Studies of the Work of W.B. Yeats

WBY 18:     Ure, Peter
TOWARDS A MYTHOLOGY: STUDIES IN THE POETRY OF W.B. YEATS (Liverpool: Liverpool University Press, 1946; 2nd edn., New York: Russell and Russell, 1967)

Ure argues that Yeats used myth to provide "a story, a framework of action and event, at once sufficiently firm to support passion and conflict, and sufficiently plastic for its meaning to be adapted to suit the personal poetic end." Discusses the Cuchulain plays, "In Memory of Major

Robert Gregory," *A Vision*, and the Crazy Jane poems.
Ure argues for the uniqueness of Yeats's poetic practice
— a practice which had little influence on his contemporaries.

WBY 19:    Henn, Thomas Rice
THE LONELY TOWER: STUDIES IN THE
POETRY OF W.B. YEATS (London: Methuen, 1950;
2nd edn., revised and enlarged, 1965) (1980)

A pioneering and still valuable study, which emphasises
both the importance of Yeats's Irish context and the
influence upon him of European sources. Presents
separate chapers on the Irish background; the theory of
the self and the anti-self; women in Yeats's poetry; Yeats
and J.M. Synge; the development of style; image and
symbol; myth and magic; *A Vision* and the interpretation
of history; Byzantium; the influence of painting on the
poems; the poetry of the plays; the mature style; and the
prophetic quality of the last poems.

WBY 20:    Winters, Yvor
THE POETRY OF W.B. YEATS (Denver, Col.: Allan
Swallow, 1960)

A sustained argument against Yeats's high standing, by
the foremost anti-modernist critic. "He has become a
standard of judgement for critics, with the result that the
work of better poets has been obscured or minimized; and
he has become a model for imitation, with the result that
the work of a good many talented poets has been damaged
beyond repair." For Winters, Yeats's poetry cannot be
separated from his irrational and anti-democratic beliefs.
His poetry must be rejected, along with the beliefs it
expresses and embodies. Throughout, his poetry is
marred by inflation and excessive dramatisation. A fine
polemical assault, well-sustained and well-argued.

WBY 21:    Engelberg, Edward
THE VAST DESIGN: PATTERNS IN
W.B. YEATS'S AESTHETIC (Toronto: University of
Toronto Press, 1964)

One of the most valuable studies on Yeats, explicating the nature of his poetics, and distinguishing his creative principles from those of the other modernists. Yeats was a European writer, with a scope derived from Goethe, Balzac and Nietzsche. The Yeatsian aesthetic was founded upon the poet's philosophy of history, which he took from the discussion of Greek and Renaissance art and culture in Walter Pater. In order to achieve (as had been the case in the greatest periods of European art) epic grandeur, with lyric intensity and dramatic tension, Yeats attempted to reconcile the three great elements of European literature: epic, drama and lyric. This attempt necessarily affected the subject matter and the treatment of his poetry and of his drama. "The single poet, still creating within a vast design which reflected, like a single image, the whole of a nation's traditions, 'the race' and 'the reality', that was Yeats's great aim as an artist. . . . To help stabilise the equilibrium of the European mind was for Yeats the responsibility of the modern poet." The study concludes with a detailed discussion of "The Statues" and of its parallelisms between ancient Greece and contemporary Ireland.

WBY 22:    Zwerdling, Alex
YEATS AND THE HEROIC IDEAL (New York: New York University Press, 1965)

Zwerdling discusses the different forms in which the hero appears in Yeats's work — the Irish hero, the aristocrat, the public hero and the visionary. An indirect approach to Yeats's supposed authoritarian leanings, it has been superseded by more recent and better studies.

WBY 23:    Bloom, Harold
YEATS (New York: Oxford University Press, 1970)

"Yeats was a poet very much in the line of vision; his ancestry in English poetic tradition were primarily Blake and Shelley, and his achievement will be judged against theirs. One of the purposes of this book is to indicate such a judgement . . . I have tried to study the major relations of Yeats's work to the English poetic tradition rather than to any of the esoteric traditions that Yeats clearly invokes." In the first six chapters, Bloom discusses the

influence of Walter Pater, William Blake and Percy
Bysshe Shelley; then, in broadly chronological order,
discusses the poetry, philosophical writings, and plays of
Yeats. For Bloom, Yeats was both the last representative,
and the betrayer, of the tradition of Blake and Shelley.
When judged against them, his achievement has been
overrated. A major and controversial study.

WBY 24:    Albright, Daniel Frank
           THE MYTH AGAINST MYTH: A STUDY OF
           YEATS'S IMAGINATION IN OLD AGE (London:
           Oxford University Press, 1972)

           A subtle study which argues that Yeats constructed his
           own personality by means of poetry, and traces the stages
           of Yeats's self as it is embodied in and created by his
           poetry. Concentrates upon "The Tower," *The Wander-
           ings of Oisin*, "News for the Delphic Oracle" and "The
           Circus Animals' Desertion."

WBY 25:    Young, Dudley
           OUT OF IRELAND: A READING OF YEATS'S
           POETRY (Cheadle Hulme, Cheshire: Carcanet Press,
           1975; New York: Persea Books, 1979)

           Yeats was a "poet-mage," experiencing that dispossess-
           sion which has been experienced by all the great
           modernist poets. "What gave his poetry such a wide
           metaphoric range was that his Irish situation was
           analogous to that of Western Europe about to shatter its
           traditional culture in the Great War." Stimulating account
           of Yeats's poetry.

# Full-length Studies of Yeats's Irish and European Context

WBY 26:    Stock, Amy Geraldine
           W.B. YEATS: HIS POETRY AND THOUGHT
           (Cambridge: Cambridge University Press, 1961)

           A detailed and cogent discussion of the thought in Yeats's

poetry and plays. The study considers "Yeats's lifelong preoccupation with his Irish inheritance"; his sense, in the early poems, that "he was recovering a way of thought very deep in himself and very ancient in the mind of Europe, although it was no longer a living reality in England"; his quest, in his middle years, for an epic voice and the political attitudes this engendered; his sense, in his later poems, of the breakdown and rebirth of civilisation. Discusses in detail *The Countess Cathleen*, *The Land of Heart's Desire*, and *A Vision*. One of the most helpful discussions of Yeats.

WBY 27:    Kain, Richard Morgan
DUBLIN IN THE AGE OF W.B. YEATS AND JAMES JOYCE (Norman: University of Oklahoma Press, 1962; Newton Abbott: David and Charles, 1972)

An informative guide to literary Dublin, which provides a lively portrait of the literary and political world in which Yeats lived and worked.

WBY 28:    Torchiana, Donald Thornhill
W.B. YEATS AND GEORGIAN IRELAND (Evanston: Northwestern University Press, 1966; London: Oxford University Press, 1966)

"This book will show his rebellion against Protestant Ireland, his return to it, his glorification of its golden age, and his continuous disappointment in its weakness and hesitation. . . . I see Yeats's identification with the Protestant nation as primarily intellectual, only partly social, and hardly at all religious." Torchiana discusses Yeats's disillusion with the patriotic literature and ideals of nineteenth-century Ireland and his ambiguous admiration for the old Protestant Ascendancy; reviews Yeats's friendship with the Gregorys; defines what in eighteenth- · century Ireland's Protestant culture so attracted Yeats; examines, in separate chapters, Yeats's enthusiasm for Swift, Burke, Berkeley, and Goldsmith; surveys the use to which Yeats put the theme of Georgian Ireland in his poetry; concludes with "an analysis of *On the Boiler*, where, in the play *Purgatory*, Yeats seems to have reached some rather grim conclusions on the progress of modern Ireland since the French Revolution and the Union."

WBY 29:    Marcus, Phillip Leduc
           YEATS AND THE BEGINNING OF THE IRISH
           RENAISSANCE (Ithaca and London: Cornell
           University Press, 1970)

           An excellent account of Yeats's activities as a writer
           between 1885 and 1899. Marcus discusses Yeats's ideals
           for Irish literature, and the controversies which followed
           with Sir Charles Gavan Duffy, Edward Dowden and John
           Eglinton. Concludes with a fine account of Yeats's
           contribution to the Irish dramatic revival.

WBY 30:    Eddins, Dwight Lyman
           YEATS: THE NINETEENTH CENTURY MATRIX
           (University, Ala.: University of Alabama Press, 1971)

           Eddins places Yeats's poetry in its late Romantic context,
           showing the development of his early poetry from a
           pictorial to a dramatic mode, and traces its relation to the
           poetry of John Keats, Percy Bysshe Shelley, Thomas
           Davis, William Allingham, Samuel Ferguson, Alfred,
           Lord Tennyson, D.G. Rossetti, William Morris, Lionel
           Johnson, Ernest Dowson and Matthew Arnold. Con-
           cludes with a discussion of Yeats's symbolism, his debt to
           the Golden Dawn and to the French Symbolists. Yeats
           dramatises the lyric, finding thereby an aesthetic machin-
           ery to express his sense of the "tragic arena" of Irish
           political and cultural life. A thorough and important study
           of Yeats's early poetry and of its cultural context.

WBY 31:    Snukal, Robert
           HIGH TALK: THE PHILOSOPHICAL POETRY OF
           W.B. YEATS (Cambridge: Cambridge University Press,
           1973)

           "Yeats's knowledge of Kant provided him with an
           epistemological theory that supported his 'romantic'
           stance, and which rejected the transcendentalism of most
           of the philosophical positions normally described as
           idealism." Provides an opening discussion of Kant;
           defines Yeats's theory of the imagination which provides
           "a key to Yeats's ideas about history, philosophy and art,
           and the phenomenal world itself." Examines, in separate

chapters, Yeats's treatment of Kantian themes: "Art, History and the Phenomenal World"; "Freedom and Necessity". Concludes with an analysis of "Among School Children." A demanding but rewarding study.

WBY 32:　Harris, Daniel Arthur
YEATS: COOLE PARK AND BALLYLEE
(Baltimore and London: Johns Hopkins University Press, 1974)

One of the few outstanding studies of Yeats, which discusses the poetry Yeats wrote about Coole Park (Lady Gregory's estate) and his own tower at Ballylee; sets it in the context of Yeats's preoccupation with the ideals of Georgian Anglo-Ireland; and examines Yeats's debt to Irish tradition and to the writings of Castiglione and Ben Jonson. "Because Byzantium could never be possessed, it could never be lost: a safe utopia. With Coole Park and Thoor Ballylee, Yeats attempted something more difficult: his territory was an incipient Eden, perpetually awaiting redemption, perpetually endangered by chaos. The twin myths of paradise regained and paradise lost go hand in hand to produce the emotion of tragic joy which . . . Yeats so relentlessly pursued. He included in his territory the West of Ireland's own psychic nemesis, the dread of physical invasion; the West had resisted English domination and thus retained its Irish character intact."

WBY 33:　Meir, Colin
THE BALLADS AND SONGS OF W.B. YEATS: THE ANGLO-IRISH HERITAGE IN SUBJECT AND STYLE (London: Macmillan, 1974; New York: Barnes & Noble, 1974)

Discusses the ballads and songs of Yeats, their origins in popular culture, and their influence upon his major poetry. An important account.

# Articles on the Work and Career of W.B. Yeats

WBY 34:　Eliot, Thomas Stearns
"Yeats," ON POETRY AND POETS (London: Faber

and Faber, 1957; New York: Farrar, Straus and Cudahy, 1957), pp. 252-62

A commemorative address delivered in 1940 to the Friends of the Irish Academy at the Abbey Theatre, Dublin. Its importance is twofold. First, Eliot declared that Yeats had no influence upon him as a young poet: "I cannot remember that his poetry at that stage made any deep impression upon me." Second, he argued — in a way which has been very influential — that 'Yeats is pre-eminently a poet of middle age." There was in his work a lack of complete emotional expression: ". . . what Yeats did in the middle and later years is a great and permanent example — which poets-to-come should study with reverence — of what I have called Character of the Artist; a kind of moral, as well as intellectual, excellence." Even so, he did not wish to give the impression "that the poetry and the plays of Yeats's earlier period can be ignored in favour of his later work. You cannot divide the work of a great poet so sharply as that." We also have to take into account the historical conditions: "Yeats was born into the end of a literary movement, and an English movement at that. . . . Born into a world in which the doctrine of 'Art for Art's sake' was generally accepted, and living on into one in which art has been asked to be instrumental to social purposes, he held firmly to the right view which is between these, though not in any way a compromise between them, and showed that an artist, by serving his art with entire integrity, is at the same time rendering the greatest service he can to his own nation and to the whole world." To some aspects of Yeats, Eliot felt unsympathetic. But he was "one of those few whose history is the history of their own time, who are part of the consciousness of an age which cannot be understood without them."

WBY 35:    Kermode, (John) Frank
THE ROMANTIC IMAGE (London: Routledge & Kegan Paul, 1957; New York: Macmillan, 1958)

Contains an important discussion of Yeats's poetry; of its Symbolist antecedents and procedures. (See MOD 7).

WBY 36:    Kenner, Hugh

"The Sacred Book of the Arts," GNOMON (New York: McDowell Obolensky, 1958), pp. 9-29

We should judge the poet by the individual volume rather than by the individual poem: "Each volume of his verse . . . is a large-scale work, like a book of the Bible."

WBY 37:     Stead, Christian Karlson
THE NEW POETIC: YEATS TO ELIOT (London: Hutchinson, 1964), pp. 7-45

Contains an important discussion of Yeats's poetic techniques; of their development; of their public rhetoric. (See MOD 127).

WBY 38:     Parkinson, Thomas
"W.B. Yeats," HISTORY OF LITERATURE IN THE ENGLISH LANGUAGE: Vol.7 THE TWENTIETH CENTURY, ed. Bernard Bergonzi (London: Barrie and Jenkins, 1970), pp. 49-74

Perhaps the best short essay on Yeats, placing him in the context of modern poetry and defining his strengths and limitations.

WBY 39:     Murphy, Sheila Ann
"William Butler Yeats: Enemy of the Irish People," *Literature and Ideology*, No.8 (1971), 15-30

Yeats's poetic vision served the interests of the British.

WBY 40:     Sage, Lorna
"Hardy, Yeats and Tradition," VICTORIAN POETRY, ed. Malcolm Bradbury and David Palmer (London: Edward Arnold, 1972), pp. 254-75

A brilliant and important essay, which compares Thomas Hardy and W.B. Yeats: "The poets of the closing years of the century resist any simply evolutionary scheme — Yeats's and Hardy's versions of the poet's role are incompatible because they both presuppose 'traditions,' very different ones, which are acts of will, not a common inheritance." Considers also the significance of the idea of "Renaissance" in Yeats's criticism.

WBY 41:     Allen, James Lovic
"The Road to Byzantium: Archetypal Criticism and Yeats," *Journal of Aesthetics and Art Criticism*, 32:1 (Fall 1973), 53-64

On the inadequacy of mythopoeic and archetypal approaches to Yeats.

WBY 42:     Allen, James Lovic
"Unity of Archetype, Myth, and Religious Imagery in the Work of Yeats," *Twentieth Century Literature*, 20:2 (April 1974), 91-5

On the motifs of Yeats's "monomyth" — the union of human being and God.

# Anthologies on the Work and Career of W.B. Yeats

WBY 43:     Hall, James and Steinmann, Martin (eds.)
THE PERMANENCE OF YEATS (New York: Macmillan, 1950)

An outstanding collection, which brings together the best of the early criticism about Yeats.
James Hall and Martin Steinmann, "The Seven Sacred Trances," pp. 1-8. Justifies the high estimation of Yeats and reviews criticism to date.
Untitled excerpts from the work of the following:
J. Middleton Murry, pp. 9-13. Discusses Yeats's failures as a poet.
Edmund Wilson, pp. 14-37. Discusses the stages of Yeats's poetic career. A poet in the Symbolist tradition, his later poetry is to be preferred.
R.P. Blackmur, pp. 38-59. Reprints a classic essay on Yeats: "The Later Poetry of W.B. Yeats." "Magic performs for Yeats the same fructifying function that Christianity does for Eliot...". But it also prevents him

from the fullest achievement as a poet of his age.

Cleanth Brooks, Jr., pp. 60-84. Discusses Yeats's *A Vision*, "the most ambitious attempt by any poet of our time to set up a 'myth'." This 'myth' is "imaginatively true. . .". Contains detailed discussions of "Sailing to Byzantium" and "Byzantium."

J.C. Ransom, pp. 85-96. "Yeats was born into a barren or irreligious age, and lived to see it become a naturalistic one. That was the background against which he had to exercise his gift of poetry which, like that of Shakespeare and Donne and Milton, was a gift for splendid metaphysical imagery. His importance to us . . . is that . . . he has saved our poetic tradition in its dignity."

Allen Tate, pp. 97-105. Yeats's poetry "is nearer the centre of our main traditions of sensibility and thought than the poetry of Eliot or of Pound." Foresees over-ingenious criticism in the future.

David Daiches, pp. 106-24. "System, order, ritual — these Yeats sought not for their own sake, not because as a man he could have chosen to subordinate his mind and body to a traditional discipline, but because he needed them as a poet, to help him achieve adequate poetic expression." Discusses very ably Yeats's early poetry.

Arthur Mizener, pp. 125-45. ". . . the greatness of the later poetry is a kind of greatness inherent in the '90's attitude."

F.R. Leavis, pp. 146-59. "Mr. Yeats's career, magnificent as the triumph was that he compelled out of defeat, is a warning. It illustrates the special disability of the poet in the last century, and impressively bears out my argument about the poetic tradition." Yeats's Irish background provided a "source of strength" unavailable to the modern English poet.

Stephen Spender, pp. 160-72. "Yeats has found no subject of moral significance in the social life of his time . . . . What one admires in Yeats's poetry is . . . its passion, its humanity, its occasional marvellous lucidity, its technical mastery, its integrity, its strength, its reality and its opportunism.... [But] Yeats's poetry is devoid of any unifying moral subject, and it develops in a perpetual search for one."

D.S. Savage, pp. 173-94. ". . . it is from the point of view of aestheticism that we must consider the career of W.B. Yeats." He "made a 'religion' of art which means in effect that he neutralised religion. His poetry, lacking an inner spiritual pressure directed upon life, developed in a vacuum."

One of the best and most subtle criticisms of Yeats's aestheticism.

Joseph Warren Beach, pp. 195-9. Short account, contrasting early and mature Yeats. "It was his weakness and misfortune that [his] discipline had . . . no common terms with the systematic knowledge and reason of his time."

Austin Warren, pp. 200-12. "Yeats needed religion less as a man than as a poet, and his need was epistemological and metaphysical; he needed to believe that poetry is a form of knowledge and power, not of amusement."

Eric Bentley, pp. 213-23. Discusses Yeats's drama; the nature of his theatre; and the reasons why he did not become a major dramatist.

Kenneth Burke, pp. 224-37. Discusses "some basic correlations of theme, or motif, in Yeats, noting how the Many are collapsed into the One and the One is ramified into the Many."

W.Y. Tindall, pp. 238-49. Discusses Yeats's debt to the European Symbolist tradition.

Donald Davidson, pp. 250-6. Discusses Yeats's relation to popular lore.

Elder Olson, pp. 257-69. Discusses "Sailing to Byzantium" as a lyric.

A. Norman Jeffares, pp. 270-6. Examines the draft versions of some of Yeats's poems to detect his methods of poetic creation.

Delmore Schwartz, pp. 277-95. Outlines the book someone should write to give a picture of the real Yeats, stressing Yeats in Europe, in Ireland, in himself, and in his lyric poetry.

T.S. Eliot, pp. 296-307. Reprints Eliot's lecture on Yeats. (WBY 34).

W.H. Auden, pp. 308-14. Discusses Yeats's legacy: "First, he transformed . . . the occasional poem . . . into a serious reflective poem." Second, "Yeats released regular stanziac poetry . . . from iambic monotony."

Morton Dauwen Zabel, pp. 315-26. "Yeats's realities are the realities of our human capacity for vitality and sincerity."

Walter E. Houghton, pp. 327-48. Discusses the heroic theme in Yeats.

The volume also contains an exhaustive bibliography of items on Yeats until 1950.

WBY 44:   Unterecker, John (ed.)
YEATS: A COLLECTION OF CRITICAL ESSAYS
(Englewood Cliffs, N.J.: Prentice-Hall, 1963)

Reprints valuable essays and excerpts from books on
Yeats by John Unterecker, "Introduction," pp. 1-6;
W.H. Auden, "In Memory of W.B. Yeats," pp. 7-9;
Hugh Kenner, "The Sacred Book of the Arts," pp. 10-22
(WBY 36); John Unterecker, "Faces and False Faces,"
pp. 23-32; Giorgio Melchiori, "The Moment of
Moments," pp. 33-6; Frank Kermode, "The Artist in
Isolation," pp. 37-42; W.Y. Tindall, "The Symbolism of
W.B. Yeats," pp. 43-53; T.S. Eliot, "Yeats," pp. 54-63
(WBY 34); R.P. Blackmur, "W.B. Yeats: Between
Myth and Philosophy," pp. 64-79; Alex Zwerdling,
"W.B. Yeats: Variations on the Visionary Quest,"
pp. 80-92; Curtis Bradford: "Yeats's Byzantium Poems:
A Study of their Development," pp. 93-130; D.J. Gor-
don and Ian Fletcher, "Byzantium," pp. 131-8; A.G.
Stock, "*A Vision*," pp. 139-54; Allen Tate, "Yeats'
Romanticism," pp. 155-62; Richard Ellmann, "Reality,"
pp. 163-74.


WBY 45:   Donoghue, Denis (ed.)
THE INTEGRITY OF YEATS (Cork: Mercier Press,
1964; Folcroft, Pa.: Folcroft, 1971)

A series of lectures by leading Yeats scholars.
   Denis Donoghue: "Yeats and Modern Poetry: An
Introduction," pp. 9-20. "Yeats, rather than Eliot or
Pound, would point the new poet towards a more 'public'
poetry, a poetry which will uphold Man's intelligence, his
reverence for human life, and his involvement in the
common life of feeling."
   A. Norman Jeffares: "Yeats the Public Man," pp.
21-32. "When a born poet decides to become a public
man, his struggle has a peculiar intensity about it, for he
must manage two personalities. . . . This pull between
public and private . . . is part of a conflict that waged
incessantly within Yeats throughout his life."
   T.R. Henn: "Yeats's Symbolism," pp. 33-46. Discusses Yeats's symbolism, with particular reference to his
tower and swan symbols.

Frank Kermode: "Players and Painted Stage," pp. 47-57. Discusses Yeats's dramatic theories and their limitations.

Donald Davie: "Yeats, the Master of a Trade," pp. 59-70. "Yeats . . . was very thoroughly and completely a *professional* poet."

WBY 46:     Donoghue, Denis and Mulryne, James Ronald (eds.) AN HONOURED GUEST: NEW ESSAYS ON W.B. YEATS (London: Edward Arnold, 1965; New York: St. Martin's, 1966)

A collection of essays, of most use to an advanced student of Yeats.

Charles Tomlinson: "Yeats and the Practising Poet," pp. 1-7. On Yeats's Nietzschean ability to remake himself and his verse.

Northrop Frye: "The Rising of the Moon: A Study of *A Vision*," pp. 8-33. On the system of *A Vision* and on its status as a work of the imagination. One of the key essays on *A Vision*.

T.R. Henn: "*The Green Helmet* and *Responsibilities*," pp. 34-53. On the context of these volumes.

Graham Martin: "*The Wild Swans at Coole*," pp. 54-72. On the two volumes published under this title.

Donald Davie: "*Michael Robartes and the Dancer*," pp. 73-87. On the treatment of the role of women in society.

John Holloway: "Style and World in *The Tower*," pp. 88-105. Yeats's supposedly "colloquial style" is in fact concerned with the philosophical relationship between the subject, language and reality.

Denis Donoghue: "On *The Winding Stair*," pp. 106-23. On the quest for value in a world of transience and death.

J.R. Mulryne: "The *Last Poems*," pp. 124-42. Discusses the themes of the sculptured image and of "tragic joy" in the *Last Poems*.

Peter Ure: "The Plays," pp. 143-64. On the principles which governed Yeats's drama and their limitations.

Ian Fletcher: "Rhythm and Pattern in *Autobiographies*," pp. 165-89. Gives an account of the ways in which Yeats attempted to pattern his life.

WBY 47:     Jeffares, Alexander Norman and Cross, Kenneth G.W.
(eds.)
IN EXCITED REVERIE: A CENTENARY
TRIBUTE TO WILLIAM BUTLER YEATS 1865-1965
(London: Macmillan, 1965; New York: St. Martin's,
1965)

An important collection of original essays, which,
accepting Yeats's status as a major modern poet,
concentrates upon his literary and historical context.

W.R. Rodgers: "William Butler Yeats: A Dublin
Portrait," pp. 1-13. Reminiscences by Yeats's contemporaries.

Lennox Robinson: "William Butler Yeats: Personality," pp. 14-23. ". . . recollections, but perhaps they help
to paint a personality, the greatest I have ever known."

A. Norman Jeffares: "John Butler Yeats," pp. 24-47.
Portrait of the poet's father. The period of his influence on
his son "extended further than the early period of
W.B. Yeats's life."

David Daiches: "The Earlier Poems: Some Themes
and Patterns," pp. 48-67.

> I do not want to make too great a claim for the quality
> and interest of Yeats's earlier poetry, but I believe that
> a fair amount of it is of real interest... . Nothing is more
> striking in Yeats's development as a poet than his
> gradual replacement of a two-term by a three-term
> dialectic. His early poems are full of simple contrasts
> between pairs, and such contrasts often provide the
> basic poetic structure: man versus nature, the domesti-
> cated versus the wild . . . the human versus the faery,
> the temporal versus the changeless, the modern versus
> the ancient.

One of the best essays on Yeats's early poetry.

Hugh MacDiarmid: "Ingenium Omnia Vincit," p. 68.

Edward Engelberg: " 'He Too Was in Arcadia': Yeats
and the Paradox of the Fortunate Fall," pp. 69-92.
Discusses Yeats's debt to Walter Pater. He refused, with
Pater, to acknowledge Death "as a destroyer of a life not
worth a conscious living . . . in this he stands on the
threshold of a kind of 'modernity' we now associate with
the name of Freud, for whom an unchallenged 'death
wish' becomes untenable, and who in later life elevated
Eros and the urge to live...". It is wrong to see the early
Yeats as a hopeless romantic or aesthete: his early poetry

is that of a 'practical visionary.' "Yeats's Arcadia, as a fallen Eden, makes mortality worth its own rewards." An important, scholarly essay on Yeats's early poetry.

A.G. Stock: "Yeats on Spenser," pp. 93-101. Discusses Yeats's changing attitudes to Spenser and his poetry.

T.R. Henn: "The Rhetoric of Yeats," pp. 102-22. "Yeats's technique seems to follow the traditional 'devices' to be found in the Renaissance textbooks of rhetoric...". He "is a professional and accomplished poet working in media where a rhetorical bent, partly native and partly traditional, is given full scope."

Discusses the formative influences, from the English tradition, from the Anglo-Irish tradition of Jonathan Swift and Bishop Berkeley; and from "the comparatively unknown popular nineteenth-century Anglo-Irish tradition...". Considers rhetorical devices — in particular, "the rhetoric of the ghost," "the rhetoric of love" and "the rhetoric of war."

Donald T. Torchiana: " 'Among School Children' and the Education of the Irish Spirit," pp. 123-50. Discusses Yeats's interest in the problem of education; his enthusiasm for the Montessori method; his debt to the writings of Giovanni Gentile on education; his relations with Maud Gonne; the profound influence of Gentile's ideas on "Among School Children", which expresses "not only Yeats's hopes for education in Ireland but also his ultimate feeling about generation and becoming."

A.D. Hope: "William Butler Yeats," p. 151.

Hazard Adams: "Some Yeatsian Versions of Comedy," pp. 152-70. "The Comic in *Autobiographies* and *A Vision* is more than casually related to Yeats's strong but peculiar sense of fate."

Jon Stallworthy: "Yeats as Anthologist," pp. 171-92. Discusses the history of, and the critical response to *The Oxford Book of Modern Verse* (1936), compiled by Yeats.

Brendan Kennelly: "Yeats," p. 193.

Russell K. Alspach: "The Variorum Edition of Yeats's Plays," pp. 194-206. The editor outlines the major editorial and bibliographical problems he encountered.

Conor Cruise O'Brien: "Passion and Cunning: An Essay on The Politics," pp. 207-78. A brilliant and provocative essay on the proto-fascist politics of Yeats, which re-kindled controversy concerning Yeats's reactionary views. "I do not believe Yeats's political activities to have been foolish . . . or his political attitudes to be detachable from the rest of his personality,

disconnected from action, or irrelevant to his poetry...".
Randolph Snow: "Anarchy," p. 279.
    S.B. Bushrui: "Yeats's Arabic Interests," pp. 280-314.
In Yeats's mind, "the East and Ancient Ireland seem to
have been linked . . . Indian philosophy, Japanese drama,
occult practices, magic and theosophy: all these things
were the background against which Yeats's intellect
worked...". Concentrates on *A Vision*; "Solomon to
Sheba"; "Solomon and the Witch": "The Gift of Harun
Al-Rashid"; *Calvary* and *The Cat and the Moon*.
    K.G.W. Cross: "The Fascination of What's Difficult:
A Survey of Yeats Criticism and Research," pp. 315-37.
Excellent bibliographical essay, outlining the critical
reception of Yeats from his death in 1939.

WBY 48:    Maxwell, Desmond E.S. and Bushrui, Suheil B. (eds.)
W.B. YEATS 1865-1965 (Ibadan, Nigeria: University of
Ibadan Press, 1965)

A first-rate collection of original essays on the art of
W.B. Yeats. The volume contains a comprehensive
bibliography of books and articles on Yeats until 1965.
    J. Kleinstück: "Yeats and Shakespeare," pp. 1-15. On
Yeats's creative response to Shakespeare.
    D.E.S. Maxwell: "Swift's Dark Grove: Yeats and the
Anglo-Irish Tradition," pp. 18-32. An important essay
which discusses the reaction of Yeats to the Easter
Rebellion and to the Civil War.

> The beginning of Yeats's interest in Swift coincides
> with his speculations about the Protestant ascendancy,
> its houses and its eighteenth-century past. It would be
> difficult to order the association of these ideas into its
> chronological sequence, but Swift, whom Yeats began
> to read extensively in the late twenties and thirties,
> gave it form and definition.

From Swift, Yeats adapted poetic modes and attitudes, of
scorn and rage, of contempt for "unprincipled politicans
and nerveless masses." Swift and the "Anglo-Irish
solitude to which he belonged" helped "to stimulate and
direct the energies of Yeats's astonishing poetic renas-
cence."
    F.F. Farag: "Oriental and Celtic Elements in the
Poetry of W.B. Yeats," pp. 33-53. Yeats freely "adapted

the ancient sagas [of Ireland] to suit the Oriental traditions which captivated his imagination early in life."

R.M. Kain: "Yeats and Irish Nationalism," pp. 54-61.

> As a country achieves independence, it faces the question of its own identity. It must re-evaluate its cultural heritage, and accept, modify, or reject elements which it cannot assimilate in its new condition. . . . At the turn of the century, Ireland confronted this problem, and W.B. Yeats was its most articulate and perceptive spokesman.

But, as the nationalist cause became narrow-minded, divided and bitter, "Yeats was soon to discover the difficulty of reconciling artistic and political aims." An illuminating essay.

Ian Fletcher: "Yeats and Lissadell," pp. 62-78. Discusses the relation of the historical Eva Gore-Booth and Constance Markiewicz to Yeats's image of them in "In Memory of Eva Gore-Booth and Con Markiewicz". "Where the facts contradicted insight, where the agents of those values in history he most cherished turned betrayers, the poet was ready with a justification that asserted tragedy against pathos; singularity against mediocrity; individuality against mob, though always with a sense of the frailty of his own myth-making." A subtle account of Yeats's poetic re-working of historical and personal experience.

D. Gerstenberger: "Yeats and Synge: 'A Young Man's Ghost'," pp. 79-87. ". . . in Synge Yeats found a symbolic figure, a man who entered into his imaginative world as a very real and substantial presence for the whole extent of Yeats's life."

E. Engelberg: "The New Generation and the Acceptance of Yeats," pp. 88-101. Accounts for the popularity of Yeats among the students of the sixties. His political attitudes do not seem outrageous to many Americans who have "begun to feel repelled by an enforced middle-brow culture and who came to regard style and grace not as undemocratic but as essential values befitting a great culture." Yeats celebrates life in an age threatened by death.

MacDonald Emslie: "Gestures in Scorn of an Audience," pp. 102-26. "Throughout his life, whatever happened to be Yeats's main interest involved an attitude of rejection, to which scorn and hatred were later additions. As man and writer he was rarely at one with his audience. Certain verbal devices that went with this position and these attitudes offered temptations that he occasionally yielded to."

B.A. King: "Yeats's Irishry Prose," pp. 127-35. Discusses the distinctively Irish style of his prose, from repetition to humour.

George Brandon Saul: "Yeats's Dramatic Accomplishment," pp. 137-53. Yeats's drama has not been taken seriously enough. "To dismiss his plays purely as poetry masquerading in dramatic guise . . . is not to realise that the finest drama depends for its power largely upon the intensity of its poetry (and lyrical concentration)."

J.R. Moore: "The Idea of a Yeats Play," pp. 154-66. Discusses the purposes of Yeats's drama as an attempt to refound tragic drama, which Henrik Ibsen and his disciples were intent on destroying.

M.J. Sidnell: "Yeats's First Work for the Stage," pp. 167-88. Discusses the early versions of *The Countess Cathleen*.

S.H. Bushrui: "*The Hour Glass*: Yeats's Revisions, 1903-1922," pp. 189-216.

R. Frechet: "Yeats's 'Sailing to Byzantium' and Keats's 'Ode to a Nightingale'," pp. 217-9. Yeats had Keats's poem in mind when he composed his own.

W.H. Stevenson: "Yeats and Blake: The Use of Symbols," pp. 219-25. "Yeats's symbolism . . . becomes more and more refined and definite, whereas Blake's symbols . . . start with a flash of inspiration and then become more and more involved and diffuse."

"A Select Bibliography," pp. 227-41. Contains over 350 items.

WBY 49:    Porter, Raymond J. and Brophy, James D. (eds.) MODERN IRISH LITERATURE: ESSAYS IN HONOUR OF WILLIAM YORK TINDALL (New York: Iona College Press/Twayne, 1972)

Contains a number of essays on Yeats, of which the most valuable are:

Samuel Hynes: "Yeats and the Poets of the Thirties," pp. 1-22. Suggests that Yeats's influence "on his younger contemporaries was great, that he was more influential than any other poet of his time; and that his influence grew during the Thirties, as things fell apart and the prophecy of 'The Second Coming' seemed to become history."

Discusses the debts of MacNeice, Spender and Auden to Yeats.

E.L. Epstein: "Yeats' Experiments with Syntax in the Treatment of Time," pp. 171-84. In his poetry, Yeats tried for "a fusion of the time-bound and the timeless. In him, it takes the form of a time-bound content expressed with a detemporalising technique." Useful contrasts with Eliot and Pound.

WBY 50:    Pritchard, William Harrison
W.B. YEATS: A CRITICAL ANTHOLOGY
(Harmondsworth, Middlesex: Penguin, 1972)

Part I gives early criticism from 1886 to 1939. Part II presents later criticism, including short extracts from sympathetic and hostile criticism of Yeats, including T.S. Eliot's lecture on Yeats (WBY 34), Yvor Winter's "The Poetry of W.B. Yeats," (WBY 20) and Conor Cruise O'Brien's "Passion and Cunning: An Essay on the Politics," (WBY 88). The other selections are from W.H. Auden, Louis MacNeice, Randall Jarrell, Arthur Mizener, L.C. Knights, George Orwell, D.S. Savage, John Crowe Ransom, Hugh Kenner, John Wain, Frank Kermode, William Empson, C.K. Stead, Donald Davie, John Holloway, Conor Cruise O'Brien, A.D. Hope, Harold Bloom, Helen Vendler and W.H. Pritchard.

WBY 51:    Keane, Patrick J. (ed.)
WILLIAM BUTLER YEATS (New York and London: McGraw-Hill, 1973)

A first-rate collection of essays, by some of the foremost recent critics of Yeats.

Patrick J. Keane: "Introduction," pp. 1-9. Presents a short and helpful guide to the extracts included in the collection.

A. Norman Jeffares: "W.B. Yeats," pp. 10-16. A biographical sketch.

Frank Kermode: "The Suffering Man, The Creative Mind," pp. 17-19. Recalls his personal response to the deaths of W.B. Yeats and T.S. Eliot.

Patrick J. Keane: "Embodied Song," pp. 20-38. Yeats's art consists of unique embodiments of certain recurrent patterns.

M.L. Rosenthal: "Poems of the Here and of the There," pp. 39-44. Discusses the interplay between reality and imagination in Yeats's poetry.

Balachandra Rajan: "Questions of Apocalypse," pp. 45-50. Discusses the theme of violent apocalypse in "No Second Troy," "The Second Coming," and "Leda and the Swan."

C.K. Stead: "Politics as Drama," pp. 51-5. "Easter 1916" employs "the terms of drama in order to stylise and objectify the world of political fact which is its subject."

Thomas R. Whitaker: "Dramatic Experience and Panoramic Vision: 'Nineteen Hundred and Nineteen'," pp. 56-65. The poem combines the perspectives of "dramatic experience and panoramic vision."

Frank Kermode: "Dancer and Tree," pp. 66-80. Emphasises Yeats's role as Symbolist.

Richard Ellmann: "Assertion Without Doctrine," pp. 81-99. "The centre of a Yeats poem is not its ideological content. It is . . . a mood . . . a state of mind."

Denis Donoghue: "The Human Image in Yeats," pp. 100-18. Yeats's focus is upon this world, living experience, the "human image."

Northrop Frye: "The Top of the Tower: A Study of the Imagery of Yeats," pp. 119-38. On archetypal symbolism in Yeats. A classic essay.

M.L. Rosenthal: "Visiting Yeats's Tower," p. 139.

Patrick J. Keane: "Epilogue" and "Reconciliation," pp. 140-3. Discusses two new poems on Yeats.

The volume concludes with an excellent selected bibliography, with notes to guide the student.

WBY 52: Jeffares, Alexander Norman
W.B. YEATS: THE CRITICAL HERITAGE (London and Boston: Routledge & Kegan Paul, 1977)

Contains criticism on Yeats until 1939, otherwise not easily available.

WBY 53: Jeffares, Alexander Norman (ed.)
YEATS, SLIGO AND IRELAND (Gerrards Cross: Colin Smythe, 1980)

A collection of essays to mark the Twenty-First Yeats International Summer School.

Lester I. Conner: "A Matter of Character: Red Hanrahan and Crazy Jane," pp. 1-16. Discusses how Yeats raised "his own characters — real people and the imaginary ones — to the same mythic level as, say, Cuchulain or Helen of Troy."

Denis Donoghue: "Romantic Ireland," pp. 17-30. "We are still annotating Yeats's sense of Romantic Ireland and the values proposed by that phrase, but the harder question turns upon Yeats's own relation to those values, not as themes of propaganda but as motifs of his own early experience."

Barbara Hardy, "The Wildness of Crazy Jane," pp. 31-53. "Like all Yeats's characters, heroic or otherwise, [Crazy Jane] is not detached and dissociated, but close to her author, resembling him and also meeting his inextricably interwound erotic and poetic needs."

Seamus Heaney: "Yeats as an Example," pp. 56-72. An important essay, reminiscent of T.S. Eliot's commemorative address on Yeats, in which a major poet discusses the example of Yeats for contemporary poets, and thereby defines his own procedures through contrast with Yeats.

T.R. Henn: "The Place of Shells," pp. 73-88. Discusses Sligo in Yeats's life and poetry. (The inaugural lecture of the Yeats International Summer School at Sligo in 1968).

John Holloway: "How Goes the Weather?" pp. 89-97. Yeats recaptures in his poetry "the West of Ireland landscape, and its rain and sun, its day and night, its living creatures, its endless wind and immense scale."

A. Norman Jeffares: "Yeats and the Wrong Lever," pp. 98-111. Discusses Charles Lever and Yeats's knowledge of his work.

F.S.L. Lyons: "Yeats and Victorian Ireland," pp. 115-38. An important essay by Yeats's official biographer: ". . . if Yeats remained . . . a Victorian to the end, he was a Victorian with a difference. The difference was largely determined by his divided allegiance. This was only partly an allegiance divided between the two islands of Britain and Ireland, it was much more an allegiance divided between the various cultures which co-existed in the country of his birth. His encounters with these cultures in his first fifteen years as a writer are the theme of this lecture." Discusses Yeats's relation to Irish nationalism and Irish Unionism.

Augustine Martin: "Hound Voices Were They All: An

Experiment in Yeats Criticism," pp. 139-52. "The most neglected of Yeats's last poems can yield one of his most explicit statements on historical and individual conviction in the poetry of the final years."

D.E.S. Maxwell: "The Scene-Changers," pp. 153-69. ". . . it is the imagination which legislates access to reality."

William M. Murphy: "Home Life Among the Yeatses," pp. 170-88. Discusses the relations between father and son.

Patrick Rafroidi: "Yeats, Nature and the Self," pp. 189-96.

Ann Saddlemyer: "The 'Dwarf-Dramas' of the Early Abbey Theatre," pp. 197-215.

Helen Vendler: "Four Elegies," pp. 216-31. Examines four of Yeats's elegies "Easter 1916," "In Memory of Eva Gore-Booth and Con Markiewicz," "Beautiful Lofty Things" and "The Municipal Gallery Revisited" in "the light of departures they exhibited from our received notions of the elegaic genre."

John S. Kelly: "Books and Numberless Dreams: Yeats's Relations with His Early Publishers," pp. 232-53.

# Full-length Studies on the Early Poetry

WBY 54:   Parkinson, Thomas Francis
W.B. YEATS SELF-CRITIC: A STUDY OF HIS EARLY VERSE (Berkeley: University of California Press, 1951) (1971)

An exemplary discussion of the development of Yeats's style; of the relation of style to content; and of the central importance of Yeats's experience as a dramatist to his writing of poetry. (See WBY 59).

WBY 55:   Grossman, Allen Richard
POETIC KNOWLEDGE IN THE EARLY YEARS (Charlottesville: University Press of Virginia, 1969)

A demanding study of *The Wind Among the Reeds*, concentrating on the sources and the background of the poems, with particular emphasis upon their debt to the occult tradition. Extremely important.

WBY 56:    Byrd, Thomas L.
THE EARLY POETRY OF W.B. YEATS: THE
POETIC QUEST (Port Washington, N.Y. and London:
Kennikat Press, 1978)

A thorough study, providing a sound perspective on the
early poetry, without "yielding to the temptation to inflate
it beyond its actual worth." "The concern here is with
Yeats's own approach to the search for reality and truth"
— a search which leads him to mysticism and symbolism.

# Full-length Studies and Articles on the Middle and Late Poetry

WBY 57:    Koch, Vivienne
W.B. YEATS: THE TRAGIC PHASE: A STUDY OF
THE *LAST POEMS* (London: Routledge & Kegan Paul,
1951; Baltimore: John Hopkins University Press, 1952)
(1969)

Presents detailed, separate analyses of the *Last Poems*.
"The pattern I have found in these great but troubled
poems derive their energy from suffering, but describe the
process of suffering, and, in the end, celebrate suffering
not only as the inevitable condition of living, but as a sign
that we truly live. . . . For Yeats, this pattern was most
observable in the paradox of sex, and . . . from the
configurations and incidents of sexual conduct he was able
to construct a field of meaning upon which he drew, in
these poems, for subject, language and imagery."

WBY 58:    Reid, Benjamin Lawrence
WILLIAM BUTLER YEATS: THE LYRIC OF
TRAGEDY (Norman: University of Oklahoma Press,
1961)

On Yeats's theory of tragedy and on the tragic theme in his
poetry. Contains some excellent discussion of the middle
and the late poems.

WBY 59:    Parkinson, Thomas Francis

W.B. YEATS: THE LATER POETRY (Berkeley and
Los Angeles: University of California Press, 1964)

"The main thesis of the book is that Yeats's poetry was
largely determined by his dramatic sense." The first
section, "Yeats and Modernity," pp. 6-72, provides an
illuminating account of Yeats's quarrel with the modernist
aesthetic of Pound and Eliot. This volume was reissued,
with Parkinson's earlier study, *W.B. Yeats Self Critic: A
Study of His Early Verse* (WBY 54) as *W.B. Yeats Self
Critic: A Study of His Early Verse and The Later Poetry*
(Berkeley and Los Angeles: University of California
Press, 1971).

WBY 60:    Garab, Arra M.
BEYOND BYZANTIUM: THE LAST PHASE OF
YEATS'S CAREER (Dekalb: Northern Illinois
University Press, 1969)

The first chapter presents a brief account of Yeats's fear
of time in the poems up to and including "Sailing to
Byzantium." Under the influence of François Villon, the
poems of the last decade, 1929-39, (which are explicated in
the body of the study) bring an acceptance of the real
world of time and of death.

WBY 61:    Perloff, Marjorie G.
"Heart Mysteries: The Later Love Lyrics of
W.B. Yeats," *Contemporary Literature*, 10:2 (Spring
1969), 266-83

Examines Yeats's lyrics between 1919 and 1939 to
challenge existing views of Yeats's poetry of old age. It is
the heart that is at the centre of his later love poems.

WBY 62:    Stallworthy, Jon Howie
YEATS: *LAST POEMS* (London: Macmillan, 1969;
Nashville: Aurora, 1970)

A collection of essays on the *Last Poems*, divided into two
parts. The first section gives contemporary opinions
1939-1940; the second section reprints essays and
excerpts from full-length studies. See: Curtis Bradford,

"On Yeats's *Last Poems*," pp. 75-97 (on the themes, metres and ordering of the poems); T.R. Henn, "The Mill of the Mind," pp. 98-114 (divides the poems into four main divisions); T.R. Henn, " 'Horseman, Pass By!'," pp. 115-21 ("The three final dated poems of *Last Poems* contain, perhaps, Yeats's *Grand Testament*"); T.R. Henn, "The Accent of Yeats's *Last Poems*," pp. 122-37 (discusses the *accent* of the poems, "a strange complexity of mire and blood; of old emotions recollected in a new dispassionate excitement, sometimes satirical, sometimes exalted"); J.R. Mulryne, "The *Last Poems*," pp. 138-59 (discusses how the poet seeks, through the poetic act, to conquer accident and tragedy); A. Norman Jeffares, "The General and Particular Meanings of 'Lapis Lazuli'," pp. 160-5 (on the "possible destruction of contemporary civilisation" which haunted Yeats in the poem); F.A.C. Wilson, " 'The Statues'," pp. 166-81 (on Yeats's theory of sculpture and its influence on the *Last Poems*); Arra M. Garab, "Times of Glory: Yeats's 'The Municipal Gallery Revisited'," pp. 182-93 (Yeats considers the role of politics and of art in shaping the nation); Jon Stallworthy, " 'The Black Tower'," pp. 194-215 (a close examination of the draft typescripts of the poem); Jon Stallworthy, " 'Under Ben Bulben'," pp. 216-44 (a close examination of the draft typescripts of the poem); Peter Ure, "*Purgatory*," pp. 245-55 (*Purgatory* is "the most successful of Yeats's . . . attempts to dramatize one stage of the progress of the soul from grave to cradle, or from grave to beatitude."); Peter Ure, "*The Death of Cuchulain*," pp. 256-62.

WBY 63:    Finneran, Richard J. (ed.)
W.B. YEATS: THE BYZANTIUM POEMS
(Columbus, Ohio: Merrill, 1970)

Presents the texts of the two poems, with an introduction, relevant passages from Yeats's poetry and prose, and selected items of previous criticism.

WBY 64:    Altieri, Charles
"From a Comic to a Tragic Sense of Language in Yeats's Mature Poetry," *Modern Language Quarterly*, 33:2 (June 1972), 156-71

In his late poems, Yeats, even while recognising the chaos of the world, still presents an affirmative vision. Therein lies his "tragic joy."

# Full-length Studies and Articles on the Plays of W.B. Yeats

WBY 65:  Ellis-Fermor, Una
THE IRISH DRAMATIC MOVEMENT (London: Methuen, 1939) (1977)

Still the best account of the Irish Dramatic Movement, with a chapter on the plays of Yeats, pp. 91-116.

WBY 66:  Williams, Raymond
"W.B. Yeats," DRAMA FROM IBSEN TO ELIOT (London: Chatto and Windus, 1952; New York: Oxford University Press, 1953), pp. 205-22

Yeats's drama placed in the context of European drama. (See MOD 166).

WBY 67:  Ure, Peter
YEATS THE PLAYWRIGHT: A COMMENTARY ON CHARACTER AND DESIGN IN THE MAJOR PLAYS (London: Routledge & Kegan Paul, 1963; New York: Barnes & Noble, 1963)

A pioneering study, which established the importance of Yeats's work as a dramatist, and outlined the areas of debate about his plays: the nature of his dramatic theory and practice; the use of myth; the realism of his drama.

WBY 68:  Nathan, Leonard E.
THE TRAGIC DRAMA OF WILLIAM BUTLER YEATS: FIGURES IN A DANCE (New York and London: Columbia University Press, 1965)

A comprehensive, chronological account, discussing almost all of Yeats's plays. Yeats was set apart as a dramatist, from traditional drama and from the realism of the new Ibsenite theatre, by his philosophical seriousness. "This quality goes a long way toward explaining both the trouble he had in finding a viable dramatic form and the eccentricity of the forms he ultimately came to." Sympathetic account of Yeats's quest to represent the spiritual dimension in dramatic art.

WBY 69:     Moore, John Rees
MASKS OF LOVE AND DEATH: YEATS AS
DRAMATIST (Ithaca: Cornell University Press, 1971)

Contains three introductory chapters on the concept of the mask, the characteristics of Yeats's drama, and the Cuchulain myth, followed by separate analyses of the plays.

WBY 70:     O'Driscoll, Robert (ed.)
THEATRE AND NATIONALISM IN
TWENTIETH-CENTURY IRELAND (Toronto:
Toronto University Press, 1971; London: Oxford
University Press, 1971)

Contains essays on Yeats and on the Abbey Theatre. See: Anne Saddlemyer, "Stars of the Abbey's Ascendancy," pp. 21-39; George Mills Harper, " 'Intellectual Hatred' and 'Intellectual Nationalism': The Paradox of Passionate Politics," pp. 40-65 (a fine discussion of Yeats's ambiguity towards nationalism); David R. Clark, "Yeats, Theatre, and Nationalism," pp. 134-55 (on Yeats's career at the Abbey); M.J. Sidnell, "Hic and Ille: Shaw and Yeats," pp. 156-78 (on the relationship of G.B. Shaw and W.B. Yeats as playwrights).

WBY 71:     MURPHY, Sheila Ann
"A Political History of the Abbey Theatre," *Literature and Ideology*, No. 16 (1973), 53-60

The Abbey Theatre fostered spiritual aspirations rather than political struggle: hence its financial backing from Unionists.

WBY 72:     Flannery, James W.
W.B. YEATS AND THE IDEA OF A THEATRE:
THE EARLY ABBEY THEATRE IN THEORY AND
PRACTICE (New Haven and London: Yale University
Press, 1976)

An important study of the technique of Yeats's drama; of
the history of the Abbey Theatre; of the Irish Dramatic
Movement, in which he played a central part; and of
Yeats's legacy to avant-garde theatre. Yeats's dramatic
theories, which were more important than his practices,
have been misconstrued.

WBY 73:     Worth, Katharine
THE IRISH DRAMA OF EUROPE FROM YEATS
TO BECKETT (London: Athlone Press, 1978; Atlantic
Highlands, N.J.: Humanities Press, 1978)

"This book offers a European perspective on the Irish
drama, bringing Yeats, Synge and Beckett, Wilde and
O'Casey under the same light with Maeterlinck and,
above all, showing how Yeats's evolution of a modern
technique of total theatre and his use of it to construct a
'drama of the interior' makes him one of the great masters
of twentieth-century theatre."

# Textual Studies

WBY 74:     Stallworthy, Jon Howie
BETWEEN THE LINES: YEATS'S POETRY IN
THE MAKING (Oxford: Clarendon Press, 1963)

Discusses Yeats's procedures in revising eighteen of his
major poems.

WBY 75:     Bradford, Curtis
YEATS AT WORK (Carbondale: Southern Illinois
University Press, 1965)

Prints and analyses the early drafts of a number of Yeats's
major poems, plays and prose pieces.

WBY 76:    Stallworthy, Jon Howie
VISION AND REVISION IN YEATS'S *LAST POEMS* (Oxford: Clarendon Press, 1969)

Discusses the various drafts (and the themes) of the *Last Poems*.

# Full-length Studies and Articles on *A Vision*

WBY 77:    Stauffer, Donald Alfred
THE GOLDEN NIGHTINGALE: ESSAYS ON SOME PRINCIPLES OF POETRY IN THE LYRICS OF WILLIAM BUTLER YEATS (London: Macmillan, 1949; New York: Hafner, 1971)

Historically important defence of *A Vision*; of Yeats's theory and practice of symbolism; and of the essential unity of his work.

WBY 78:    Seiden, Morton Irving
WILLIAM BUTLER YEATS: THE POET AS MYTHMAKER 1865-1939 (East Lansing: Michigan State University Press, 1962)

Argues that *A Vision* is the centre of Yeats's work, discusses its esoteric sources, explicates the work in its two versions, and suggests its influence on Yeats's poetry and plays. "Over and over again, he explained to his contemporaries his self-appointed religious and political mission. . . . Through his poetic rediscovery of forgotten religions, Yeats believed that he might draw back into Ireland and the whole Western world those moral, social and religious values everywhere being destroyed (he thought) by science, decadent Christianity, or Philistine temperaments. He also wanted, he continually said, metaphors or symbols for his poetry — lovely images, those not yet corrupted by a civilisation which, as he saw, was hysterically dashing itself to the ground."

WBY 79:    Vendler, Helen Hennessy
YEATS'S *A VISION* AND THE LATER PLAYS (Cambridge, Mass.: Harvard University Press, 1963; London: Oxford University Press, 1963)

"To understand most of the essays and a good part of the poetry it is not essential to know *A Vision*, but for the late plays I think it is." *A Vision* (of which Vendler gives a detailed and illuminating account) must not "be taken literally, but as an arrangement of experience." Its five books "all bear principally on poetry and the poetic process." She then presents a reading of the later plays, and of "Byzantium," "Cuchulain Comforted," "Leda and the Swan," and "The Second Coming."

WBY 80:     Whitaker, Thomas Russell
SWAN AND SHADOW: YEATS'S DIALOGUE WITH HISTORY (Chapel Hill: University of North Carolina Press, 1964)

An important and rewarding study of Yeats's view of history: "history was for Yeats a mysterious interlocutor, sometimes a bright reflection of the poet's self, sometimes a shadowy force opposed to that self. . . . This visionary and paradoxical dialogue — both strikingly individual and highly traditional — was a central fact underlying Yeats's complex and sustained growth." Discusses Yeats's *A Vision* and related poetry. The study contains two outstanding chapters on the Anglo-Irish background: "The Living Heritage and The Measured Way," pp. 133-62; "Poet of Anglo-Ireland," pp. 188-221.

WBY 81:     Ronsley, Joseph
YEATS'S *AUTOBIOGRAPHY*: LIFE AS SYMBOLIC PATTERN (Cambridge, Mass.: Harvard University Press, 1968; London: Oxford University Press, 1968)

Discusses the symbolic patterning which transformed personal experience in *The Autobiography*. "Seeing himself as the product of an heritage linked intimately with Ireland's history and culture, he also saw his personal history blended with that of his country, and he began to think of his own image as a kind of symbol of Ireland." Examines in this context Yeats's notion of the Unity of Culture and the Unity of Being. Includes many perceptive comments on *A Vision*.

# Full-length Studies of Yeats and the Occult

WBY 82:    Wilson, Francis Alexander Charles
W.B. YEATS AND TRADITION (London: V.
Gollancz, 1958; New York: Macmillan, 1958)

"The highroad to proper understanding of Yeats's poetry
lies through his symbolism, and this in turn requires a
knowledge of the tradition on which it is based." Yeats is a
religious poet, drawing upon the tradition of "heterodox
mysticism" of Neo-Platonism found in the works of
Plotinus, Porphyry, Proclus and Julian. To understand
Yeats's poetry, it is necessary to refer to the structures of
symbolism antecedent to and exterior to the poetry. Yeats
was a decorator of received ideas traditionally associated
with Neo-Platonic icons. A controversial study, the
American edition contains a brief reply to his first
reviewers.

WBY 83:    Wilson, Francis Alexander Charles
YEATS'S ICONOGRAPHY (London: V. Gollancz,
1960; New York: Macmillan, 1960)

Continues the above (WBY 82) dealing with a different
range of Yeats's poetry and drama.

WBY 84:    Bachchan, Harbans Rai
W.B. YEATS AND OCCULTISM: A STUDY OF
HIS WORK IN RELATION TO INDIAN LORE,
THE CABBALA, SWEDENBORG, BOEHME AND
THEOSOPHY (Delhi: Motilal Banarsidass, 1965)

Useful discussion of Yeats's occult influences, particularly the Eastern ones. Concludes that "Yeats found a
'system' from which to draw inspiration for his poetry, but
failed to provide one that could be accepted as a
tradition."

WBY 85:    Harper, George Mills
YEATS'S GOLDEN DAWN (London and New York:
Macmillan, 1974)

A comprehensive account of Yeats's membership of the
Hermetic Order of the Golden Dawn.

WBY 86:     Flannery, Mary Catherine
            YEATS AND MAGIC: THE EARLIER WORK
            (Gerrards Cross: Colin Smythe, 1977; New York: Barnes
            & Noble, 1977)

            Discusses the "vital relationship between Yeats's ideas
            about poetry and his belief and practice of magic." Yeats
            "saw a subtle but important difference between being a
            mystic and being a magician: the mystic passionately
            submits to a system while the magician is a creator, a
            controller of systems. The distinction between mysticism
            and magic is central to our understanding of Yeats
            because his idea of a magician is strikingly similar to his
            idea of a poet: all poets share some of the power of the
            magician and the greater the poet the more conscious he
            will be of the links between magic and poetry." A
            comprehensive account, which explains the attractions of
            Theosophy, Cabbalism and Indian lore for Yeats in a way
            which makes them seem neither self-indulgent nor
            eccentric.

# Full-length Studies and Articles on Yeats's Political and Social Thought

WBY 87:     Knights, Lionel Charles
            "Poetry and Social Criticism: The Work of W.B. Yeats,"
            EXPLORATIONS (London: Chatto and Windus, 1946;
            New York: Stewart, 1947), pp. 170-85

            Discusses the importance of the aristocratic concept in
            Yeats's life and thought.

WBY 88:     O'Brien, Conor Cruise
            "Passion and Cunning: An Essay on the Politics," IN
            EXCITED REVERIE, ed. A. Norman Jeffares and
            K.G.W. Cross (London: Macmillan, 1965; New York:
            St. Martin's, 1965), pp. 207-78

            A brilliant, provocative and pioneering essay on Yeats's
            politics. Yeats's poetry was never detached from his
            politics, which were opportunistic, ambiguous, and,
            finally, authoritarian. Stresses the effect of the First

World War on Yeats's political attitudes.

WBY 89:     Harrison, John Raymond
"W.B. Yeats," THE REACTIONARIES: A STUDY
OF THE ANTI-DEMOCRATIC INTELLIGENTSIA
(London: V. Gollancz, 1966; New York: Schocken,
1966), pp. 39-73

A succinct survey of Yeats's political attitudes during his
career as a writer. Particularly good on Yeats's attitude to
violence and to authoritarianism. (See MOD 54).

WBY 90:     Rajan, B.
"Yeats and the Renaissance," *Mosaic*, 5:4 (Summer
1972), 109-18

On the importance of the Renaissance, with its attainment
of Unity of Being, for Yeats's system and political views.

WBY 91:     Cullingford, Elizabeth
YEATS, IRELAND AND FASCISM (London:
Macmillan, 1981; New York: New York University
Press, 1981)

The most thorough examination yet of the links between
Yeats's poetic and his political vision, particularly useful
in examining Yeats's relation to Irish fascism. "Yeats's
poetry escapes simple political labels because it is
essentially dialectical, while his practical choices reveal
the inappropriateness of the label 'fascist'."

# Full-length Studies and Articles on Yeats and Other Writers

WBY 92:     Adams, Hazard
BLAKE AND YEATS: THE CONTRARY VISION
(Ithaca: Cornell University Press, 1955; London:
Cumberlege, 1956)

A valuable study of Yeats's aesthetics and symbolism, defined through contrast with William Blake's: "The important relationship" between Yeats and Blake lay in "the modes or forms of experiencing and creating poetic worlds."

WBY 93:  Faulkner, Peter
WILLIAM MORRIS AND W.B. YEATS (Dublin: Dolmen Press, 1962)

On Yeats's biographical connections with Morris and his influence upon Yeats's social thinking.

WBY 94:  Salvadori, Corinna
YEATS AND CASTIGLIONE: POET AND COURTIER (Dublin: Figgis, 1965)

"A study of some fundamental concepts of the philosophy and poetic creed of W.B. Yeats in the light of Castiglione's *Il Libro del Cortegiano*." Draws interesting parallels between Coole Park and Urbino, Lady Gregory and the Duchess of Urbino.

WBY 95:  McAlindon, Thomas
"Yeats and the English Renaissance," *PMLA*, 82:2 (May 1967), pp. 157-69

An important essay, stressing the influence of Edmund Spenser, William Shakespeare and Ben Jonson (as well as Friedrich Nietzsche) in shaping Yeats's aristocratic attitudes.

WBY 96:  McAlindon, Thomas
"The Idea of Byzantium in William Morris and W.B. Yeats," *Modern Philology*, 64:4 (May 1967), 307-19

Important discussion of Morris's view of Byzantium and its influence on Yeats's cultural theories and *A Vision*.

WBY 97:  Lentricchia, Frank Richard
THE GAIETY OF LANGUAGE: AN ESSAY ON

THE RADICAL POETICS OF W.B. YEATS AND
WALLACE STEVENS (Berkeley: University of
California Press, 1968)

Yeats rejected the Romantic and Symbolist theories of
poetry in favour of a "poetics of will and impersonation"
which "framed in tragic awareness," found freedom in the
act of poetic creativity. Discusses the early stories, the
Byzantium poems and "Lapis Lazuli."

WBY 98:    Bornstein, George Jay
YEATS AND SHELLEY (Chicago and London:
University of Chicago Press, 1970)

A balanced account, showing both the extent of Percy
Bysshe Shelley's influence on Yeats and the degree to
which Yeats reacted against Shelley. Yeats's changing
view of Shelley deepens our appreciation of Yeats's work
at every stage.

WBY 99:    Fullwood, Daphne
"The Influence on W.B. Yeats of Some French Poets,"
*Southern Review*, 6:2 (April 1970), 356-79

Convincing account of the influence of Stéphane Mallarmé, Paul Verlaine and Paul Claudel.

WBY 100:    Reguerio, Helen
THE LIMITS OF IMAGINATION:
WORDSWORTH, YEATS AND STEVENS (Ithaca
and London: Cornell University Press, 1976)

The modernity of William Wordsworth, W.B. Yeats and
Wallace Stevens is seen to lie in their recognition of the
dialectical relationship of imagination and reality and of
the dangers — of solipsism, of silence — which lie in the
dealings of the imagination with the exterior world.

WBY 101:    Olney, James
THE RHIZOME AND THE FLOWER: THE
PERENNIAL PHILOSOPHY — YEATS AND
JUNG (Berkeley and London: University of California
Press, 1980)

Examines the similarities between W.B. Yeats and Carl
Jung, and argues that Yeats was an original and important
modern thinker.


# Yeats and the Visual Arts

WBY 102:   Melchiori, Giorgio
THE WHOLE MYSTERY OF ART: PATTERN
INTO POETRY IN THE WORK OF W.B. YEATS
(London: Routledge & Kegan Paul, 1960) (1979)

The most important and detailed study on Yeats's visual
sources, which investigates the pictorial sources of
Yeats's symbolism — and suggests why Yeats used them
as he did. Discusses Yeats's unicorn symbolism, and the
symbols of the egg, sphere and gyre. Contains fascinating
readings of "Leda and the Swan," *A Vision* and the
Byzantium poems.


WBY 103:   Gordon, Donald James and Fletcher, Ian (eds.)
W.B. YEATS: IMAGES OF A POET, MY
PERMANENT OR IMPERMANENT IMAGES
(Manchester: University of Manchester Press, 1961; 2nd
edn., Manchester: Manchester University Press, 1970;
New York: Barnes & Noble, 1970)

An exhibition catalogue of photographs and pictures of
Yeats, which contains a series of fine essays by the editors
and others on Yeats in the 1890s. "The Image of the
Poet," pp. 7-14 (on Yeats's views of portraits of him);
"Persons and Places," pp. 25-44 (on Yeats's Irish
friends, particularly Robert Gregory); "The Poet and the
Theatre," pp. 56-65 (on the Noh Theatre and its influence
in England); "Byzantium," pp. 81-9 (an outstanding
study of Yeats's sources and of the interest of the 1890s in
Byzantine art); "Symbolic Art and Visionary Land-
scape," pp. 91-107 (on Yeats's views of English painting
in the 1890s). The volume concludes with brief essays by
Frank Kermode, "The Dancer," pp. 120-3 and Robin
Skelton, "Books and Manuscripts," pp. 129-150.

# Part III
# PERCY WYNDHAM LEWIS
# 1882-1957

# Bibliographical Information

For the most extensive bibliography of the writings of Wyndham Lewis, see Bradford Morrow and Bernard Lafourcade, A BIBLIOGRAPHY OF THE WRITINGS OF WYNDHAM LEWIS (Santa Barbara, Calif.: Black Sparrow Press, 1978). For a full descriptive bibliography of Lewis's writings (including his scripts for radio), see Omar S. Pound and Philip Grover, WYNDHAM LEWIS: A DESCRIPTIVE BIBLIOGRAPHY (Hamden, Conn.: Shoe String Press, 1978; Folkestone: Dawson, 1978).

There is no complete bibliography of criticism of Wyndham Lewis. Geoffrey Wagner's WYNDHAM LEWIS: A PORTRAIT OF THE ARTIST AS THE ENEMY (New Haven: Yale University Press, 1957; London: Routledge & Kegan Paul, 1957) contains an unusually full bibliography, not only of the writings of Lewis, but also of writings on Lewis, until 1957. For a brief (and somewhat sketchy) checklist of more recent criticism, see THE ENGLISH NOVEL: FROM CONRAD TO THE PRESENT, compiled by Paul L. Wiley (Northbrook, Ill.: AHM Publishing, 1973), pp. 78-80.

The most detailed bibliographical essay on criticism of Lewis is by Bernard Lafourcade, "Wyndham Lewis: du purgatoire au panorama," *Etudes anglaises*, 26:2 (April-June 1973), 195-211. Lafourcade reviews (in French) the articles, journals, biographies and critical studies, which have, in his opinion, given Lewis his current high standing among advanced critics of literature, art and philosophy.

# Memoirs and Biographies

WL1:     Wagner, Geoffrey
         WYNDHAM LEWIS: A PORTRAIT OF THE
         ARTIST AS THE ENEMY (New Haven: Yale
         University Press, 1957; London: Routledge & Kegan
         Paul, 1957) (1973)

Still the only critical biography of Lewis, providing indispensable information on the continental sources of his ideas. Particularly good on Lewis's hostile relationship to (and parody of) James Joyce. Argues that Lewis was an exponent of creative individualism, for the creative individual established the values by which a culture might live.

WL2:    Meyers, Jeffrey
THE ENEMY: A BIOGRAPHY OF WYNDHAM
LEWIS (London: Routledge & Kegan Paul, 1980)

A well-researched and thoughtful biography which is set to become the standard account of Lewis's life and career.

# Full-length Studies of the Work of Wyndham Lewis

WL3:    Porteus, Hugh Gordon
WYNDHAM LEWIS: A DISCURSIVE
EXPOSITION (London: D. Harmsworth, 1932)

The first, full-length study of Lewis, who is seen as a satirist practising necessary surgery upon a corrupt body politic.

WL4:    Grigson, Geoffrey
A MASTER OF OUR TIME: A STUDY OF
WYNDHAM LEWIS (London: Methuen, 1951;
Folcroft, Pa.: Folcroft, 1951)

As an artist, Lewis sought to create something permanent out of the wreckage of modern history.

WL5:    Kenner, Hugh
WYNDHAM LEWIS (Norfolk, Conn.: New
Directions, 1954)

A subtle, brief introduction to Lewis's life and work, which are seen (almost in existentialist fashion) as "a career of performances.'' The multiple Lewis asserts the need for significant creative and personal action in the face of modern, mass society. Emphasises Lewis's central importance to English Modernism.

WL6:        Tomlin, Eric Walter Frederic
WYNDHAM LEWIS (London and Toronto: Longmans, Green, 1955)

Short, adulatory British Council pamphlet on Lewis.

WL7:        Pritchard, William Harrison
WYNDHAM LEWIS (New York: Twayne, 1968)

An excellent introductory study, sympathetic to Lewis, which examines Lewis's fiction in detail (including *The Human Age*), and emphasises the philosophical and political focus of his fiction and his other writings. Contains a useful bibliography.

WL8:        McLuhan, Marshall
COUNTERBLAST (New York: Harcourt Brace, 1969; London: Rapp and Whiting, 1970)

McLuhan's ''homage to Lewis,'' who in his fiction set in, and essays on, North America had described the new world, ''the pendant cradle of the New Man,'' out of which post-European civilisation was to shape itself. Lewis, multi-media artist, is seen to provide both the technical means and the inspiration to shape that new civilisation.

WL9:        Chapman, Robert T.
WYNDHAM LEWIS: FICTIONS AND SATIRES (London: Vision Press, 1973; New York: Barnes & Noble, 1973)

A fine analysis of Lewis's mode of writing, described as ''imaginative polemics.'' ''Often reading like modern Socratic dialogues, Lewis's fictions are peopled with characters who represent attitudes or philosophies. Action becomes a function of a particular world-view and in this way ideas are evaluated according to the behaviour of their embodiment." Lewis's work "can be read as a defence of Western Man against the forces of the anti-Enlightenment which, he felt, so many of his contemporaries espoused." A comprehensive account of Lewis's imaginative and theoretical writings throughout his career.

WL10:     Materer, Timothy
          WYNDHAM LEWIS THE NOVELIST (Detroit, Michigan: Wayne State University Press, 1976)

Lewis's fiction is essentially dramatic, embodying a satirico-tragic vision of the modern world which Lewis encapsulated in his interpretation of Shakespeare. As a satirist, Lewis presents characters who are "deformed by the violence of their desires or the brutality of their experiences"; as a tragedian, he presents characters in an irrational world of violence in which "few things can be rescued from the destructive progress of the century." Concludes that Lewis is closer to the philosophical and emotional intensity of Kurt Vonnegut and Thomas Pynchon than to English social fiction.

# Articles and Chapters from Books on Wyndham Lewis's Work and Career

WL11:     Frye, Northrop
          "Neo-Classical Agony," *Hudson Review*, 10:4 (Winter 1957-8), 592-8

On the biographical motive in Lewis's art. We understand Lewis when we realise that "he is an almost solipsistic writer, whose hatreds are a part of him because he understands nothing of what goes on outside his own mind."

WL12:     Elliott, Robert Carl
          THE POWER OF SATIRE: MAGIC, RITUAL, ART (Princeton, N.J.: Princeton University Press, 1960)

An anthropological account of satire, with its origins in the
magical curse and the expulsion of the scapegoat, which
contains an account of Lewis's career as a satirist.

WL13:        Holloway, John
"Wyndham Lewis: The Massacre and the Innocents,"
THE CHARTED MIRROR: LITERARY AND
CRITICAL ESSAYS (London: Routledge & Kegan
Paul, 1960; New York: Horizon, 1962), pp. 118-36

No one has seen more clearly or explained more forcefully
than Lewis the violence at the heart of modern life.

WL14:        Allen, Walter
"Lonely Old Volcano: The Achievement of Wyndham
Lewis," *Encounter*, 11:9 (September 1963), 63-70

Sympathetic survey of Lewis's life and achievement.

WL15:        Pritchard, William H.
"On Wyndham Lewis," *Partisan Review*, 35:2 (Spring
1968), 253-67

A fine account of Lewis's views of the "men of 1914,"
expounding his critical principles and insights.

WL16:        Schneidau, Herbert N.
EZRA POUND: THE IMAGE AND THE REAL
(Baton Rouge: Louisiana State University Press, 1969)

Discusses *passim* the role of Lewis and of Vorticism in
early Modernism.

WL17:        Holloway, John
"From Between the Dragon's Teeth," *Critical
Quarterly*, 13:4 (Winter 1971), 367-76

An appreciation of Lewis's centrality. "Lewis committed
himself in respect of one of the radical intellectual — or
rather psychic — choices articulating the civilisation of
the modern world."

WL18:    Mayne, Richard
"Wyndham Lewis," *Encounter*, 38:2 (February, 1972),
42-51

An appreciative assessment of Lewis, greatly indebted to
Geoffrey Wagner (See WL1).

WL19:    Regnery, Henry
"Eliot, Pound and Lewis: A Creative Friendship,"
*Modern Age*, 16:2 (Spring 1972), 146-60

The most significant writers of the century were all from
North America, linked by their hostility to the shallow
liberalism of the age.

WL20:    Jameson, Fredric
"Wyndham Lewis as Futurist," *Hudson Review*, 26:2
(Summer 1973), 295-329

Brilliant structuralist discussion of Lewis's prose style.
Lewis's prose is a democratic practice, disarming, on the
level of language and its organisation of individual
consciousness, those forms which are habitual, mechanical, ideological. Concentrates upon "Cantleman's
Spring-Mate" and *The Childermass*.

WL21:    Wilson, Colin
"Wyndham Lewis: A Refracted Talent?" *Books and
Bookmen*, 19:5 (February 1974), 44-8; 19:6 (March 1974),
51-2; 19:7 (April 1974), 39-42

Three short articles, which argue that Lewis, for all his
intellectual abilities, failed completely as a literary artist.

WL22:    McMillan, Dougald
"*transition* in the Wake: Friends and the Enemy,"
*TRANSITION*: THE HISTORY OF A LITERARY
ERA 1927-1938 (London: Calder and Boyars, 1975; New
York: Braziller, 1976), pp. 204-31

On Lewis's parody of James Joyce in *The Childermass*
and Joyce's parody of Lewis in *Finnegans Wake*.

WL23:          Pritchard, William Harrison
SEEING THROUGH EVERYTHING: ENGLISH
WRITERS 1918-1940 (London: Faber and Faber, 1977;
New York: Oxford University Press, 1977)

An account of English literary history in which the
objectivity and insight of Wyndham Lewis are counterposed to the subjectivism, self-deception and lack of
creativity of his contemporaries. Contains full (if too
adulatory) accounts of *Tarr, The Revenge for Love* and
*Men Without Art*.

WL24:          Mitchell, Judith
"Women and Wyndham Lewis," *Modern Fiction
Studies*, 24:2 (Summer 1978), 223-31

Lewis's early fiction satirises women, particularly feminists. But, after his characterization of Margot in *The
Revenge for Love*, there enters a sympathetic note in his
portrayal of women. "Lewis was not, we may conclude, a
woman-hater. What he disliked was the exploitation of
women by their division into robot-classes, the feminist
class on one hand and the feminine class on the other."

WL25:          Russell, John
STYLE IN MODERN BRITISH FICTION
(Baltimore: Johns Hopkins University Press, 1978),
pp. 123-57

Demanding technical analyses of Lewis's style.

# Articles and Chapters from Books on the Early, Middle and Late Fiction

WL26:          Spender, Stephen
"The Great Without," THE DESTRUCTIVE
ELEMENT (London: Jonathan Cape, 1935; New York:
Houghton Mifflin, 1936), pp. 201-16 (1970)

Detailed discussion of *The Apes of God* as satire. (See
MOD 2).

WL27:  Carter, Thomas
"Rationalist in Hell," *Kenyon Review*, 18:2 (Spring 1956), 326-36

A fine reading of *The Human Age*, stressing both its metaphysical content and its critique of the Welfare State.


WL28:  Kenner, Hugh
"The Devil and Wyndham Lewis," GNOMON (New York: McDowell Obolensky, 1958), pp. 215-41

A comprehensive discussion of *The Human Age*.


WL29:  Maes-Jelinek, Hena
"Wyndham Lewis," CRITICISM OF SOCIETY IN THE ENGLISH NOVEL BETWEEN THE WARS (Paris: Société d'Editions "Les Belles Lettres," 1970), pp. 159-230

First-rate account of Lewis's interwar fiction.


WL30:  Materer, Timothy
"The Short Stories of Wyndham Lewis," *Studies in Short Fiction*, 7:4 (Fall 1970), 615-24

On the unity of the stories in *The Wild Body*; on Lewis's view of peasant life; on his Bergsonian theory of humour.


WL31:  Chapman, Robert T.
"Satire and Aesthetics in Wyndham Lewis' *Apes of God*," *Contemporary Literature*, 12:2 (Spring 1971), 133-45

The novel is a Swiftian satire and an exposition of Lewis's ideas about satire and the effect of art upon life.


WL32:  Materer, Timothy
"Wyndham Lewis: Satirist of the Machine Age," *Satire Newsletter*, 10:1 (Fall 1972), 9-18

Lewis's *Snooty Baronet* is superior to the satire of Aldous

Huxley and Evelyn Waugh because its central figure acquires self-understanding.

WL33:    Parker, David
"The Vorticist, 1914: The Artist as a Predatory Savage,"
*Southern Review* (Adelaide), 8:1 (March 1975), 3-21

On the history of *Blast* and on Lewis's creation of the ideal vorticist self: the artist as savage and as hunter, abstract, anti-pacifist and anti-feminist.

WL34:    Parker, David
"*Tarr* and Wyndham Lewis's War-time Stories: The Artist as Prey," *Southern Review* (Adelaide), 8:2 (June 1975), 166-79

*Tarr*, "Cantleman's Spring-Mate" and "The War Baby" which all show the masculine hero defeated by Nature in the form of women, provide a more human corrective to the inhuman, masculine figure projected by Lewis in *Blast*.

# Full-length Studies, Articles and Chapters from Books on Lewis's Political and Social Thought

WL35:    Kirk, Russell
"Wyndham Lewis's First Principles," *Yale Review*, 44:4 (Summer 1955), 520-34

Lewis's political views, hostile to state-power, expounded (and applauded).

WL36:    Harrison, John Raymond
"Wyndham Lewis," THE REACTIONARIES: A STUDY OF THE ANTI-DEMOCRATIC INTELLIGENTSIA (London: V. Gollancz, 1966; New York: Schocken, 1966), pp. 77-108

The most sustained criticism of Lewis's politics. "Lewis's ideas about power are clearly related to fascist ideology. His desire for the separation of the creative man

and the average man, which we have noticed, is also close
to certain fascist ideals.'' (See MOD 54).

WL37:     Smith, Rowland
          ''The Spanish Civil War and the British Literary Right,''
          *Dalhousie Review*, 51:1 (Spring 1971), 60-176

          In retrospect, Wyndham Lewis and Roy Campbell were
          more accurate in their insight into the Spanish Civil War
          than those on the Left.

WL38:     Wagner, Geoffrey
          ''Wyndham Lewis (1886-1957),'' THE POLITICS OF
          TWENTIETH-CENTURY NOVELISTS, ed.
          George A. Panichas (New York: Hawthorn Books,
          1971), pp. 51-64

          A succinct and subtle analysis of Lewis's politics. ''We
          cannot accept Lewis's own estimate of Lewis.'' Despite
          his later denials, Lewis did support Mussolini and Hitler;
          he did echo anti-Semitic sentiments; he did, in his attacks
          upon ''group rhythm'' assume an extremist position.
          ''The terms of Lewis's excesses are extremely uncon-
          genial to the academic mind, and there is something
          unpleasantly unworthy of the man in the craven nature of
          his rapid rewritings. Wyndham Lewis called his 'the
          politics of the intellect,' but it was, for many, a strangely
          emotional elite he championed in his lifetime as his 'ideal
          giant' for society.''

WL39:     Bridson, Douglas Geoffrey
          THE FILIBUSTER: A STUDY OF THE
          POLITICAL IDEAS OF WYNDHAM LEWIS
          (London: Cassell, 1972)

          The most detailed defence to date of Lewis's political
          views. He was (with the exception of a temporary
          aberration in the early thirties) an internationalist,
          opposed to nationalism.

WL40:     Currie, Robert
          ''The Modernism of Wyndham Lewis,'' GENIUS: AN

IDEOLOGY IN LITERATURE (London: Chatto and Windus, 1974; New York: Schocken, 1974), pp. 116-42

A philosophico-literary essay, tracing within Lewis's fiction and political thought the illiberal tendencies inherent in Modernism and traceable to the degenerate Romanticism from which Modernism issues. (See MOD 27).

WL41:    Jameson, Fredric
FABLES OF AGGRESSION: WYNDHAM LEWIS, THE MODERNIST AS FASCIST (Berkeley, Los Angeles and London: University of California Press, 1979)

Scintillating Marxist — structuralist and neo-Freudian analysis of the transformations in Lewis's work, from the democratic prose of the early stories to the static, death-filled figuration of his later fiction. Jameson seeks to describe and explain the social, political and literary choices by which early modernists became, after the First World War, supporters of fascism. Contains some of the best criticism of "Cantleman's Spring-Mate," *The Childermass* and *The Human Age*.

WL42:    Manganiello, Dominic
"The Reaction to Fascism," JOYCE'S POLITICS (London and Boston: Routledge & Kegan Paul, 1980), pp. 227-34

Illuminating discussion of James Joyce's satire in *Finnegans Wake* of Lewis's fiction and politics.

# Anthologies of Articles on Wyndham Lewis

WL43:    Wyndham Lewis Special Issue
*Agenda*, 7:3/4; 8:1 (Autumn-Winter 1969-70)

A collection of essays on Lewis's life and career as a writer and as a painter, with reviews of works on Lewis, reminiscences of Lewis, and unpublished pieces by Lewis himself.

Martin Seymour-Smith: "Wyndham Lewis as Imaginative Writer," pp. 9-15. On the polemical nature of Lewis's imagination. Owing to illness in mid-career, his view of humanity became misanthropic. Only in *The Human Age* did he achieve a truly tragic vision.

I.A. Richards: "A Talk on *The Childermass*," pp. 16-21. Admits himself baffled by "this dismaying and entrancing book."

Penelope Palmer: "*The Human Age*," pp. 22-30. *The Human Age* is "an immensely intelligent vision," whose metaphysics Palmer brilliantly explicates. Concludes that it is not an aesthetic success.

Peter Dale: "*Self Condemned*," pp. 31-6. Harding is meant to be the tragic hero of the novel, but our sympathies lie with his wife, whose sufferings are greater.

Julian Symons: "The Thirties Novels," pp. 37-48. Lewis's novels, written with a popular audience in mind, seek to expose the false political and social values of the time. For that reason, their characters do not evoke our sympathy.

Ezra Pound: "Argument of the Novel," pp. 49-56. James Joyce's *Ulysses*, E.E. Cummings's *Eimi*, and Lewis's *The Apes of God* diagnose the corrupt state of contemporary society.

Timothy Materer: "The Great English Vortex," pp. 57-65. Places *The Apes of God* in its social and literary context.

Rebecca West: "*Tarr*," pp. 67-9. Early review of *Tarr* as a Dostoevskyian work.

Peter Dale: "*The Revenge for Love*," pp. 71-7. Lewis's obtrusiveness ruins the credibility of his fiction.

Walter Michel: "Wyndham Lewis the Painter," pp. 78-84. A brief survey of his career as a painter.

Ezra Pound: "The War Paintings of Wyndham Lewis," pp. 85-7.

Edmund Gray: "Wyndham Lewis and the Modern Crisis of Painting," pp. 88-92. On the successes and failures of Lewis's paintings.

E.W.F. Tomlin: "Reflections on *Time and Western Man*," pp. 97-108. Argues that this is one of the major works of the century, which seeks to defend the values of the intellect, under threat from the philosophers and psychologists of the present century.

C.H. Sisson: "The Politics of Wyndham Lewis," pp. 109-16. A review of Lewis's political writings, which advocate the aloofness of the intellectual. In the thirties,

Lewis was not always true to his own stated position.

W.K. Rose: "Pound and Lewis: the Crucial Years," pp. 117-33. On the relations between the two men.

Kenneth Cox: "Dualism and Les Autres," pp. 134-9. Lewis recognised the weakness of Modernism, which came from its lack of interest in social and political theory, and attempted to rectify it.

William H. Pritchard: "Lawrence and Lewis," pp. 140-7. On the similarity of their critical reception.

Alan Bold: *"One-Way Song,"* pp. 148-55. An exposition and defence of the poem: "Lewis managed to produce one of the few outstanding long poems in the English language this century."

Annamaria Sala: "Some Notes on Vorticism and Futurism," pp. 156-62. A brief history of the two movements which stresses their differences.

D.G. Bridson: "The Making of *The Human Age*," pp. 163-71. Reminiscences by the producer of *The Human Age*, first written for broadcast on the BBC.

Hugh Gordon Porteus: "A Man Apart," pp. 172-9. Reminiscences of Lewis in the thirties.

WL44:     Meyers, Jeffrey (ed.)
WYNDHAM LEWIS: A REVALUATION (London: Athlone Press, 1980; Montreal: McGill-Queen's University Press, 1980)

A first-rate collection of original essays on Lewis, covering the span of his literary career.

John Holloway: "Machine and Puppet: A Comparative View," pp. 3-14. An outstanding essay which examines the links between Lewis's work as a painter and as a writer.

Robert Chapman: "Letters and Autobiographies," pp. 15-28. On the multiple masks of the letters and autobiographies.

E.W.F. Tomlin: "The Philosophical Influences," pp. 29-46. On Schopenhauer, Nietzsche, Sorel and Bergson.

Timothy Materer: "Lewis and the Patriarchs: Augustus John, W.B. Yeats, T. Sturge Moore," pp. 47-63. On Lewis's friendship with Augustus John, W.B. Yeats and T. Sturge Moore. Valuable for placing Lewis in relation to English Idealism.

Marshall McLuhan: "Lewis's Prose Style," pp. 64-7.

"Lewis the painter turned to literature in an age of passive mechanical photography. As a writer he set out to educate the eye by means of deft organization of gestures."

Bernard Lafourcade: "The Taming of the Wild Body," pp. 68-84. In the writing of "The Wild Body" Lewis "achieved a sort of self-analysis, which . . . brought him face to face with the absurd."

Hugh Kenner: "*Mrs. Dukes' Million*: The Stunt of an Illusionist," pp. 85-91. ". . . semblance and manifold illusion were thoroughly familiar to Lewis well before 1914." It was in 1914, however, (after the writing of the novel) that he learned how deadly were the illusionist's tricks.

Wendy Stallard Flory: "*Enemy of the Stars*," pp. 92-106. "*Enemy of the Stars* shows that the fear of mortality lies at the heart of all Arghol's problems and this play provides us with a crucial insight into Lewis's own thinking that helps us to understand the nature of the satire in his other works."

Alistair Davies: "*Tarr*: A Nietzschean Novel," pp. 107-19. "*Tarr* has been found wanting in structure and characterization because it has been judged by conventions of tragic or dramatic action which are inappropriate. Lewis, who had spent several months of study in Munich in 1905, makes use of and adapts to his own ends as a novelist the form employed by the two leading German avant-garde writers of the period, the Nietzschean novella."

Alan Munton: "A Reading of *The Childermass*," pp. 120-32. "Lewis exposes the working of an ideology in *The Childermass*, which is a radical and humane work, having none of the reactionary tendencies usually attributed to Lewis."

Paul Edwards: "*The Apes of God*: Form and Meaning," pp. 133-48. "*The Apes of God* is one of the major pessimistic achievements of literary modernism."

William M. Chace: "On Lewis's Politics: The Polemics Polemically Answered," pp. 149-65. The hostile judgement of Lewis's politics is deserved.

C.J. Fox: "Lewis as Travel Writer: The Forgotten *Filibusters in Barbary*," pp. 166-80.

Rowland Smith: "*Snooty Baronet*: Satire and Censorship," pp. 181-95. Explores the circumstances surrounding the writing and publication of the novel; and discusses its "strengths as satire," typical of Lewis's work in the thirties.

William H. Pritchard: "Literary Criticism as Satire,"
pp. 196-210. On the virtues and limitations of Lewis's
literary criticism, which deserves more attention than it
has received.

Valerie Parker: "Enemies of the Absolute: Lewis, Art
and Women," pp. 211-25. "Lewis was not hostile to
women but found it necessary to adopt this stance because
he was trying to reject the ideology and structure of the
English nineteenth-century novel."

Jeffrey Meyers: "*Self Condemned,*" pp. 226-37.
"Lewis's finest novel remains extraordinarily close to his
personal experience, and gains enormous power by the
self-lacerating exposure of his most intimate feelings and
deepest suffering. Yet Lewis also maintained the requisite
aesthetic distance... ".

D.G.Bridson: "*The Human Age* in Retrospect,"
pp. 238-51. Observations by the producer of the radio
dramas from which the final version of *The Human Age*
was fashioned.

# Wyndham Lewis and the Visual Arts

WL45:    Michel, Walter (ed.)
WYNDHAM LEWIS: PAINTINGS AND
DRAWINGS (Berkeley and Los Angeles: University of
California Press, 1971; London: Thames and Hudson,
1971)

Reproduces Lewis's major works, with an expository
essay by Hugh Kenner.

WL46:    Wees, William C.
VORTICISM AND THE ENGLISH
AVANT-GARDE (Toronto: University of Toronto
Press, 1972; Manchester: Manchester University Press,
1972)

First-rate contextual study, describing Vorticism as a
movement and analysing the social forces which shaped it.

WL47:    Cork, Richard

VORTICISM AND ABSTRACT ART IN THE
FIRST MACHINE AGE (2 Vols.) (London: Gordon
Fraser, 1976; Berkeley and Los Angeles: University of
California Press, Vol.1, 1976; Vol.2, 1977)

Monumental study of English Vorticism, showing the
breadth and variety of the movement. Lewis (by no means
pre-eminent as an artist) was pre-eminent as a propa-
gandist.

# Part IV
# DAVID HERBERT LAWRENCE
# 1885-1930

# Bibliographical Information

For the standard bibliography of Lawrence's writings, see Warren Roberts, A BIBLIOGRAPHY OF D.H. LAWRENCE (London: Rupert Hart-Davis, 1963). Omissions and additions are given in the *Times Literary Supplement*, November 3, 1966, 1012; November 10, 1966, 1023; and November 17, 1966, 1052. For a comprehensive calendar of Lawrence's works, see Keith Sagar, D.H. LAWRENCE: A CALENDAR OF HIS WORKS (Austin: University of Texas Press, 1979; Manchester: Manchester University Press, 1979). The same volume contains a checklist, compiled by Lindeth Vasey, of Lawrence's manuscripts, giving their locations, and an appendix giving the locations of Lawrence's major paintings.

There is no adequate bibliography of criticism on Lawrence. See, for criticism until 1959, Maurice Beebe and Anthony Tommasi, "Criticism of D.H. Lawrence: A Selected Checklist of Criticism with an Index to Studies of Separate Works," *Modern Fiction Studies*, 5:1 (Spring 1959), 83-98. For criticism from 1959 to 1968, see the checklist compiled by R.D. Beards and G.B. Crump, "Ten Years of Criticism, 1959-1968," *D.H. Lawrence Review*, 1:3 (Fall 1968), 245-85. Since 1968, the spring volume of the *D.H. Lawrence Review* has contained an annual checklist of D.H. Lawrence criticism and scholarship, providing the fullest bibliographical information about criticism on Lawrence in English and in other languages.

# Memoirs and Biographies

DHL 1:     Lawrence, Frieda
           "NOT I BUT THE WIND..." (New York: Viking Press, 1934; London: W. Heinemann, 1935) (1974)

           The autobiography of Lawrence's wife.


DHL 2:     Lawrence, Frieda
           FRIEDA LAWRENCE: THE MEMOIRS AND CORRESPONDENCE, ed. E.W. Tedlock, Jr. (London: W. Heinemann, 1961; New York: Alfred A. Knopf, 1964)

DHL 3:     E.T. (Chambers, Jessie)
           D.H. LAWRENCE: A PERSONAL RECORD
           (London: Jonathan Cape, 1935; revised 2nd edn.,
           London: Frank Cass, 1965; New York: Barnes & Noble,
           1965) (1980)

           Invaluable account of Lawrence's early intellectual
           development, by the model for Miriam in *Sons and
           Lovers*. Although the account of their relationship is
           widely regarded as unreliable, the work is useful for its
           account of the rich and wide reading of the young
           Lawrence in late nineteenth-century materialist science,
           theology, and the French, Russian and English novel.
           Originally published under a pseudonym, E.T., the work
           was republished under the name of its author.

DHL 4:     Moore, Harry Thornton
           THE INTELLIGENT HEART: THE STORY OF
           D.H. LAWRENCE (New York: Grove Press, 1954;
           London: W. Heinemann, 1955)

           The first major biography of Lawrence, which attempted
           to present his life and work sympathetically, as that of a
           great creative spirit.

DHL 5:     Moore, Harry Thornton
           THE PRIEST OF LOVE: A LIFE OF
           D.H. LAWRENCE (New York: Farrar, Straus and
           Giroux, 1974; London: W. Heinemann, 1974)

           The above (DHL 4) revised and enlarged.

DHL 6:     Nehls, Edward (ed.)
           D.H. LAWRENCE: A COMPOSITE BIOGRAPHY
           (3 Vols.) (Madison: University of Wisconsin Press,
           1957-9)

           Brief fragments of biographical detail from Lawrence's
           family, friends, and associates, arranged to compose a
           many-sided portrait of Lawrence. Invaluable as a
           source-book and useful as a reminder of the partiality and
           bias of Lawrence's friends and associates.

DHL 7:    Weiss, Daniel A.
OEDIPUS IN NOTTINGHAM: D.H. LAWRENCE
(Seattle: University of Washington Press, 1962;
Nottingham: University of Nottingham Press, 1962)

Psycho-biography of Lawrence, who, according to Weiss, suffered from the Oedipus complex all his life. "*Sons and Lovers* is a coin whose reverse is the remainder of Lawrence's fiction."

DHL 8:    Corke, Helen
D.H. LAWRENCE: THE CROYDON YEARS
(Austin: University of Texas Press, 1965)

Portrait of Lawrence from 1909 to 1910 by the heroine of *The Trespasser*, most valuable for its account of Lawrence's reading at this time. Contains an account of Lawrence's discussion with her of the Apocalypse, which needs to be treated with caution.

DHL 9:    Moore, Harry T. and Roberts, Warren
D.H. LAWRENCE AND HIS WORLD (New York: Viking Press, 1966)

A critical biography, with 160 excellent photographs.

DHL 10:    Callow, Philip
SON AND LOVER: THE YOUNG LAWRENCE
(London: Bodley Head, 1975; New York: Stein and Day, 1975)

Biography of Lawrence's early life — until his departure from England in 1919.

DHL 11:    Delany, Paul
D.H. LAWRENCE'S NIGHTMARE: THE WRITER AND HIS CIRCLE IN THE YEARS OF THE GREAT WAR (New York: Basic Books, 1978; Hassocks, Sussex: Harvester Press, 1979)

Detailed, informative and convincing biographical study. Perhaps the best account of Lawrence's relationship with

Katherine Mansfield and John Middleton Murry; his
reactions to the First War; the writing of *Women in Love*.
Essential reading.

DHL 12:    Sagar, Keith
           THE LIFE OF D.H. LAWRENCE: AN
           ILLUSTRATED BIOGRAPHY (London: Eyre
           Methuen, 1980; New York: Pantheon, 1980)

           Composite biography, interesting mainly for its photo-
           graphs.

# Guides and Glossaries

DHL 13:    Gerard, David E.
           "Glossary of Eastwood Dialect Words Used by
           D.H. Lawrence in His Poems, Plays and Fiction,"
           *D.H. Lawrence Review*, 1:3 (Fall 1968), 215-37

DHL 14:    Holderness, Graham
           WHO'S WHO IN D.H. LAWRENCE (London: Elm
           Tree Books, for Hamish Hamilton, 1976; New York:
           Taplinger, 1976)

           "This book is not a crib for those seeking plot summaries,
           for it provides no facile synopses. It is rather a key to the
           understanding of the men, women, children (and animals)
           who appear in his fiction."

# Introductory Studies

DHL 15:    Draper, Ronald Philip
           D.H. LAWRENCE (New York: Twayne, 1964)

           Succinct, rich and comprehensive discussion, both of
           Lawrence's background and ideas, and of his fiction, tales
           and poems. Draper sympathetically analyses Lawrence's
           themes, his technique, his relation to realism, and judges
           his achievement within English literature. "Wholeness of

being is Lawrence's great theme, and to have gone at least part of the way towards discovering a mode of writing that would not merely advocate but communicate wholeness is his chief contribution to the English novel. The more particular achievement — the integration of the Romantics' visionary world with the world of the naturalist novel; his revaluation of the concept of 'character,' and his extension of the subject matter of the novel to include an inward portrayal of working-class life, and a serious treatment of man's sexual experience — all these are part of the over-riding and unifying theme of wholeness.'' Perhaps the best introductory study of Lawrence, with an interesting final chapter on Lawrence's reputation and influence. Contains a short annotated bibliography.

DHL 16:    Goode, John
           "D.H. Lawrence," HISTORY OF LITERATURE IN
           THE ENGLISH LANGUAGE: Vol.7 THE
           TWENTIETH CENTURY, ed. Bernard Bergonzi
           (London: Barrie and Jenkins, 1970), pp. 106-52

One of the best recent essays on Lawrence, placing him within his cultural and social context, and tracing the ideological contradictions revealed in his development as an artist.

DHL 17:    Kermode, (John) Frank
           LAWRENCE (London: Fontana/Collins, 1973; New
           York: Viking Press, 1973 under the title
           *D.H. LAWRENCE*)

A fine introductory study of Lawrence's life and work, which, in detailing Lawrence's recourse to apocalyptic thinking, voices anxiety about the incapacity of modernist fiction to accept and render radical contingency.

# Full-length Studies on Lawrence's Work and Career

DHL 18:    Murry, John Middleton
           SON OF WOMAN (London: Jonathan Cape, 1931; New
           York: J. Cape and H. Smith, 1931)

The first (and the best) psycho-biography of Lawrence. *The Rainbow* was "radically the history of Lawrence's final sexual failure." Thereafter, his fiction presented a series of aggressive fantasies in which "the unsatisfactory, demanding female" was annihilated by the man who could not satisfy her.

DHL 19:     Eliot, Thomas Stearns
AFTER STRANGE GODS: A PRIMER OF
MODERN HERESY (New York: Harcourt Brace,
1933; London: Faber and Faber, 1934)

The most sustained, early critique of Lawrence. Influenced by the degenerate Protestantism of his youth, educated on an inadequate fare of eccentric English literature, Lawrence lacked "the critical faculties which education should give." He appealed only to "the sick and debile and confused."

DHL 20:     Tindall, William York
D.H. LAWRENCE AND SUSAN HIS COW
(Columbia: Columbia University Press, 1939) (1973)

Amusing and often derogatory account of Lawrence, written under the inspiration of T.S. Eliot. "Lawrence's Protestant departure from Christian ways led to strange places and stranger notions." Tindall provides one of the first, full-scale analyses of *The Plumed Serpent*, and of Lawrence's illiberal politics which it revealed. Lawrence, whose individualism made him resistant to totalitarianism, believed in theocracy, "like the Puritans of Massachusetts and the Fifth Monarchy rebellions." The study contains important research on Lawrence's reading in esoterica, in anthropology, in books on ancient civilisations, and on New World antiquities. "I have shown the sources upon which Lawrence drew for his Egyptian, Mexican and Etruscan wanderings." His Hinduism might lead him to venerate his cow, Susan.

DHL 21:     Young, Kenneth
D.H. LAWRENCE (London, New York and Toronto:
Longmans, Green, 1952)

British Council pamphlet on Lawrence, which is now only of interest because of the well-deserved derision it attracted from F.R. Leavis.

DHL 22:  Leavis, Frank Raymond
D.H. LAWRENCE NOVELIST (London: Chatto and Windus, 1955; New York: Alfred A. Knopf, 1956)

The single most important study of Lawrence, responsible for the establishment of Lawrence's reputation in English and American letters as "not only . . . our last great writer" but as "the great writer of our phase of civilisation." In a series of essays on *St. Mawr*, *The Rainbow*, *Women in Love* and *Lady Chatterley's Lover*, Leavis argues for Lawrence's greatness both as an artist and as a moralist, and does so in explicit response to the views of John Middleton Murry (DHL 18) and T.S. Eliot (DHL 19). Leavis's study is not only an outstanding appreciation of Lawrence's work and achievement. It is also the work from which much subsequent criticism of Lawrence, in agreement and in disagreement, has taken its starting-point.

DHL 23:  Spilka, Mark
THE LOVE ETHIC OF D.H. LAWRENCE
(Bloomington: Indiana University Press, 1955; London: Dennis Dobson, 1958)

Spilka, in a study which began the serious appraisal of Lawrence in American criticism, relates the "religious dimension in his fiction" to the "mana" concept as defined by Ernst Cassirer in *Language and Myth*: "Lawrence was a religious artist . . . and his work was governed by religious ends. To understand Lawrence properly, we need some adequate definition of his central religious impulse. Because of his belief in the life-force, he has generally been called 'a vitalist.' But 'organicist' would come closer to the mark, since the goal of life, for Lawrence, was organic wholeness." Furthermore, "the art of the novel was *the* religious art for Lawrence," for "in the novel he could speak for the whole man about wholeness." His novels "body forth that general pattern of experience which I would call his love ethic — and by using that phrase 'love ethic,' I would emphasise his radical commitment to spontaneous life and to 'phallic marriage' as the fount of life itself.'' Discusses *Sons and Lovers, The Rainbow, Women in Love, Lady Chatterley's Lover* and *The Man Who Died.*

DHL 24:    Hough, Graham
THE DARK SUN: A STUDY OF D.H. LAWRENCE
(London: Duckworth, 1956; New York: Macmillan, 1957)
(1972)

The first complete critical survey of Lawrence's fiction and poetry by a critic who was not an advocate of Lawrence. Not only does it contain generally excellent expositions of Lawrence's work, it also conveys a sense of the doctrinal unity which underlies Lawrence's creative achievement.

DHL 25:    Vivas, Eliseo
D.H. LAWRENCE: THE FAILURE AND
TRIUMPH OF ART (Evanston: Northwestern
University Press, 1960)

''The first and most difficult problem that the critic of Lawrence has to face is that of distinguishing . . . poetry from prophecy.'' When Lawrence is examined in this light, it becomes clear that ''after *Women in Love*, Lawrence is not able to inform the matter of his experience with the success he had achieved earlier.'' The study begins with ''a detailed examination of the work that Lawrence did after *Women in Love* (*Aaron's Rod, Kangaroo, The Plumed Serpent*, and *Lady Chatterley's Lover*) which will show that, whatever its many incidental aesthetic excellences and whatever its ideological value, on the whole it does not come up to the purity exhibited in his two greatest works, *The Rainbow* and *Women in Love*.'' The study ends with a discussion of those works, attempting to define ''the constitutive symbols'' through which Lawrence grasps and expresses the complexity of the world.

DHL 26:    Widmer, Kingsley
THE ART OF PERVERSITY: D.H. LAWRENCE'S
SHORTER FICTIONS (Seattle: University of
Washington Press, 1962)

"The subjects of this essay are the art and attitude of the more than sixty short stories and novellas of D.H. Lawrence. These fictions, I believe, constitute Lawrence's central writings." Widmer presents "an apologia for perversity" in Lawrence's fiction: "Lawrence's negative ways to his affirmations provide the cruxes of understanding." For Widmer, "the perverse view, which may well be an inadequately acknowledged part of our common sensibility, uses angry intelligence and sophisticated art to achieve relations to reality that, apparently, certain primitive and mystics attain by less tortuous means." Still a controversial study.

DHL 27:     Goodheart, Eugene
THE UTOPIAN VISION OF D.H. LAWRENCE
(Chicago: University of Chicago Press, 1963)

Goodheart's study, inspired by Karl Jaspers, argues that Lawrence's imagination, in his fiction as well as in his other writings, was neither diabolist nor nihilist. It was, while creatively drawing upon the past, turned toward the future. Underlying his whole career was a religious-creative quest for transcendence. Its characteristic impulse was to discover the new forms of life immanent, though not actual, in the world. Lawrence's fiction extended beyond the level of social and psychological realism: his career was "a repudiation of art which is content to imitate already enacted life." His principal discovery was the bodily life that man had once possessed in his pre-civilised past, and must now fully recover if future, civilised life is to be possible. Accordingly, Lawrence's symbolism is seen as an attempt to recreate the pre-civilised, mythic consciousness which modern man had lost.

As a social theorist, Lawrence tried to overcome the division between self and society, accepted by the English social novel and legitimised by Sigmund Freud, through the notion of spontaneous being. Society was not to be a system of obligation. It was to be the fulfilment of the human impulse toward community with others. Lawrence sought to describe the quest for oneness with the cosmos, a position which at times led him to "erotic solipsism" in his novels, and to the cult of power in his political novels. But his distrust of coercion, of anything which prevented autonomy, kept Lawrence "firmly away from totalitarian temptations."

To stress the revolutionary implications of Lawrence's utopianism, Goodheart argues, against F.R. Leavis, that his work was not exclusively derived from the English non-conformist tradition. Lawrence, a "tablet-breaker and visionary" in the manner of Blake, Dostoevsky and Nietzsche, rejected traditional Christian morality (and its influences within English fiction), in order to renew the possibilities of religious experience in the post-Christian era. One of the key studies of Lawrence.

DHL 28:     Moynahan, Julian
THE DEED OF LIFE: THE NOVELS AND TALES OF D.H. LAWRENCE (Princeton, N.J.: Princeton University Press, 1963; London: Oxford University Press, 1963)

"This book is a study of Lawrence's works of fiction as works of art." Lawrence, inspired by developments in modern painting, extended the tradition of the novel. "The task of the writer is to invent a new world within the known world, the 'known world' standing here for the developed form at any given moment of its history, the 'new world' standing for what has been innovated by any given major novelist." Lawrence's career involved the search for a form adequate to show the effect of the impersonal and the vital, and to represent the integration of the social and the inhuman self. "*Sons and Lovers, Women in Love, The Lost Girl* and *Lady Chatterley's Lover* stand out superior in interest and achievement and are given the more extended treatment. *Aaron's Rod, Kangaroo, The Plumed Serpent* are treated in a single chapter. The assumption is that they are unsuccessful books." The study contains outstanding analyses of *Women in Love* and *Lady Chatterley's Lover* and provides one of the best discussions to date of Lawrence's techniques of fiction.

DHL 29:     Tedlock, Ernest Warnock
D.H. LAWRENCE: ARTIST AND REBEL (Albuquerque: University of New Mexico Press, 1963)

Lawrence's art is inseparable from "rebellion, in the sense in which Camus used it in his history and analysis of the perilous position of so many modern intellectuals . . . between the reformist side of their radical discontent and the disastrous nihilism that often resulted." Lawrence avoided nihilism, maintaining a tension between his religious "apprehension of the wonder and evolutionary purpose of natural life, and his revulsion against the modern civilisation that he feels to be at cross-purposes with." Contains a comprehensive discussion of the novels and short stories.

DHL 30:     Panichas, George Andrew
ADVENTURE IN CONSCIOUSNESS: THE
MEANING OF D.H. LAWRENCE'S RELIGIOUS
QUEST (The Hague and Paris: Mouton, 1964)

Lawrence is a writer with a religious vision. Discusses Lawrence and Dostoevsky; *David*; Lawrence and the War; *Last Poems*; and Lawrence and Christianity.

DHL 31:     Daleski, Herman M.
THE FORKED FLAME: A STUDY OF
D.H. LAWRENCE (Evanston: Northwestern
University Press, 1965)

The first study to give prominence to Lawrence's essays, particularly the *Study of Thomas Hardy*. "It is wise to regard the expository writings not as laboratory reports on experiments successfully concluded but as signposts to a road which is finally travelled only in the 'art'." Daleski explores "a central feature of Lawrence's thought — its dualism," particularly that of male and female, in *Sons and Lovers, The Rainbow, Women in Love, Aaron's Rod, The Plumed Serpent*, and *Lady Chatterley's Lover*. "It is my contention that Lawrence, though believing in himself as a male, was fundamentally identified with the female principle as he himself defines it in the essay on Hardy. The consequent breach in his nature made it imperative for him to try to reconcile the opposed elements within himself, and I have viewed his work as a lifelong attempt to effect such a reconciliation." One of the best discussions both of the structure and the development of Lawrence's thought and writing.

DHL 32: Ford, George H.
DOUBLE MEASURE: A STUDY OF THE NOVELS
AND STORIES OF D.H. LAWRENCE (New York:
Holt, Rinehart and Winston, 1965)

"In the essay on Poe the opposition described is not only
between life and death forces, but between two contrary
drives in human relations, the one impelling us toward
isolation, the other toward union." Lawrence's fiction
explores the forces of life and of sickness, of togetherness
and of solitude, at work in individual and communal life.
But Lawrence, extending the realist tradition of English
fiction, finds also a method to explore these contraries in a
structural double measure, discourse and image. "His
best fiction portrays conflicts . . . in which a dramatic
testing is more significant than a simplified evaluation."
The major part of the study concerns *The Rainbow* and
*Women in Love*, Lawrence's "greatest fictions." In *The
Rainbow*, despite the instrusion of individualism, the
setting is predominantly of farm and village. In *Women in
Love*, the setting is of crumbling contemporary civilisation, "Cities of the Plain, from which the hero and the
heroine must make their hard won escape." One of the
best discussions of these two novels, particularly of their
biblical and apocalyptic themes.

DHL 33: Sagar, Keith
THE ART OF D.H. LAWRENCE (Cambridge and
New York: Cambridge University Press, 1966)

"Dr. Leavis' approach yields countless valuable insights
and the most definitive account yet of Lawrence's art.
This study will be largely a matter of confirming Dr.
Leavis' findings, though from a somewhat different
approach. . . . By concentrating more on Lawrence's
reaction *against* the English realist tradition, and on his
search for an access to a deeper and more permanent
reality, I hope to contribute some insights complementary
to those of Dr. Leavis, and to bring us a little nearer to
understanding the nature and magnitude of Lawrence's
achievement." Particularly good on Lawrence's poetry.
Contains a very full bibliography.

DHL 34: Clarke, Colin Campbell
RIVER OF DISSOLUTION: D.H. LAWRENCE

AND ENGLISH ROMANTICISM (London:
Routledge & Kegan Paul, 1969; New York: Barnes &
Noble, 1969)

Current Lawrence criticism is moralistic, either denying
the theme of decadence in Lawrence, or criticising
Lawrence for his satanism, finding beauty in the
phosphorescence of decay. "Virtually nothing has been
written on Lawrence's debt to the English Romantic
poets." They express views that have "close affinities
with the ones I have been considering — the ambivalence
of Lawrence's attitude to corruption." In *The Rainbow*
and *Women in Love*, which the study examines, the
process of dissolution, which breaks down the ego, is seen
to be positive, leading to a "creative-destructive fullness
of being." A demanding and historically important study.

DHL 35:   Yudhistar
CONFLICT IN THE NOVELS OF
D.H. LAWRENCE (Edinburgh: Oliver and Boyd, 1969;
New York: Barnes & Noble, 1969)

Lawrence explored the relations between men and
women, but became concerned with defining man's need
for self-possession, for freeing men and women for
"isolate self-responsibility." Accordingly, Lawrence's
fiction after *Women in Love* should not be judged as
inferior to his earlier work. Contains an exemplary
discussion of *Aaron's Rod*.

DHL 36:   Baruch, Hochman
ANOTHER EGO: THE CHANGING VIEW OF
SELF AND SOCIETY IN THE WORK OF
D.H. LAWRENCE (Columbia: University of South
Carolina Press, 1970)

Lawrence moves from a radical individualism to what "I
term a radical (if qualified) communalism." Lawrence
"stands between the Romantic visionaries, who turned
their attention to the workings of the deepest subjectivity,
and such contemporary thinkers as Herbert Marcuse and
Norman O. Brown, who envision possibilities of a
non-represssive mode of being that would free man from
the negative, destructive burden of civilisation... . Assum-

ing the natural sociality of man, he trusts that conception
of sociality to suit his immediate ends." Good on
Lawrence's response to the First World War.


DHL 37:     Alldritt, Keith
            THE VISUAL IMAGINATION OF
            D.H. LAWRENCE (London: Edward Arnold, 1971;
            Evanston: Northwestern University Press, 1971)

"One of the most important conditions of Lawrence's
genius was that it grew to maturity during one of those rare
periods in which the visual arts in England retained a
European significance. The writings of Ruskin and of
Pater, the works of the pre-Raphaelites, and of William
Morris . . . constitute a tradition . . . which had a
powerful effect throughout Europe." Lawrence was able
to modify and enlarge the drab outlook of realism "by a
pictorial vision that introduces a new, simultaneously
moral and visual quality into his fictional art." This
quality is one of the factors which accounts for the epic
quality of *The Rainbow*, a work which is epic by "virtue of
the kind of vision which informs the writing." *Women in
Love*, in its prose style and subject matter, records
Lawrence's reaction to the aestheticist, primitivist and
futurist traditions of Modernism in painting and sculpture
from a perspective derived from Lawrence's study of
Cézanne. "The seen world is a subject of doubt —
pervading the structure of the novel as a whole. It is there
in the simultaneous manysidedness, in the depiction of
English society, which contrasts so strongly with the
traditional linearity of the narrative of *The Rainbow*."
Alldritt's argument is Lukacsian: vision is as much
cultural as retinal. "In the early prose it is easy to see the
presence . . . of certain images and configurations that we
associate with Blake, the English landscape painters,
Rossetti and some of the Italian painters commended by
Ruskin himself." Lawrence's mind was marked by the
particular visual sensibility of the Victorian period, but
*Women in Love* reveals "the abrupt superannuation of
this tradition of seeing. For all its power, there is a
diminution of cultural density in subject matter and an
enforced experimentation in style. It is the major
representation of a momentous crisis in English culture."
Lawrence's art appears to lose contact with its native
culture, as the epic vision becomes a fragmentary one.

After *Women in Love*, there are no new themes or perspectives in Lawrence's novels.

Alldritt's brilliant study contributes greatly to an understanding of the nature of Lawrence's prose style. By drawing attention to Lawrence's critique of John Ruskin and William Morris as social thinkers in *The Rainbow*, he also clarifies Lawrence's relationship to the tradition of social and cultural revolt from which his best work comes. An indispensable study.

DHL 38:    Miko, Stephen J.
TOWARD *WOMEN IN LOVE*: THE EMERGENCE OF A LAWRENTIAN AESTHETIC (New Haven and London: Yale University Press, 1971)

An account of Lawrence's first five novels, from *The White Peacock* and *The Trespasser*, which are discussed in detail, to *Women in Love*. "All the first five novels present evidence of a search for the most fundamental kinds of consistency, a basic search for coherence, not just of the world of the novels, stories and poems, but of human life itself. . . . It is ambitious to articulate such a search in novels. . . . But this sort of writing only emerged once he had found himself as a novelist, at the time when his novels were becoming more distinctly Lawrentian." Miko analyses the changes from realism to "the symbolic scene" in Lawrence's fiction, as the author finds means to express and to represent a dualistic metaphysic. "To our comprehension, the world is everywhere divided, even when we consider it metaphysically. The closest we can come to describing the ultimate unity is to call it a relation, especially a relation between man and his universe. And when pressed to show when such a relation exists, we can point, or at least Lawrence pointed, towards works of art as living things, insisting that an ultimate balance could be intuited, though it was grounded in a 'fourth dimension'." A difficult study, which is throughout concerned with Lawrence's style and technique. One of the key books on Lawrence, most suitable for advanced students.

DHL 39:    Pritchard, Ronald Edward
D.H. LAWRENCE: BODY OF DARKNESS (London: Hutchinson, 1971; Pittsburgh: University of Pittsburgh Press, 1971)

The author devotes particular attention to Lawrence's psychological problems and development, believing a true appreciation of these essential to an understanding of Lawrence's response to life. "Like all artists, especially perhaps Romantic artists, he projected his own agonies on to the world he saw; but like all great artists, his courageous exploration of his own nature enabled him to become a profound and prophetic analyst of the crisis in the culture of his own time." Discusses the fiction, poetry and social writings of Lawrence.

DHL 40:    Stoll, John E.
THE NOVELS OF D.H. LAWRENCE: A SEARCH FOR INTEGRATION (Columbia: University of Missouri Press, 1971)

A study of dualism in Lawrence's work, exploring the split between the known and the vital self; between the conscious and the unconscious; between realism and symbolism in his fiction. "A response to the split, the novels are as a whole conditioned by a basic quest for the wholeness of being." References to Sigmund Freud and Carl Jung, *passim*.

DHL 41:    Sanders, Scott
D.H. LAWRENCE: THE WORLD OF THE MAJOR NOVELS (London: Vision Press, 1973; New York: Viking Press, 1974)

A structuralist analysis of the relationship between Nature and Culture in Lawrence's major novels, "viewing the ideas as parts of a social system."

DHL 42:    Leavis, Frank Raymond
THOUGHT, WORDS AND CREATIVITY: ART AND THOUGHT IN D.H. LAWRENCE (London: Chatto and Windus, 1976)

A series of combative yet elegaic essays which "attempt to characterize the distinctive Laurentian genius" in its creative response to the problems of modern, mass-industrial society. Concerned with the demise of an "educated public," Leavis acknowledges elegaically that "a new Lawrence has certainly been made impossible by the changed conditions." Discusses *The Plumed Serpent, Women in Love, The Captain's Doll* and *The Rainbow*.


DHL 43:     Niven, Alastair
            **D.H. LAWRENCE: THE NOVELS** (Cambridge and
            New York: Cambridge University Press, 1978)

A solid study of Lawrence's fiction, incorporating a general assessment of his cultural and historical significance with a close analysis of his method. Niven discusses the ten major novels, believing that *The White Peacock* and *The Trespasser* are central to an understanding of Lawrence's later development, and that *Kangaroo* is "the most undervalued of all Lawrence's novels." By contrast, "*Aaron's Rod* seems a negative work, and *The Plumed Serpent* too inflexibly positive. . . . All three have been criticised for being bitty and broken-backed, but I have attempted to show the necessity for this." Niven concludes that outrage, vigour, self-righteousness and scorn can be found throughout Lawrence's work, but they are tempered by his constant desire to press on beyond the immediate perception or the apparently obvious truism. "Doubt and enquiry are far more typical of Lawrence's fiction than dogmatism."


DHL 44:     Worthen, John
            **D.H. LAWRENCE AND THE IDEA OF THE
            NOVEL** (London: Macmillan, 1979; New York:
            Rowman, 1979)

"Lawrence knew, as an imaginative writer as well as an ordinary man, that someone of his own upbringing was almost inevitably caught between a social isolation created by an uneasily divided upbringing and an often nostalgic attachment to the very idea of community." Lawrence's theory and practice of the novel changed as his relationship to his audience changed.

# Articles and Chapters from Books on Lawrence's Work and Career

DHL 45:     Raleigh, John Henry
"Victorian Morals and the Modern Novel," *Partisan Review*, 25:2 (Spring 1958), 241-65

Brief account of Lawrence's "protesting voice against literary tradition." James Joyce represents the novel of middle-class consciousness, "Lawrence the counter-attack from below." He was an anarchist, "one of the shakers who can revitalise the tradition."

DHL 46:     Walsh, William
THE USE OF THE IMAGINATION:
EDUCATIONAL THOUGHT AND THE
LITERARY MIND (London: Chatto and Windus, 1959)

This includes "The Writer as Teacher: The Educational Ideas of D.H. Lawrence," pp. 199-228 and "The Writer and The Child," pp. 163-74, a discussion of Ursula's relation to her father in *The Rainbow*.

DHL 47:     Baldanza, Frank
"D.H. Lawrence's Song of Songs," *Modern Fiction Studies*, 7:2 (Summer 1961), 106-14

Biblical prosody, representing the oldest and most primitive emotional expression of the Jewish people, had a special influence on Lawrence's style.

DHL 48:     Hoffman, Frederick John
THE MORTAL NO: DEATH AND THE MODERN
IMAGINATION (Princeton, N.J.: Princeton
University Press, 1964), pp. 406-23

Lawrence's fiction and poetry discussed in terms of the three major patterns which define the move towards the literature of violence in our century: "the ambiguities of 'reason' in its application to social definition; the growth towards secularization of literary metaphor; and the importunate, disturbing pressure of violence upon established literary forms." Concentrates upon *Women in Love*.

DHL 49: Lerner, Laurence
"D.H. Lawrence," THE TRUTHTELLERS: JANE AUSTEN, GEORGE ELIOT AND
D.H. LAWRENCE (London: Chatto and Windus, 1967; New York: Schocken, 1967), pp. 172-235

Lucidly expressed reservations, from a liberal viewpoint, about Lawrence's sexual and political doctrines, as they emerge in his fiction and poetry.

DHL 50: Friedman, Alan
"The Other Lawrence," *Partisan Review*, 37:2 (1970), 239-53

Compares the techniques of James Joyce and D.H. Lawrence in rendering the unconscious, finding Lawrence a more radical innovator.

DHL 51: Garcia, Reloy
"The Quest for Paradise in the Novels of
D.H. Lawrence," *D.H. Lawrence Review*, 3:2 (Summer 1970), 93-114

On the conflict of the country and the city, (on the quest for sanctuary) in Lawrence's fiction.

DHL 52: Bedient, Calvin
"D.H. Lawrence," ARCHITECTS OF THE SELF: GEORGE ELIOT, D.H. LAWRENCE AND
E.M. FORSTER (Berkeley, Los Angeles and London: University of California Press, 1972), pp. 115-95

The study presents four outstanding and judicious chapters on the vital self, the politics of being, *Lady Chatterley's Lover*, and on the writings of Lawrence and E.M. Forster about Italy. Lawrence is seen, through a contrast with George Eliot, to reverse Victorian values: "from the doctrine of living for others, conscience and

faith . . . to the doctrine of living out of all the
'promptings' of the self."

DHL 53:    Donoghue, Denis
           "Prometheus in Straits," *Times Literary Supplement*,
           November 10, 1972, 1371-3

           Lawrence is Promethean in valuing energy and violence.
           Yet his fiction offers a critique of these values. Discusses
           T.S. Eliot's quarrel with Lawrence.
           Reprinted in Denis Donoghue, THIEVES OF FIRE
           (New York: Oxford University Press, 1974), pp. 111-39.

DHL 54:    Craig, David
           THE REAL FOUNDATION: LITERATURE AND
           SOCIAL CHANGE (London: Chatto and Windus 1973;
           New York: Oxford University Press, 1974)

           Contains two essays on Lawrence: "Shakespeare,
           Lawrence, and Sexual Freedom," pp. 17-38 (on *Measure
           for Measure* and Lawrence's short stories); and "Law-
           rence and Democracy," pp. 143-67 (on Lawrence's
           "seriously mistaken and unjust reaction to the movement
           for democracy" in *Women in Love*).

DHL 55:    Sale, Roger
           "D.H. Lawrence, 1910-1916," MODERN HEROISM:
           ESSAYS ON D.H. LAWRENCE, WILLIAM
           EMPSON AND J.R.R. TOLKIEN (Los Angeles and
           London: University of California Press, 1973),
           pp. 16-106

           Lawrence was a writer "driven to become a historian of
           the Myth of Lost Unity who then refused to accept the
           generally held attitudes toward the Myth." This period of
           defiance was followed by another, of retreat, into "a
           personally needed code or dogma." Discusses Law-
           rence's whole career, with particular emphasis on *The
           Rainbow* and *Women in Love*.

DHL 56:    Adamowski, T.H.
           "Character and Consciousness: D.H. Lawrence,

Wilhelm Reich, and Jean-Paul Sartre,'' *University of Torono Quarterly*, 43:4 (Summer 1974), 311-34

Presents similarities and differences in the views of these three writers relating to freedom and the self.

DHL 57:    Spender, Stephen
''English Threnody, American Tragedy,'' LOVE-HATE RELATIONS: A STUDY OF ANGLO-AMERICAN SENSIBILITIES (London: Hamish Hamilton, 1974; New York: Random House, 1974), pp. 159-202

Presents a subtle and convincing comparison of D.H. Lawrence and E.M. Forster. ''Lawrence had a revivalist temperament and he had more faith in a resurgence of England than had Forster.''

DHL 58:    Stewart, Garrett
''Lawrence, 'Being', and the Allotropic Style,'' *Novel*, 9:3 (Spring 1976), 217-42

Lawrence's style attempts to present an underlying reality.

DHL 59:    Wilt, Judith
''D.H. Lawrence: Ghosts in the Daylight,'' GHOSTS OF THE GOTHIC: AUSTEN, ELIOT AND LAWRENCE (Princeton, N.J.: Princeton University Press, 1980), pp. 231-92

Brilliant and suggestive discussion of Lawrence as a Gothic novelist, in the tradition of Jane Austen and George Eliot.

# Anthologies on Lawrence's Work and Career

DHL 60:    Moore, Harry T. and Hoffman, Frederick J. (eds.)
THE ACHIEVEMENT OF D.H. LAWRENCE
(Norman: University of Oklahoma Press, 1953)

The first anthology of criticism of Lawrence, now of most interest for its presentation of the dispute between T.S. Eliot and F.R. Leavis over the stature of Lawrence as a writer and thinker.

DHL 61:    Moore, Harry T. (ed.)
A D.H. LAWRENCE MISCELLANY (Carbondale: Southern Illinois University Press, 1959; London: W. Heinemann, 1961)

A collection of critical essays, reminiscences, memoirs, and textual studies. See: Marvin Mudrick: "The Originality of *The Rainbow*," pp. 54-81 (DHL 80); Angelo P. Bertocci, "Symbolism in *Women in Love*," pp. 82-101 (an important study of the dense, symbolic texture of the novel); Robert E. Gajdusek, "A Reading of *The White Peacock*," pp. 188-203 (an excellent discussion of its symbolism and of its autobiographical origins); Jascha Kessler, "Descent in Darkness: The Myth of *The Plumed Serpent*," pp. 239-61 (on the quest structure of the novel); Frederick R. Karl, "Lawrence's 'The Man Who Loved Islands': The Crusoe Who Failed," pp. 265-79 (argues that the work, unduly neglected, links the early and late fiction); Raymond Williams, "The Social Thinking of D.H. Lawrence," pp. 295-311 (on his Victorian antecedents); Richard Foster, "Criticism as Rage: D.H. Lawrence," pp. 312-25 (on the "felt quality" of Lawrence's critical response); Herbert Lindenberger: "Lawrence and the Romantic Tradition," pp. 326-40 (considers Lawrence's Romantic departure from "the novel of society"); A. Alvarez: "D.H. Lawrence: The Single State of Man," pp. 341-58 (a classic essay on Lawrence's achievement as a poet); Harold Bloom, "Lawrence, Blackmur, Eliot, and the Tortoise," pp. 359-68 (defends Lawrence's poetry against its detractors).

DHL 62:    Spilka, Mark (ed.)
D.H. LAWRENCE: A COLLECTION OF CRITICAL ESSAYS (Englewood Cliffs, N.J.: Prentice-Hall, 1963)

A well-balanced collection of essays, giving attention to Lawrence's hitherto neglected short stories and to his social views.

Mark Spilka: "Introduction," pp. 1-14. A fine bibliographical essay on Lawrence's critical reception.

Dorothy Van Ghent: "On *Sons and Lovers*," pp. 15-28. Discusses how the controlling idea "of an organic disturbance in the relationships of men and women" governs the structure and symbol of the novel.

Marvin Mudrick: "The Originality of *The Rainbow*," pp. 29-49. "*The Rainbow* is recording a community in its last flare of vitality." A classic essay.

Mark Schorer: "*Women in Love* and Death," pp. 50-60. Explores how the novel's new conception of "character as fate," its new themes of integration and disintegration of being, necessitate a new structure and a new prose.

Harry T. Moore: "*The Plumed Serpent*: Vision and Language," pp. 61-71. On the strengths and weakness of the novel. The failures of Lawrence's attempts to set up an ideal community in New Mexico must account "to some extent for the dichotomy between language and vision" in the novel.

Julian Moynahan: "*Lady Chatterley's Lover*: The Deed of Life," pp. 72-92. On the struggle between death-in-life and the vital realm in the novel. One of the best accounts of the work.

Monroe Engel: "The Continuity of Lawrence's Short Novels," pp. 93-100. ". . . these short novels constitute an extraordinary body of imaginatively realised thesis fiction." Discusses *The Fox, The Captain's Doll, The Ladybird, St. Mawr, The Man Who Died*.

Graham Hough: "Lawrence's Quarrel with Christianity: *The Man Who Died*," pp. 101-11. For Lawrence, the post-Christian era would not be pagan: "If a new order is to come into being, it will in its splendour and joy be the inheritor of Christian abnegation and suffering."

Mark Spilka: "Ritual Form in 'The Blind Man'," pp. 112-16. Describes how the "kinetic transformation of being" in Lawrence's short stories affects their form.

W.D. Snodgrass: "A Rocking-Horse: The Symbol, the Pattern, the Way to Live," pp. 117-26. On the masturbatory sexual symbolism in "The Rocking-Horse Winner."

V. de S. Pinto: "Poet Without a Mask," pp. 127-41. An excellent essay on Lawrence's career as a poet. His were "experiments of a major poet groping his way towards the discovery of a new kind of poetic art."

Arthur E. Waterman: "The Plays of D.H. Lawrence," pp. 142-50. "The magnificence of Lawrence lies partly in this continuous qualification as abstractions are

tested against the reality of art and life. The plays of
D.H. Lawrence show this qualification in dramatic
action." However, the plays do not "stand up very well
under conventional dramatic criticism."

Richard Foster: "Criticism as Rage: D.H. Lawrence," pp. 151-61. A fine account of the range and style
of his criticism.

Raymond Williams: "Lawrence's Social Writings,"
pp. 162-74. On the continuity of Lawrence's social
criticism with English thinkers of the last century; on its
anti-industrial substance; on the consequences of his
social mobility and exile.

DHL 63:     Draper, Ronald Philip (ed.)
            D.H. LAWRENCE: THE CRITICAL HERITAGE
            (London and Boston: Routledge & Kegan Paul, 1970)

A comprehensive collection of the most important
contemporary reviews of Lawrence's work, largely by
fellow novelists and poets in England and America,
1909-1932. The collection includes: Ezra Pound's review
of *Love Poems and Others* (1913), pp. 53-4; Lascelles
Abercrombie's review of *Sons and Lovers* (1913),
pp. 67-8; Virginia Woolf's essay on *The Lost Girl* (1920),
pp. 141-3; John Middleton Murry's review of *Women in
Love* (1921), pp. 168-72; Stuart P. Sherman's review of
*St. Mawr* (1923), pp. 250-57; T.S. Eliot's unfavourable
comments on Lawrence from his "The Contemporary
English Novel," *La Nouvelle Revue Française*, (1927),
pp. 275-7; André Malraux's essay on *Lady Chatterley's
Lover* (1932), pp. 293-7; the obituaries of Lawrence by
Arnold Bennett and E.M. Forster, pp. 340-7. Draper also
includes a wide selection of criticism from contemporary
literary journalism, showing the extreme hostility to
Lawrence among the traditional men of letters.

DHL 64:     Andrews, Wyndham Thomas (ed.)
            CRITICS ON D.H. LAWRENCE (London: George
            Allen and Unwin, 1971; Coral Gables, Fla.: University of
            Miami Press, 1971)

Contains brief extracts from critics on Lawrence,
1911-1930 and from 1930-1950 (including Woolf, Auden,
Joyce and Huxley); essays from specialist journals.

Roger Dataller: "Elements of D.H. Lawrence's Prose Style," pp. 52-7. As Lawrence becomes more estranged from his subject, he loses the close texture of his writing.

T.B. Tomlinson: "Lawrence and Modern Life: *Sons and Lovers, Women in Love,*" pp. 58-66. Highlights the importance of Walter Morel and Gerald Crich in Lawrence's diagnosis of modern sickness.

Edward Engelberg: "Escape from the Circles of Experience: D.H. Lawrence's *The Rainbow* as a Modern *Bildungsroman,*" pp. 67-80. The novel is a modern *Bildungsroman*, "a trial and error warfare with experience, which allows finally a glimpse of the ideal that rises inevitably out of experience." Defends the conclusion to the novel.

F.H. Langman: "*Women in Love,*" pp. 81-6. "*Women in Love* places Lawrence in the line of European writers who, from Dostoevsky on, have made the novel the medium of at once the most deeply felt social awareness and the most urgent philosophical speculation."

Curtis Atkinson: "Was there Fact in D.H. Lawrence's *Kangaroo*?," pp. 87-8. Lawrence drew, but too loosely, upon actual events.

G.B. McK. Henry: "Carrying on: *Lady Chatterley's Lover,*" pp. 89-104. A fine defence of the substance of the novel, marred as a novel by its "intrusive didacticism."

H.M. Daleski: "The Tiger and the Lamb: The Duality of Lawrence," pp. 105-8. On the male-female duality in Lawrence.

Eugene Goodheart: "*The Man Who Died,*" pp. 109-16. *The Man Who Died* seen as a tale of Dionysian resurrection.

George A. Panichas: "Voyage of Oblivion," pp. 117-23. On the *Last Poems*, which show that "death is a continuing part of a great mystery."

DHL 65: Coombes, Henry (ed.)
D.H. LAWRENCE: A CRITICAL ANTHOLOGY
(Harmondsworth, Middlesex: Penguin, 1973)

A wide and representative selection from Lawrence's letters, with a narrow selection of criticism from the writing of F.R. Leavis and the *Scrutiny* group.

DHL 66: Hamalian, Leo (ed.)
D.H. LAWRENCE: A COLLECTION OF

CRITICISM (New York and London: McGraw-Hill, 1973)

Contains an introduction by the editor; short memoirs by Lawrence and his wife; Alfred Kazin, "Sons, Lover, and Mothers," pp. 22-32 (on Lawrence's openness to experience and his heightening of consciousness in *Sons and Lovers*); and excerpts from the full-length studies of Colin Clarke, "Reductive Energy in *The Rainbow*," pp. 33-53, David Cavitch, "On *Women in Love*," pp. 54-64, Yudhistar, "The Changing Scene in *Aaron's Rod*," pp. 65-80, Anthony Beal, "On *Kangaroo*," pp. 81-6, Keith Sagar, "The Lost Trail: *The Plumed Serpent*," pp. 87-96, Graham Hough, "On *Lady Chatterley's Lover*," pp. 97-108. The collection ends with three essays: Monroe Engel, "The Continuity of Lawrence's Short Stories," pp. 109-17; Kenneth Rexroth's important, "The Poetry of D.H. Lawrence," pp. 118-32; Dan Jacobson, "D.H. Lawrence and Modern Society," pp. 133-43.

DHL 67:  Spender, Stephen (ed.)
NOVELIST POET PROPHET (London: Weidenfeld and Nicolson, 1973; New York: Harper & Row, 1973)

Uneven collection of essays by distinguished liberal critics, many still troubled by Lawrence's apparent status as an "irrational prophet," including John Carey's dismissive account of Lawrence's doctrine. The most useful essays provide reminiscences of Lawrence. Contains:

Diana Trilling: "D.H. Lawrence and the Movements of Modern Culture," pp. 1-7. Attitudes to Lawrence change with our attitudes to normative social and political structures.

Barbara Weekley Barr: "Memoir of D.H. Lawrence," pp. 8-36. Fascinating account by the daughter of Frieda and, her first husband, Ernest Weekley.

David Garnett: "Frieda and Lawrence," pp. 37-41.

Alan Sillitoe: "D.H. Lawrence and His District," pp. 42-70. On Eastwood, Nottingham and its environs.

Stephen Spender: "D.H. Lawrence, England and the War," pp. 71-6. Brief but illuminating account.

Frank Kermode: "The Novels of D.H. Lawrence," pp. 77-89. Judges Lawrence's literary career and his achievements.

Barbara Hardy: "Women in D.H. Lawrence's Novels," pp. 90-121. "Lawrence never faced the question of the identity of man and woman's political predicament, except perhaps intuitively, but he recorded their common struggle to survive in the industrial world."

John Carey: "D.H. Lawrence's Doctrine," pp. 122-34 Wholehearted critique of Lawrence's doctrine: ". . . separated from his warm, intense, wonderfully articulate being, it becomes the philosophy of any thug or moron."

Jeffrey Meyers: "D.H. Lawrence and Homosexuality," pp. 135-58. In *Women in Love*, Lawrence "substitutes anal marriage for homosexual love."

Clive James: "D.H. Lawrence in Transit," pp. 159-69. On Lawrence's travel-literature.

Tony Tanner: "D.H. Lawrence and America," pp. 170-96. On his period at Taos and its influence on *St. Mawr*.

Denis Donoghue: " 'Til the Fight is Finished': D.H. Lawrence in his Letters," pp. 197-209.

A. Alvarez: "Lawrence's Poetry: The Single State of Man," pp. 210-23. One of the best essays on Lawrence's poetry, arguing for "its originality, delicacy, wit and, above all, its honesty and intelligence...".

Edward Lucie-Smith: "The Poetry of D.H. Lawrence — With a Glance at Shelley," pp. 224-33.

John Russell: "D.H. Lawrence and Painting," pp. 234-43.

DHL 68:    Gomme, Andor Harvey (ed.)
D.H. LAWRENCE: A CRITICAL STUDY OF THE MAJOR NOVELS AND OTHER WRITINGS
(Hassocks, Sussex: Harvester Press, 1978; New York: Barnes & Noble, 1978)

A collection of "new essays by critics who accept the stature of Lawrence and seek, through close and detailed analysis of his texts, to distil his meanings and significance."

Ian Robinson: "D.H. Lawrence and English Prose," pp. 13-29. On the nature and the significance of Lawrence's transformation of English prose.

A.H. Gomme: "Jessie Chambers and Miriam Leivers," pp. 30-52. As a novelist, Lawrence achieved distance in *Sons and Lovers* from his autobiographical experience.

Jacques Berthoud: "*The Rainbow* as Experimental

Novel," pp. 53-69. "Lawrence's experimental orienta-
tion is the direct product of Lawrence's new concept of
the self."

Richard Drain: "*Women in Love*," pp. 70-93. On the
"dislocations of mood" which the novel practises and its
hidden centre.

R.E. Pritchard: "The Way to Freedom . . . Furtive
Pride and Slinking Singleness," pp. 94-119. On Lawrence's quest, in his life and art, for "proud singleness."

D. Kenneth M. MacKenzie: "Ennui and Energy in
*England, My England*," pp. 120-41. On the short stories
published under this title.

H.M. Daleski: "Aphrodite of the Foam and *The
Ladybird Tales*," pp. 142-58. On the strengths and
shortcomings of "The Ladybird" and "The Fox."

G.R. Strickland: "The First *Lady Chatterley's
Lover*," pp. 159-74. Lawrence lost control, in the
subsequent versions, of what he had said effectively in the
first version.

R.T. Jones: "D.H. Lawrence's Poetry: Art and the
Apprehension of Fact," pp. 175-89. Lawrence's
strengths as a poet lie in his "attentive curiosity about the
world."

John and Ann Remsbury: "Lawrence and Art,"
pp. 190-218. "The sharpening effect of this painterly
enthusiasm on the philosophical and discursive side of
Lawrence's thinking should not be underestimated."
Lawrence's writing on art and aesthetics should be ranked
with those of Hegel and Wittgenstein.

# Articles on *The White Peacock* and *The Trespasser*

DHL 69:     Hinz, Evelyn J.
           "Juno and *The White Peacock*: Lawrence's English
           Epic," *D.H. Lawrence Review*, 3:2 (Summer 1970),
           115-35

           Stimulating account of the structure and the themes of
           Lawrence's first novel, which, combining the mythic and
           the historical, Hinz argues, presented an epic vision of
           England.

DHL 70:    Hinz, Evelyn J.
"*The Trespasser*: Lawrence's Wagnerian Tragedy and
Divine Comedy," *D.H. Lawrence Review*, 4:2 (Summer
1971), 122-41

The characters in the story represent the clash of cultures,
Greek, Germanic, Christian. An excellent discussion of
an unduly neglected novel.

DHL 71:    Mason, H.A.
"D.H. Lawrence," *Cambridge Quarterly*, 7:3 (1977),
216-30

Lawrence's earliest novel, *The White Peacock*, discloses
his essential strengths and weaknesses.

# Full-length Studies, Articles and Anthologies on *Sons and Lovers*

DHL 72:    Beebe, Maurice
"Lawrence's Sacred Font: The Artist Theme of *Sons and
Lovers*," *Texas Studies in Literature and Language*, 4:4
(Winter 1963), 539-52

On the dilemmas of the modern artist: Paul Morel
embraces life and art through sexual experience and
through his mother's death.

DHL 73:    Tedlock, Ernest Warnock (ed.)
D.H. LAWRENCE AND *SONS AND LOVERS*:
SOURCES AND CRITICISM (New York: New York
University Press, 1965; London: London University
Press, 1966)
A collection of essays divided into three parts: (1) the
biographical origins of the novel; (2) its Freudian
connections and approaches: Alfred Booth Kuttner, "A
Freudian Appreciation," pp. 76-100; Frederick J. Hoff-
man, "Lawrence's Quarrel with Freud," pp. 101-11;
Daniel A. Weiss, "The Mother in the Mind," p. 112-36;
Frank O'Connor, "D.H. Lawrence, *Sons and Lovers*,"
pp. 137-44; (3) its techniques and values: John Middleton

Murry, "Son and Lover," pp. 151-63; Mark Schorer, "Technique as Discovery," pp. 164-9 (on the artistic failure of the novel); Dorothy Van Ghent, "On *Sons and Lovers*," pp. 170-87 (the novel is too much dominated by its idea); Mark Spilka: "How to Pick Flowers," pp. 188-99; Mark Spilka, "Counterfeit Loves," pp. 200-16 (on the symbolism and life-impulse of the novel); Louis Fraiberg, "The Unattainable Self," pp. 217-37 (the novel does not successfully combine its Freudian ideas with "Lawrence's mystique of sexual experience"); Alfred Kazin: "Sons, Lovers and Mothers," pp. 238-50 (on the novel as social documentary).

DHL 74: Salgado, (Ramsay) Gamini N.
D.H. LAWRENCE: *SONS AND LOVERS* (London: Edward Arnold, 1966)

Sympathetic and intelligent introductory essay.

DHL 75: Salgado, (Ramsay) Gamini N. (ed.)
*SONS AND LOVERS*: A SELECTION OF CRITICAL ESSAYS (London: Macmillan, 1969; Nashville: Aurora, 1970)

The best anthology of criticism on the novel. Contains an introduction by the editor; extracts from the letters of D.H. and Frieda Lawrence; the original foreword to the novel; early reviews; early critical essays, Alfred Booth Kuttner's "A Freudian Appreciation" (1916), pp. 69-94 and J. Middleton Murry's psycho-biographical analysis from *Son of Woman*, pp. 95-105; essays and extracts from studies by recent critics:

Mark Schorer: "Technique as Discovery," pp. 106-11. On the form of the novel. Judged a failure.

Dorothy Van Ghent: "On *Sons and Lovers*," pp. 112-29. The problems of the central character are unresolved. The novel ends with a drift towards death. Too much dominated by its controlling idea.

Seymour Betsky: "Rhythm and Theme: D.H. Lawrence's *Sons and Lovers*," pp. 130-43. On the sense of communal disintegration and sickness due to industrialism which underlies the novel.

Frank O'Connor: "*Sons and Lovers*," pp. 145-51. The shortcomings of the novel are traced to Lawrence's break with his roots.

Graham Hough: "Adolescent Love," pp. 152-9. The importance of the novel lies in its "psychological adventurousness" which prefigures his later masterpieces.

Simon Lesser: "Form and Anxiety," pp. 160-3. On the way in which Lawrence's fiction, as fiction, conveys feelings which the conscious mind would repress.

David Daiches: "Lawrence and the Form of the Novel," pp. 164-70. On the way in which Lawrence's wish to make statements about modern civilisation affected the traditional form of the English novel.

Eliseo Vivas: "The Triumph of Art," pp. 171-6. On the discrepancy between Lawrence's "intention and the intention of the novel."

Maurice Beebe: "The Artist Theme," pp. 177-90. On Lawrence's (and Paul Morel's) acceptance of the transforming power of art.

H.M. Daleski: "The Release: The First Period," pp. 191-207. On the struggle between the male and female principles.

Keith Sagar: "The Bases of the Normal," pp. 208-15. On the role of Clara in the novel.

Laurence Lerner: "Blood and Mind: The Father in *Sons and Lovers*," pp. 216-20. "Throughout the whole of Lawrence runs a contrast between two kinds of men," men of instinct and men of intellect.

DHL 76:   Farr, Judith (ed.)
TWENTIETH CENTURY INTERPRETATIONS
OF *SONS AND LOVERS* (Englewood Cliffs, N.J.:
Prentice-Hall, 1970)

Contains an introduction by the editor; an essay by Virginia Woolf, "Notes on D.H. Lawrence," pp. 24-8 (on Lawrence's insufficiency in comparison to Proust as an autobiographical novelist); excerpts from the full-length studies of Daniel A. Weiss (DHL 7), Keith Sagar (DHL 33), Mark Spilka (DHL 23), and George H. Ford (DHL 32); an essay by Alfred Kazin, "Sons, Lovers and Mothers," pp. 74-84 (stressing the value of the novel as social documentary); and short excerpts from the letters of D.H. Lawrence, from the foreword to the novel, from the letters of Frieda Lawrence and Edward Garnett, and from the criticism of Wyndham Lewis, Ernest Seillière, Karl Menninger, Mark Schorer, Father William Tiverton, Frank O'Connor, and Kingsley Widmer. The collection concludes with a selection from the papers of Mary Chambers Holbrook, the elder sister of Jessie Chambers Wood, Lawrence's "Miriam Leivers", pp. 106-15.

DHL 77:     Rossman, Charles
"The Gospel According to D.H. Lawrence: Religion in *Sons and Lovers*," *D.H. Lawrence Review*, 3:1 (Spring 1970), 31-41

On the religious significance of eating in the novel.

DHL 78:     Hinz, Evelyn J.
"*Sons and Lovers*: The Archetypal Dimensions of Lawrence's Oedipal Tragedy," *D.H. Lawrence Review*, 5:1 (Spring 1971), 26-53

A brilliant analysis of the controlling historical, religious, and social symbolic patterns of the novel.

# Full-length Studies, Articles and Anthologies on *The Rainbow*

DHL 79:     Sale, Roger
"The Narrative Technique of *The Rainbow*," *Modern Fiction Studies*, 5:1 (Spring 1959), 83-98

A brilliant account of the means by which Lawrence creates the effect of timelessness in the novel.

DHL 80:     Mudrick, Marvin
"The Originality of *The Rainbow*," *Spectrum*, 3:4 (Winter 1959), 3-28

"The revolutionary nature of *The Rainbow* is twofold: it is the first English novel to record the normality and significance of physical passion; and it is the only English novel to record, with a prophetic awareness of the consequences, the social revolution whereby Western man lost his sense of community and whereby men — and more especially women — learned, if they could, that there is no help any longer except in the individual and in his capacity for a passional life." Still one of the best discussions of the novel.

DHL 81:   Goldberg, S.L.
"*The Rainbow*: Fiddle-Bow and Sand," *Essays in Criticism*, 11:4 (Winter 1961), 418-34

A classic article, which argues that the prophetic conclusion to *The Rainbow* is a creative failure.

DHL 82:   Gloversmith, Frank
D.H. LAWRENCE: *THE RAINBOW* (London: Edward Arnold, 1971)

A fine and detailed introductory essay.

DHL 83:   Kinkead-Weekes, Mark (ed.)
TWENTIETH-CENTURY INTERPRETATIONS OF *THE RAINBOW* (Englewood Cliffs, N.J.: Prentice-Hall, 1971)

In addition to a helpful introduction by the editor, this collection includes two classic essays on *The Rainbow* by Marvin Mudrick (DHL 80) and Mark Kinkead-Weekes (DHL 101), revised chapters on *The Rainbow* from the full-length studies of Herman M. Daleski (DHL 31), Keith Sagar (DHL 33), George H. Ford (DHL 32), and articles from the studies of William Walsh (DHL 46) and Laurence Lerner (DHL 49). Marvin Mudrick, "The Originality of *The Rainbow*," pp. 11-32; H.M. Daleski, "The First and Second Generation," pp. 32-57; Keith Sagar, "The Third Generation," pp. 58-72; George H. Ford, "*The Rainbow* and the Bible," pp. 73-82; William Walsh, "The Childhood of Ursula," pp. 82-91; Laurence Lerner, "Lawrence's Carbon," pp. 91-5; Mark Kinkead-Weekes, "The Marble and the Statue," pp. 96-120.

DHL 84:     Wallace, Kay
            "Lawrence and *The Rainbow*: Apollo and Dionysus in
            Conflict," *Southern Quarterly*, 10:3 (April 1972), 209-22

            On the polarities between Dionysus, associated with the
            earliest Brangwen men, and Apollo, associated with the
            women.

DHL 85:     Adamowski, T.H.
            "*The Rainbow* and 'Otherness'," *D.H. Lawrence
            Review*, 7:1 (Spring 1974), 58-78

            Lawrence's terms have been misused by modern psycho-
            therapeutic culture and have lost their profundity. His
            ideas and insight are akin to those of Jean-Paul Sartre.

DHL 86:     Balbert, Peter
            D.H. LAWRENCE AND THE PSYCHOLOGY OF
            RHYTHM: THE MEANING OF FORM IN *THE
            RAINBOW* (The Hague and Paris: Mouton, 1974)

            "The elemental repetitive rhythms of syntax, symbol, and
            character in the novel provide Lawrence with the
            aesthetic form Lawrence *must* employ to remain true to
            his belief in the repetitively rhythmic form of life
            experience."

DHL 87:     Brown, Homer O.
            "The Passionate Struggle into Being: D.H. Lawrence's
            *The Rainbow*," *D.H. Lawrence Review*, 7:3 (Fall 1974),
            275-90

            The movement of the novel shows how some of the
            characters transcend the narrow circle of consciousness
            which constrains modern humanity.

DHL 88:     Smithson, Isaiah
            "Structuralism as a Method of Literary Criticism,"
            *College English*, 37:2 (October 1975), 145-59

            A definition of Structuralism, with a lengthy "structural"
            analysis of *The Rainbow*.

DHL 89:     Gill, Stephen
            "Lawrence and Gerald Crich," *Essays in Criticism*, 28:3
            (July 1977), 231-46

Lawrence is not in the tradition of the nineteenth century
novelists. Twentieth-century men, he believes, want to be
enslaved by the machine. Gerald Crich is used to embody
Lawrence's despairing vision of the cost of mass
industrialism — except that his complexity resists his
creator's attempts to make him embody undemonstrable
generalisations. While *Women in Love* presents an
industrialised and mechanised England beyond redemption, *The Rainbow* embodies a myth about an England
seen now to be destroyed. A stimulating and important
essay.

DHL 90:     Tobin, Patricia Dreschel
            "The Cycle Dance: D.H. Lawrence, *The Rainbow*,"
            TIME AND THE NOVEL: THE GENEALOGICAL
            IMPERATIVE (Princeton, N.J.: Princeton University
            Press, 1978), pp. 81-106

A luminous discussion of the way in which *The Rainbow*
subverts the patriarchal and the dynastic values of the
family novel.

# Full-length Studies, Articles and
# Anthologies on *Women in Love*

DHL 91:     Gray, Ronald Douglas
            "English Resistance to German Literature from
            Coleridge to D.H. Lawrence," THE GERMAN
            TRADITION IN LITERATURE 1871-1945
            (Cambridge and New York: Cambridge University Press,
            1965), pp. 327-54

"*Women in Love* is a novel which must strike every reader
familiar with German literature as almost cast in a
German mould." Lawrence satirises the yearning for
oneness. He must "have been aware of the implications
his novel had for Germany. It is unlikely to be mere
chance that the novel moves from England in the final
chapters towards Germany — to the Austrian Tyrol."

DHL 92:  Langman, F.H.
"Women in Love," *Essays in Criticism*, 17:2 (April 1967), 183-206

Contrasts the "corrosive pessimism" of Joseph Conrad with Lawrence's "positive scepticism." While Conrad fears the breakdown of social rules and values, Lawrence sees how they can be revived. The article contains an important analysis of the essentially "open" structure of the novel form in *Women in Love*, comparing the hopeful story of Ursula and Birkin with the "closed" and doomed story of Gerald and Gudrun.

DHL 93:  Miko, Stephen J. (ed.)
TWENTIETH CENTURY INTERPRETATIONS OF *WOMEN IN LOVE* (Englewood Cliffs, N.J.: Prentice-Hall, 1969)

Contains an introduction by the editor; extracts from the full-length studies of George H. Ford (DHL 32), Alan Friedman (MOD 157), David J. Gordon (DHL 161), Julian Moynahan (DHL 28), Mark Spilka (DHL 23), and Eliseo Vivas (DHL 25), which discuss the relationship between Lawrence's ideas and the form in which they are embodied; and short excerpts from essays and studies by Robert B. Heilman, Edwin Honig, Leone Vivante and Daniel A. Weiss (DHL 7).

DHL 94:  Rudrum, Alan
"Philosophical Implication in Lawrence's *Women in Love*," *Dalhousie Review*, 51:2 (Summer 1971), 240-50

Lawrence subverted the traditional forms of fiction to show the failure of the fixed moral and social order of Western civilisation.

DHL 95:  Remsbury, John
"*Women in Love* as a Novel of Change," *D.H. Lawrence Review*, 6:2 (Summer 1973), 149-72

The drama of the novel lies in the struggle for Gudrun — between Loerke, who represents the new century of change and Gerald, who represents the nineteenth century. The novel suggests "the dramatic difference between the 19th and 20th centuries."

DHL 96: Reddick, Bryan D.
"Point of View and Narrative Tone in *Women in Love*: The Portrayal of Interpsychic Space," *D.H. Lawrence Review*, 7:2 (Summer 1974), 156-71

On the different techniques and strategies of narration in the novel.

DHL 97: Bersani, Leo
"Lawrentian Stillness," *Yale Review*, 65:1 (October 1975), 38-60

Subtle account of the contrast between motion, which seeks peace and ultimately death, and stillness, which seeks spiritual unity and life, in the language, characterisation, plot and themes of *Women in Love*.
Reprinted in Leo Bersani, A FUTURE FOR ASTYANAX: CHARACTER AND DESIRE IN LITERATURE (Boston: Little, Brown and Co., 1976; London: M. Boyars, 1978), pp. 156-85.

DHL 98: Kestner, Joseph
"Sculptural Character in Lawrence's *Women in Love*," *Modern Fiction Studies*, 21:4 (Winter 1975), 543-52

A spatial sense derived from Futurism led to a neglect of the necessarily temporal dimension of fiction. The units of the story are *spectacular*.

DHL 99: Reddick, Bryan D.
"Tension at the Heart of *Women in Love*," *English Literature in Transition*, 19:2 (1976), 73-86

A fine exploration of the techniques involved in presenting the relationships between the two couples in *Women in Love*.

# Full-length Studies, Articles and Anthologies on *The Rainbow* and *Women in Love*

DHL 100:  Kermode, Frank
"Lawrence and the Apocalyptic Types," *Critical Quarterly*, 10:1/2 (Spring-Summer 1968), 14-38

Lawrence "believed himself to be living in a time of cosmic crisis, and partly justified this conviction by archaic typologising." Discusses apocalyptic notions in Lawrence; the influence of Joachitism, of the Book of Revelation upon his thinking; and *The Rainbow* and *Women in Love* as apocalyptic fictions.

DHL 101:  Kinkead-Weekes, Mark
"The Marble and the Statue: The Exploratory Imagination of D.H. Lawrence," IMAGINED WORLDS: ESSAYS ON SOME ENGLISH NOVELS AND NOVELISTS IN HONOUR OF JOHN BUTT, ed. Maynard Mack and Ian Gregor (London: Methuen, 1968), pp. 317-40

The classic essay on *The Rainbow* and *Women in Love*, which analyses the different versions of *The Rainbow* and *Women in Love*; the influence of the *Study of Thomas Hardy* on *The Rainbow*; the influence of *The Crown* on *Women in Love*. Concludes with a luminous discussion of the nature of Lawrence's imagination.

DHL 102:  Ruthven, K.K.
"The Savage God: Conrad and Lawrence," *Critical Quarterly*, 10:1/2 (Spring-Summer 1968), 39-54

*The Rainbow* and *Women in Love* set in the context of late-Romantic primitivism and decadence. "This is hardly surprising, seeing that war in Europe had turned *fin du globe* prophecy into fact; but what is peculiar to Lawrence's treatment of this theme is the way it merges with the ancient belief in resurrection." Hence, Lawrence's *fin de siècle* pessimism is qualified by *nouveau siècle* optimism.

DHL 103:  Clarke, Colin Campbell (ed.)
*THE RAINBOW* AND *WOMEN IN LOVE* (London: Macmillan, 1969; Nashville: Aurora, 1970)

Contains letters by Lawrence relating to the novels; the prologue and the foreword to *Women in Love*; early reviews by John Middleton Murry; essays by Roger Sale (DHL 79) S.L. Goldberg (DHL 81), G. Wilson Knight, and Frank Kermode (DHL 100); revised chapters from the studies of Mary Freeman (DHL 135), Julian Moynahan (DHL 28), Herman M. Daleski (DHL 31), George H. Ford (DHL 32), Ronald Gray (DHL 91) and Colin Clarke (DHL 34). Mary Freeman, "Lawrence and Futurism," pp. 91-103; Roger Sale, "The Narrative Technique of *The Rainbow*," pp. 104-16; S.L. Goldberg, "*The Rainbow*: Fiddle-Bow and Sand," pp. 117-34; G. Wilson Knight, "A Comment on *Women in Love*," pp. 135-41; Julian Moynahan, "Ritual Scenes in *The Rainbow*," pp. 142-50; H.M. Daleski, "*Women in Love*: 'Firm Singleness and Melting Union'," pp. 151-66; George H. Ford, "*Women in Love*: the Disintegration of Western Man," pp. 167-87; Ronald Gray, "*Women in Love* and the German Tradition in Literature," pp. 188-202; Frank Kermode, "Lawrence and the Apocalyptic Types," pp. 203-18; Colin Clarke, " 'Living Disintegration': a Scene from *Women in Love* Reinterpreted," pp. 219-34.

DHL 104:  Kleinbard, David J.
"D.H. Lawrence and Ontological Insecurity," *PMLA*, 89:1 (January 1974), 154-63

Characterisation in *The Rainbow* and *Women in Love* is best understood through R.D. Laing's concept of ontological insecurity and Erik Erickson's analysis of identity confusion.

# D.H. Lawrence and the New World: the Literature of Travel, *St. Mawr* and *The Plumed Serpent*

DHL 105:  Arnold, Armin
D.H. LAWRENCE AND AMERICA (London:

Linden Press, 1958; New York: Philosophical Press,
1959)

An uninspired account of Lawrence's interest in America
and his involvement with Americans; a discussion of the
various versions of his essays on American literature; a
survey of critical opinion in America about the value of
*Studies in Classic American Literature*. Contains a
valuable bibliography of criticism of Lawrence in American books and journals until 1958.

DHL 106: Vickery, John B.
"*The Plumed Serpent* and the Eternal Paradox,"
*Criticism*, 5:2 (Spring 1963), 119-34

The novel is structured around a quest-motif: its central
male and female characters seek fulfilment in rites of
self-knowledge.

DHL 107: Clark, L.D.
DARK BODY OF THE NIGHT (Austin: University of
Texas Press, 1964)

A biographical account of Lawrence in Mexico, "The
Man and the Continent"; a discussion of his reading in
esoteric sources, in Mexican history and anthropology; an
analysis of *The Plumed Serpent* as a "ritual work of art,"
with particular emphasis upon the spiritual journey of
Kate Leslie, its heroine. By far the most scholarly and
comprehensive work on *The Plumed Serpent*.

DHL 108: Cavitch, David
D.H. LAWRENCE AND THE NEW WORLD (New
York: Oxford University Press, 1969)

"Lawrence's writing was always guided by his desire to
break down the barriers to spontaneity and to reintegrate
our submerged, fundamental selves with our overt lives.
He felt that art could serve man's urgent need to reclaim
his essential being. Apart from the possibly restorative
powers of passional experience, as in sexual intercourse
or deeply felt encounters with death, only the strong
feelings of an aesthetic response can renew man's

awareness of his sensual identity and direct him towards acceptance of his whole self.'' But Lawrence's attempt to break free from a dying world into a fuller life, a process which impelled him to leave Europe for America, was inextricably bound up with his own homosexual desires. Contains an important re-reading of *Women in Love*, which gives full attention to its homosexual content.

DHL 109:   Cowan, James Costello
D.H. LAWRENCE'S AMERICAN JOURNEY: A STUDY IN LITERATURE AND MYTH (Cleveland and London: Press of Case Western Reserve University, 1970)

Lawrence came to America ''in fulfilment of his own role as an artist of the post-Christian myth,'' seeking ''the means to religious, political and cultural regeneration for society.'' Lawrence's pilgrimage to America ''follows the pattern of the quest of the hero of romance, a paradigm which becomes the dominant structural and thematic image in his fiction.'' Provides an excellent discussion of *Movements in European History, Studies in Classic American Literature*, and of Lawrence's ''quarrel with Christianity.''

DHL 110:   Swigg, Richard
LAWRENCE, HARDY AND AMERICAN LITERATURE (London and New York: Oxford University Press, 1972)

''Because I believe that Lawrence's development as a novelist cannot be considered without an understanding of his relationship to tragedy, I have tried to make clear in the course of this study the connections between various areas of his creative interest — areas which in the past have usually been discussed separately or only in relation to his criticism. If tragedy was a crucial issue for Lawrence the novelist, then equally so were the expressions of tragic dilemma which he found in other writers whose work he needed in order to focus his perceptions, to crystallise his sense of the 'passional problem'. It was this need, above all, which brought Lawrence to an imaginative engagement with the work of Hardy, Poe, Hawthorne, Melville and Cooper. Through them Lawrence defined his own evolving purposes as a novelist. Without the other writers as a sharpening force in Lawrence's imagination, *The Rainbow* and *Women in Love* would probably not have emerged in the form in which we have them today." A difficult, but rewarding study.

DHL 111:   Ragussis, Michael
"The False Myth of *St. Mawr*: Lawrence and the Subterfuge of Art," *Papers on Language and Literature*, 11:2 (Spring 1975), 186-96

A subtle essay, which argues that *St. Mawr* contains a critique of its own apparent resolution.

## Textual Studies and Histories

DHL 112:   Littlewood, J.C.F.
"D.H. Lawrence's Early Tales," *Cambridge Quarterly*, 1:2 (Spring 1966), 107-24

Discusses the revisions to the early short stories.

DHL 113:   Joost, Nicholas and Sullivan, Alvin
D.H. LAWRENCE AND *THE DIAL* (Carbondale and Edwardsville: Southern Illinois University Press, 1970; London: Feffer and Simons, 1970)

An excellent account of Lawrence's literary career, 1913-1930, and of his poetry and short stories published in *The Dial*.

DHL 114:   Strickland, Geoffrey
"The First *Lady Chatterley's Lover*," *Encounter*, 36:1 (January 1971), 44-52

On the superiority of the first version.

DHL 115:   Widmer, Kingsley
"The Pertinence of Modern Pastoral: The Three

Versions of *Lady Chatterley's Lover*," *Studies in the
Novel*, 5:3 (Fall 1973), 298-313

Discusses the virtues and limitations of the final version of
the novel.

DHL 116:  Ross, Charles L.
"The Composition of *Women in Love*: A History,
1913-1919," *D.H. Lawrence Review*, 8:2 (Summer 1975),
198-212

On the problems of analysing the stages of composition of
*Women in Love* because of the different transcriptions
circulated among Lawrence's friends.

DHL 117:  Ross, Charles L.
"The Revisions of the Second Generation in *The
Rainbow*," *Review of English Studies*, New Series, 37
(1976), 277-95

The intense violence, shown in the revised version,
between Anna and Will, reflects the violence of the First
World War.

DHL 118:  Cushman, Keith
D.H. LAWRENCE AT WORK: THE EMERGENCE
OF *THE PRUSSIAN OFFICER* STORIES
(Charlottesville: University Press of Virginia, 1978;
Hassocks, Sussex: Harvester Press, 1978)

Discusses the revision of the early short stories.

DHL 119:  Ross, Charles L.
THE COMPOSITION OF *THE RAINBOW* AND
*WOMEN IN LOVE*: A HISTORY (Charlottesville:
University Press of Virginia, 1980)

The most important study of the composition and revision
of Lawrence's two major novels. (See DHL 116 and 117).

# Full-length Studies, Articles and Chapters from Books on the Poetry of D.H. Lawrence

DHL 120:    Hughes, Glenn
"D.H. Lawrence, The Passionate Psychologist,"
IMAGISM AND THE IMAGISTS (Stanford: Stanford
University Press, 1931), pp. 167-96

"So far as I can determine there was no radical change in
Lawrence's poetry as a result of his association with the
Imagists. Even the poems by which he is represented in
the anthologies are only occasionally Imagistic. The
strongest influence in his work . . . is Whitman."

DHL 121:    Blackmur, Richard Palmer
"D.H. Lawrence and Expressive Form," THE
DOUBLE AGENT (New York: Arrow Editions, 1935),
pp. 103-20. Reprinted in R.P. Blackmur, LANGUAGE
AS GESTURE (New York: Harcourt Brace, 1952),
pp. 286-300

The most sustained and the most influential rejection of
Lawrence's poetry. Lawrence was "a deracinated,
unsupported imagination . . . a mind without rational
structure." Accordingly, he failed to make effective use of
the formal device of the art of poetry. Writing out of "a
tortured Protestant sensibility and upon the foundation of
an incomplete, uncomposed mind," he was "an extreme
victim" of the "plague of expressive form."

DHL 122:    Rexroth, Kenneth
SELECTED POEMS OF D.H. LAWRENCE (New
York: New Directions, 1947)

With this edition, and Rexroth's positive introduction,
began the revival of interest in Lawrence as a poet.

DHL 123:    Alvarez, Alfred
"D.H. Lawrence: the Single State of Man," THE
SHAPING SPIRIT (London: Chatto and Windus, 1958),
pp. 140-61. Published in America as STEWARDS OF
EXCELLENCE (New York: Charles Scribner's Sons,
1958)

The best single essay on Lawrence's poetry to date. Lawrence was the only mature poet of importance to survive the First War. His best poems are marked by complete truth to feeling, since his "controlling standard" as an artist was "delicacy: a constant fluid awareness, nearer the checks of intimate talk than those of regular prosody." His was an integrity to experience rather than to the traditional and inherited forms of language. Modern poetry is in need of Lawrence's discipline of accurate feeling. He was "the foremost emotional realist of the century."

DHL 124:  Pinto, Vivian de Sola
"Poet Without A Mask," *Critical Quarterly*, 3:1 (Spring 1961), 5-18

Refuting Blackmur (DHL 121), Pinto argues that Lawrence was a poet who dispensed with a defunct tradition of poetry. "In his poetry we must look for the 'insurgent naked throb of the instant moment'." His early autobiographical poems and his Whitmanesque poems were the experiments of "a major poet groping his way towards the discovery of a new poetic art." Reprinted in Mark Spilka (DHL 62). See also the counter-argument, Henry Gifford, "The Defect of Lawrence's Poetry," *Critical Quarterly*, 3:3 (Autumn 1961), pp. 268-70.

DHL 125:  Spender, Stephen
THE STRUGGLE OF THE MODERN (London: Hamish Hamilton, 1963; Berkeley: University of California Press, 1963), pp. 100-09.

First-rate discussion of Lawrence as a modern poet.

DHL 126:  Garcia, Reloy and Karabastos, James (eds.)
A CONCORDANCE TO THE POETRY OF D.H. LAWRENCE (Lincoln: University of Nebraska, 1970)

DHL 127:  Marshall, Tom
THE PSYCHIC MARINER: A READING OF THE POEMS OF D.H. LAWRENCE (London: W. Heinemann, 1970; New York: Viking Press, 1970)

Perhaps the best book-length study of Lawrence's poems. "One cannot appreciate fully the course of Lawrence's development as a poetic craftsman unless one understands what it was that motivated that development." Having diagnosed his own and civilisation's disease, Lawrence "wished his poems not only to propose but to embody the cure. The urgency of his quest for a poetic form was one with the urgency of his need to communicate his vision." Not only does the study contain an excellent close analysis of Lawrence's poetry, it also presents a fair account of the critical debate about his poetry.

DHL 128:    Spender, Stephen
"Form and Pressure in Poetry," *Times Literary Supplement*, October 23, 1970, 1226-8

A fine discussion of Lawrence's free verse.

DHL 129:    Gilbert, Sandra Mortola
ACTS OF ATTENTION (Ithaca and London: Cornell University Press, 1972)

Lawrence's best qualities as a poet are "manifest in those poems in which the poet fulfils his own condition of true thought: 'a man in his wholeness wholly attending,' and makes a successful 'act of attention' a kind of meditation on a subject that reveals it as wholly itself. The way Lawrence succeeds in doing this accounts for the peculiarly 'free' form of his verse which is, in his best poems, merely the emotion defining its proper and unique shape." Lawrence distrusted formalism, for it was against life. Gilbert argues that Lawrence is greatest as a religious poet in his *Last Poems*.

DHL 130:    Oates, Joyce Carol
"The Hostile Sun: the Poetry of D.H. Lawrence," *Massachusetts Review*, 13:4 (Autumn 1972), 639-53

Lawrence, as a poet of the psyche, is enthralled by the drama of the self and "its totally Other," a force symbolised by the sun. A comprehensive discussion.

DHL 131: Solomon, Gerald
"The Banal and the Poetry of D.H. Lawrence," *Essays in Criticism*, 23:3 (July 1973), 254-67

Lawrence's fear of self-questioning and self-knowledge seems to have had a disastrous impact upon his poetry, whose inadequacies he never questioned.

DHL 132: Vickery, John B.
"D.H. Lawrence's Poetry: Myth and Matter,"
*D.H. Lawrence Review*, 7:1 (Spring 1974), 1-18

Lawrence's best poetry reconciles the two trends of modern poetry, "the mythic" (T.S. Eliot) and "the phenomenologically concrete" (William Carlos Williams).

DHL 133: Shakir, Evelyn
" 'Secret Sin': Lawrence's Early Verse,"
*D.H. Lawrence Review*, 8:2 (Summer 1975), 155-75

On the confessional nature of his early verse, which he revised to emphasise the masculine rather than the feminine perspectives.

# Full-length Studies of the Plays of D.H. Lawrence

DHL 134: Sklar, Sylvia
THE PLAYS OF D.H. LAWRENCE: A BIOGRAPHICAL AND CRITICAL STUDY
(London: Vision Press, 1975; New York: Barnes & Noble, 1975)

The most detailed single account of Lawrence's work as a dramatist, and of his debt to Chekhov, with separate chapers on: *A Collier's Friday Night; The Widowing of Mrs. Holroyd; The Daughter-in-Law; The Merry-go-Round; The Fight for Barbara; Touch and Go; Attitude* and *Noah's Flood; David.*

# Full-length Studies and Articles Placing Lawrence in his Intellectual Context

DHL 135:    Freeman, Mary
D.H. LAWRENCE: A BASIC STUDY OF HIS
IDEAS (Gainesville: University of Florida Press, 1955)

Still one of the best studies of Lawrence, seen from the
point of view of the writings of Erich Fromm. Lawrence is
presented as a major, and coherent, modern thinker. His
social theory was original and important, dealing with, but
repudiating fascism. Indeed, Lawrence was an acute
analyst of the compulsions towards fascism. His work as a
whole was the testimony of a man responding to the horror
of the First World War and its aftermath. A wide-ranging
account, covering not only his theoretical work, but also
his novels, plays and poetry, the study convincingly
supports a libertarian reading of Lawrence. Deserves to
be more widely known than it is.

DHL 136:    Williams, Raymond
"D.H. Lawrence," CULTURE AND SOCIETY
1780-1950 (London: Chatto and Windus, 1958; New
York: Columbia University Press, 1958), pp. 199-215

"The thinker of whom one is most often reminded, as one
goes through Lawrence's social writings, is Carlyle."

DHL 137:    Rieff, Philip
"The Therapeutic as Mythmaker: Lawrence's True
Christian Philosophy," THE TRIUMPH OF THE
THERAPEUTIC: USES OF FAITH AFTER FREUD
(New York: Harper & Row, 1966; London: Chatto and
Windus, 1966), pp. 189-231

On Lawrence's importance as a modern philosopher.

DHL 138:    Nahal, Chaman
D.H. LAWRENCE: AN EASTERN VIEW (South
Brunswick and New York: A.S. Barnes, 1970; London:
Thomas Yoseloff, 1970)

"Lawrence was a Yogi who has missed his way and come into a European body to work out his difficulties." Discusses the similarities and differences between Eastern and Western forms of self-realisation.

DHL 139: Delavenay, Emile
D.H. LAWRENCE AND EDWARD CARPENTER: A STUDY IN EDWARDIAN TRANSITION (London: W. Heinemann, 1971; New York: Taplinger, 1971)

"This study is not meant to be a search for 'sources' of the works of D.H. Lawrence so much as an attempt to define a mental climate, to connect historically and in detail, the works of a great creative writer with ideas and conceptions detected in them yet never hitherto specifically related to his immediate surroundings." Lawrence followed Edward Carpenter and Havelock Ellis in revolting against "the crippling social and religious conditioning of his Victorian adolescence, against middle-class patterns of behaviour which his generation and he himself had imitated in their aspiration towards social elevation." But through these figures, he also came into contact with the racial mysticism of Houston Stewart Chamberlain and the anti-Semitism of Otto Weininger.

DHL 140: Zytaruk, George J.
D.H. LAWRENCE'S RESPONSE TO RUSSIAN LITERATURE (The Hague and Paris: Mouton, 1971)

Lawrence's reading of Russian literature helped him to extend the possibilities of the Victorian novel. Discusses his role as translator; his response to Tolstoy; the Dostoevsky cult; the phallic vision of V.V. Rozanov. A major contribution to an important and hitherto neglected area in Lawrence studies.

DHL 141: Delavenay, Emile
D.H. LAWRENCE: THE MAN AND HIS WORK: THE FORMATIVE YEARS 1885-1919, trans. Katherine Delavenay (London: W. Heinemann, 1972; Carbondale: Southern Illinois University Press, 1972)

Originally published in French, this is the most extensive intellectual biography of Lawrence to date, relating his "writings to the ideas which he had absorbed from reading and conversations and examining the works of fiction and the ideas together as a part of the whole man at work in the creative process." Delavenay presents a detailed account of Lawrence's family, his childhood, adolescence and early manhood in England; his travels in Europe; his life with Frieda von Richthofen. After his honeymoon with Frieda in Germany in 1912, his reading and his ideas changed as he became acquainted with the racial mysticism of Houston Stewart Chamberlain. "It is impossible for my generation to forget that some of the ideas which attracted Lawrence as early as 1915 were subsequently mobilized in the service of the worst crimes against mankind." The study relates Lawrence "to the change of climate from the 19th to the 20th century, which, with him, not only coincides with his new life with a German wife, but corresponds to something much wider and more general at the end of the Edwardian age." The most substantial, and still the most controversial, account of Lawrence's ideas and their context.

DHL 142:   Vickery, John B.
THE LITERARY IMPACT OF *THE GOLDEN BOUGH* (Princeton, N.J.: Princeton University Press, 1973)

Chapter 8, "D.H. Lawrence: The Evidence of the Poetry," pp. 280-93, discusses the influence of anthropology on Lawrence's poetry; Chapter 9, "D.H. Lawrence: The Mythic Elements," pp. 294-325, its influence on his fiction and discursive prose.

DHL 143:   Green, Martin Burgess
THE VON RICHTHOFEN SISTERS: THE TRIUMPHANT AND THE TRAGIC MODES OF LOVE (London: Weidenfeld and Nicolson, 1974; New York: Basic Books, 1974)

An account of the intellectual, political and social milieu of the von Richthofen sisters, Frieda, (whom Lawrence married), and Else (the lover of Max Weber). Green argues that Lawrence's debt as a writer and as a thinker was to the ideas of the radical intelligentsia of Munich. In particular, Lawrence took from it the terms by which to expound, first, an essentially matriarchal system of values, and then, in his leadership fiction, a patriarchal system of values. Not only is Green's study rich and suggestive, it is also a repudiation of Emile Delavenay's thesis (DHL 141) that Lawrence took from his German sources racist, anti-Semitic and authoritarian views.

DHL 144: Humma, John B.
"D.H. Lawrence and Friedrich Nietzsche," *Philological Quarterly*, 53:1 (January 1974), 110-20

Although Lawrence criticises Nietzsche, they share the same view of the Dionysian and the instinctual, and deprecate the harmful effects of idealism.

DHL 145: Green, Eleanor H.
"Schopenhauer and D.H. Lawrence on Sex and Love," *D.H. Lawrence Review*, 8:3 (Fall 1975), 329-45

On the similarities of their theories.

DHL 146: Burns, Aidan
NATURE AND CULTURE IN D.H. LAWRENCE
(London: Macmillan, 1980; New York: Barnes & Noble, 1980)

The author presents Lawrence as a philosophical, as an anti-idealist novelist, emphasising his debt to philosophical contemporaries and predecessors. Discusses *The White Peacock* and *Sons and Lovers*; *The Rainbow*; *Women in Love*; and *Lady Chatterley's Lover*.

# Articles and Chapters from Books on Lawrence's Political and Social Thought

DHL 147: Guttmann, Allan
"D.H. Lawrence: The Politics of Irrationality," *Wisconsin Studies in Contemporary Literature*, 5:2 (Summer 1964), 151-63

A fine essay on the growth and development of Lawrence's anti-democratic views. Discusses *Kangaroo* and *The Plumed Serpent*.

DHL 148:     Harrison, John Raymond
"D.H. Lawrence," THE REACTIONARIES: A STUDY OF THE ANTI-DEMOCRATIC INTELLIGENTSIA (London: V. Gollancz, 1966; New York: Schocken, 1966), pp. 168-89

The fullest recent elaboration of the charge that Lawrence's politics were anti-democratic. His "homicidal tendencies and his belief in 'blood' are reminiscent of the worst features of German fascism." (See MOD 54).

DHL 149:     Fairbanks, N. David
" 'Strength Through Joy' in the Novels of
D.H. Lawrence," *Literature and Ideology*, No.8, 1971, 67-78

Lawrence seeks not to change society but to regenerate his characters through racist and anti-feminist modes of fulfilment.

DHL 150:     Pinto, Vivian de Sola
"D.H. Lawrence 1885-1930," THE POLITICS OF TWENTIETH-CENTURY NOVELISTS, ed. George A. Panichas (New York: Hawthorn Books, 1971), pp. 30-49

The most sustained defence of Lawrence's politics. "Lawrence was not a trained philosopher and his thinking about politics and society is not systematic but full of contradictions and paradoxes. What we find in his works when he deals with these subjects is the penetrating criticism and probings of a powerful and free intelligence illuminated by the richness and vitality of a poet's vision. To speak of the thought of such a writer as 'leading to Auschwitz' is sheer nonsense, and it is equally beside the point to class him with Pound and Yeats as part of a reactionary 'swerve to the right.' He was a freer and saner spirit than either Pound or Yeats. Unlike Pound, he never surrendered to fascism, and unlike Yeats, he was never misled by an obsolete aristocratic ideal. He was a prophetic poet like Blake, whose wisdom and vision were beyond the reach of his contemporaries and are now only beginning to be understood as he recedes in time."

DHL 151:    Wilding, Michael
POLITICAL FICTIONS (London and Boston: Routledge & Kegan Paul, 1980)

In Chapters 4 and 5, Wilding discusses *The Rainbow* and *Kangaroo* as "revolutionary fictions." "How can a traditional and conventional novel form deal with what is new in politics?" Since it cannot, the twentieth-century novelist needs to reject nineteenth-century modes.

# Articles, Chapters from Books, and Anthologies of Articles on Lawrence's Views on Sexuality and on Women

DHL 152:    Kinkead-Weekes, Mark
"Eros and Metaphor: Sexual Relationships in the Fiction of Lawrence," *Twentieth-Century Studies*, 1:2 (November 1969), 3-19

Lawrence not only used sexual consciousness and activity to investigate relationships within and between individuals. He "saw in artistic creation and in the language of fiction itself, an analogy with the sexual act." Discusses *Sons and Lovers*, *The Rainbow*, *Women in Love*, and *Lady Chatterley's Lover*.

DHL 153:    Millett, Kate
SEXUAL POLITICS (New York: Doubleday, 1970; London: R. Hart-Davis, 1971), pp. 237-83

Millett's detailed argument that Lawrence's misogyny led him to represent women in fiction as objects to be dominated, has stimulated discussion ever since of Lawrence's sexual attitudes, his representation of women and his representation of men.

DHL 154:   Mailer, Norman
THE PRISONER OF SEX (Boston: Little, Brown and
Co., 1971; London: Weidenfeld and Nicolson, 1971)

Rebuts Kate Millett (DHL 153) and defends Henry Miller
and D.H. Lawrence *passim*: Lawrence "understood
women as they had never been understood before."

DHL 155:   Blanchard, Lydia
"Love of Power: A Reconsideration of Sexual Politics in
D.H. Lawrence," *Modern Fiction Studies*, 21:3
(Autumn 1975), 431-45

Disputing Kate Millett's thesis (DHL 153), the article
argues that "Lawrence has described the destruction that
inevitably occurs when one person tries to dominate or
control another."

DHL 156:   Harris, Janice
"Sexual Antagonism in D.H. Lawrence's Early
Leadership Fiction," *Modern Language Studies*, 7:1
(Spring 1977), 43-52

Women in Lawrence's leadership fiction serve as a foil to
correct the assertiveness of men. Discusses *The Plumed
Serpent*.

DHL 157:   Rossman, Charles
" 'You are the Call and I am the Answer':
D.H. Lawrence and Women," *D.H. Lawrence Review*,
8:3 (Fall 1975), 255-328

Lawrence, far from being a 'chauvinist' writer, presented
subtle and complex relationships, with an awareness of
the concerns now discussed by feminists.

DHL 158:   Meyers, Jeffrey
"D.H. Lawrence," HOMOSEXUALITY AND
LITERATURE (London: Athlone Press, 1977;
Montreal: McGill-Queen's University Press, 1977),
pp. 131-61

"Lawrence's inner struggle with repressed homosexual desires results in an ambiguity of presentation, for none of his heroes can commit himself completely to homosexuality, although it is portrayed as a 'higher' form of love. Though this ambiguity has artistic functions, it also exposes Lawrence's doubts about the ultimate validity of homosexual experience." Discusses *The White Peacock; Women in Love; Aaron's Rod; The Plumed Serpent*.

DHL 159:   Smith, Anne (ed.)
LAWRENCE AND WOMEN (London: Vision Press, 1978; New York: Barnes & Noble, 1978)

A collection of new articles which attempt to "understand the experience of the relationship between men and women as Lawrence presents it in his work."

Anne Smith: "A New Adam and a New Eve — Lawrence and Women: A Biographical Overview," pp. 9-48. Composes an excellent psycho-biography of Lawrence from the extant biographies of Lawrence by friends and by critics.

Faith Pullin: "Lawrence's Treatment of Women in *Sons and Lovers*," pp. 49-74. "Lawrence's main objective was always to examine the male psyche and to use his women characters to that end." Consequently women are not fully rounded characters but diagrams.

Lydia Blanchard: "Mothers and Daughters in D.H. Lawrence: *The Rainbow* and Selected Shorter Works," pp. 75-100. "Lawrence has helped to fill the void of [a] great untold story, the story of mother and daughter." Discusses *The Rainbow, St. Mawr* and "Mother and Daughter."

Mark Kinkead-Weekes: "Eros and Metaphor: Sexual Relationships in the Fiction of Lawrence," pp. 101-21. "Lawrence saw in artistic creation, and in the language of fiction itself, an analogy with the sexual act." Discusses *Sons and Lovers, The Rainbow, Women in Love* and *Lady Chatterley's Lover*. (See DHL 152).

Julian Moynahan: "Lawrence, Woman, and the Celtic Fringe," pp. 122-35. "It appears that whenever we examine the Celt-woman link in Lawrence, we find associated with it the notion of rebellion and of removal from the European and industrialised world." Discusses *St. Mawr* and *The Plumed Serpent*.

Philippa Tristram: "Eros and Death (Lawrence, Freud

and Women)'', pp. 136-55. *The Rainbow, Women in Love* and *Aaron's Rod* seen both as ''the account of personal crisis'' and as ''an account of Europe itself'' in the traumatic period 1913-1918. Lawrence's conclusions are often similar to those of Sigmund Freud.

T.E. Apter: ''Let's Hear What the Male Chauvinist is Saying: *The Plumed Serpent*,'' pp. 156-77. A fine and perceptive essay. Lawrence seeks to reforge the notion of the ''male'' and the ''female'' degraded by industrial society.

Harry T. Moore: ''Bert Lawrence and Lady Jane,'' pp. 178-88. Discusses Kate Millett on Lawrence (DHL 153). ''Essentially Lawrence regarded love — and women — in a way that can only be called religious.''

Mark Spilka: ''On Lawrence's Hostility to Wilful Women: The Chatterley Solution,'' pp. 189-91. A man's concern with the male identity, as opposed to male dominance, is seen to be crucial to his capacity for tenderness. A wide-ranging account of Lawrence's fiction.

DHL 160:  Dix, Carol
LAWRENCE AND WOMEN (London: Macmillan, 1980; New York: Rowman, 1980)

Sympathetic to Lawrence's account of women, but somewhat slight.

# Full-length Studies and Articles on Lawrence's Criticism

DHL 161:  Gordon, David J.
D.H. LAWRENCE AS A LITERARY CRITIC (New Haven and London: Yale University Press, 1966)

Drawing upon the work of Northrop Frye, Gordon argues that Lawrence's criticism is that of a Romantic individualist in an apocalyptic-demonic age.

DHL 162:  Salter, K.W.
''Lawrence, Hardy and 'The Great Tradition','' *English*, 22:113 (Summer 1973), 60-5

On Lawrence's *Study of Thomas Hardy* and on his superiority to Hardy.

DHL 163:     Colacurcio, Michael J.
"The Symbolic and the Symptomatic: D.H. Lawrence in Recent American Criticism," *American Quarterly*, 27:4 (October 1975), 486-501

It is perhaps time to admit that Lawrence's literary and cultural insights in his *Studies in Classic American Literature* form received critical wisdom.

DHL 164:     Ulmer, Gregory L.
"D.H. Lawrence, Wilhelm Worringer, and the Aesthetics of Modernism," *D.H. Lawrence Review*, 10:2 (Summer 1977), 165-81

An outstanding essay on the philosophical origins and purposes of Lawrence's culture-criticism, in his writing on literature and on art, which is placed in the context of "German art history as represented by such men as Alois Riegl and Wilhelm Worringer, whose works played an important role in the shaping of modernist aesthetics. Hegel, of course, stands at the head of this tradition."

# Lawrence and the Visual Arts

DHL 165:     Merrild, Knud
A POET AND TWO PAINTERS: A MEMOIR OF D.H. LAWRENCE (London: Routledge & Kegan Paul, 1938; New York: Viking Press, 1939)

Interesting for its account of Lawrence's views on modern painting.

DHL 166:     Levy, Mervyn (ed.)
PAINTINGS OF D.H. LAWRENCE (London: Cary, Adams, Mackay, 1964; New York: Viking Press, 1964)

Reproduces twenty-six of Lawrence's paintings, with essays by Harry T. Moore, "D.H. Lawrence and His

Paintings," pp. 17-34 (Lawrence's work as a painter exemplifies his great creative delight in the world); Jack Lindsay, "The Impact of Modernism on Lawrence," pp. 35-53 (on Lawrence's relationship to Cézanne, Futurism and Dada); Herbert Read, "Lawrence as a Painter," pp. 55-64 ("Lawrence was an expressionist, an extreme example of that type of artist who seeks a direct correspondence between feelings and representation...").

DHL 167:	Meyers, Jeffrey
PAINTING AND THE NOVEL (Manchester: Manchester University Press, 1975; New York: Barnes & Noble, 1975)

Discusses some of the painters mentioned by D.H. Lawrence in his novels — Maurice Greiffenhagen and *The White Peacock*; Fra Angelico and *The Rainbow*; Mark Gertler and *Women in Love*, pp. 46-82.

# Part V
# THOMAS STEARNS ELIOT
# 1888-1965

# Bibliographical Information

For the standard bibliography of Eliot's writings, see the revised and extended edition of Donald Gallup's T.S. ELIOT: A BIBLIO-GRAPHY (London: Faber and Faber, 1969; New York: Harcourt Brace, 1969). For a listing of works by Eliot, and of the major critical studies of them until 1970, see Bradley Gunter, THE MERRILL CHECKLIST OF T.S. ELIOT (Columbus, Ohio: Merrill, 1970).

For the fullest bibliography of criticism of T.S. Eliot, until 1965, see Mildred Martin, A HALF-CENTURY OF ELIOT CRITIC-ISM: AN ANNOTATED BIBLIOGRAPHY OF BOOKS AND ARTICLES IN ENGLISH 1916-1965 (Lewisburg, Pa.: Bucknell University Press, 1972; London: Kaye and Ward, 1972). Martin provides an exhaustive bibliography of criticism in English, arranged chronologically and cross-indexed by subject, author and title. For a more recent bibliography, see Beatrice Ricks, T.S. ELIOT: A BIBLIOGRAPHY OF SECONDARY WORKS (Metuchen, N.J. and London: Scarecrow Press, 1980).

The best bibliographical essay on criticism of Eliot is still Richard M. Ludwig's "T.S. Eliot," in SIXTEEN MODERN AMERICAN AUTHORS: A SURVEY OF RESEARCH AND CRITICISM, edited by Jackson R. Bryer (Durham, North Carolina: Duke University Press, 1974), pp. 181-222. For an excellent checklist of essential criticism of Eliot until 1977, see GUIDE TO AMERICAN LITERATURE FROM EMILY DICKINSON TO THE PRES-ENT, edited by James T. Callow and Robert J. Reilly (New York and London: Barnes & Noble, 1977), pp. 223-5. For a detailed review of criticism of Eliot from 1970 to 1975, see Audrey T. Rogers, "Eliot in the 70s: A Mosaic of Criticism," *T.S. Eliot Review*, 2:1 (Spring 1975), 10-15.

# Memoirs and Biographies

TSE 1:     March, Richard and Tambimuttu, M.J. (eds.)

T.S. ELIOT: A SYMPOSIUM FOR HIS SIXTIETH
BIRTHDAY (London: Editions Poetry, 1948; Chicago:
Regnery, 1949)

An uneven collection of forty-seven essays and poems,
providing "reminiscences from those who were intimately
associated with Mr. Eliot at various times." Includes
contributions by Wyndham Lewis, W.H. Auden,
Stephen Spender, Edith Sitwell and John Betjeman.

TSE 2:    Sencourt, Robert
T.S. ELIOT: A MEMOIR, ed. Donald Adamson
(London: Garnstone Press, 1971; New York: Dodd,
Mead, 1971)

An affectionate memoir, giving Sencourt's recollections
and impressions.

TSE 3:    Matthews, Thomas Stanley
GREAT TOM: NOTES TOWARDS THE
DEFINITION OF T.S. ELIOT (New York: Harper &
Row, 1974; London: Weidenfeld and Nicolson, 1974)

Sadly, the fullest biographical account of Eliot's life to
date. Matthews outlines the contents (and gives the
flavour) of his book in the foreword: "In the pages that
follow, some awkward questions will have to be asked,
whether or not they can be satisfactorily answered. These
are some of them: Who was T.S. Eliot? Why did he want
to keep his private life a secret? . . . Is there less, or more,
in his poetry than meets the eye? To what extent does his
poetry depend on plagiarism and parody? Did he have a
'fine ear'? Was he a phony scholar? A phony saint? What
sort of American was he? Was he a Christian? Why did he
take Ezra Pound's editing of *The Waste Land* so meekly?
Did Pound create Eliot? Were his plays any good? Why
was Eliot's first marriage so unhappy? Was he a
homosexual? Did Bertrand Russell seduce Vivienne
Eliot? Why was *Ode* published once and then dropped?
Why did Eliot abandon his first wife? Because she was
mad? Was she mad? Should he have abandoned her, in
any case? Was he a great poet or a monstrous clever
fellow? Did late happiness rescue him from horror but
turn him into a dullard... . This is a biography, of a sort."
Of a sort.

TSE 4:    Gordon, Lyndall
ELIOT'S EARLY YEARS (London and New York:
Oxford University Press, 1977)

Lacking competition, this is the most complete interpreta-
tive biography of Eliot. "As more is gradually known of
Eliot's life, the clearer it seems that the 'impersonal'
facade of his poetry — the multiple faces and voices —
masks an often quite literal reworking of personal
experience.... . This book is an attempt to elicit the
autobiographical element in Eliot's poetry by measuring
the poetry against the life." Gordon argues that the
determining point in Eliot's life was "not when he was
baptized in 1927 but in 1914 when he first interested
himself in the motives, the ordeals and the achievements
of saints. In his later years Eliot seemed to beg off
personally in favour of a routine life of prayer and
observance, but the early manuscripts suggest that for a
time in his youth he dreamed of the saint's ambitious task,
of living by his own vision beyond the imaginative
frontiers of his civilization."

# Guides to the Poetry

TSE 5:    Williamson, George
A READER'S GUIDE TO T.S. ELIOT: A
POEM-BY-POEM ANALYSIS (New York: Noonday
Press, 1953; London: Thames and Hudson, 1955) (1974)

Still one of the best studies, not only of Eliot's allusions
and references, but also of his allusive technique.

TSE 6:    Smith, Grover Cleveland
ELIOT'S POETRY AND PLAYS: A STUDY IN
SOURCES AND MEANINGS (Chicago: University of
Chicago Press, 1956; revised 2nd edn., 1974)

The best guide to Eliot's works, which not only provides a
comprehensive survey of sources and influences in the
poetry and the plays, but also suggests possible interpretations.

TSE 7:     Southam, Brian Charles
A STUDENT'S GUIDE TO THE SELECTED
POEMS OF T.S. ELIOT (London: Faber and Faber,
1968; New York: Harcourt Brace, 1968) (1981)

Factual notes on the early poems, *The Waste Land* and
the religious poems, detailing Eliot's references and
allusions.

TSE 8:     Blamires, Harry
WORD UNHEARD: A GUIDE THROUGH
ELIOT'S *FOUR QUARTETS* (London: Methuen,
1969; New York: Barnes & Noble, 1969)

Not only a superb guide to *Four Quartets*, this study also
provides illuminating insights into the nature of poetic
Modernism. At times, however, it may seem over-
ingenious. Nevertheless, an indispensable aid.

# Introductory studies

TSE 9:     Unger, Leonard
T.S. ELIOT (Minneapolis: University of Minnesota
Press, 1961)

A brief introductory survey of Eliot's poetry, with a
particular emphasis upon language and style, which is still
one of the finest accounts of Eliot's work.

TSE 10:     Frye, Northrop
T.S. ELIOT (London and Edinburgh: Oliver and Boyd,
1963; New York: Barnes & Noble, 1966) (1981)

A short and subtle introduction to Eliot's work, which is
widely thought to be the best single short study of Eliot.
"An American moving to Europe to live is likely to be the
more sharply aware of the 'Western' context and origin of
his cultural tradition." Frye discusses Eliot's engagement
with that tradition; his attraction to theory about its
sources, development and renewal. "A thorough knowledge of Eliot," he concludes, "is compulsory for anyone
interested in contemporary literature."

TSE 11:     Headings, Philip Ray
T.S. ELIOT (New York: Twayne, 1964)

A first-rate introductory discussion of Eliot's poetry and drama. Emphasising Eliot's lifelong debt to Dante, the author interprets Eliot's early poems and *The Waste Land* in "much less negative terms" than usual.

TSE 12:     Spender, Stephen
ELIOT (London: Fontana/Collins, 1975; New York: Viking Press, 1976, under the title, *T.S. ELIOT*)

A succinct and comprehensive survey of Eliot's life and works, showing how his work reveals "the search for the merging of individual consciousness within some wider objective truth — at first the tradition, next the idea of the supernatural, and finally the dogmas of the Catholic church (Eliot considered the Church of England to be Catholic)." A balanced, illuminating study.

# Full-length Studies of the Work of T.S. Eliot

TSE 13:     Matthiessen, Francis Otto
THE ACHIEVEMENT OF T.S. ELIOT: AN ESSAY ON THE NATURE OF POETRY (New York: Houghton Mifflin, 1935; revised 2nd edn., New York: Oxford University Press, 1947; 3rd edn., revised and enlarged, with an afterword by C.L. Barber, New York and London: Oxford University Press, 1958)

The classic study of Eliot's poetic method, which was revised as Eliot's own poetry developed and changed. Matthiessen's double aim was "to evaluate Eliot's method and achievement as an artist, and in so doing to emphasise certain fundamental elements in the nature of poetry which are in danger of being obscured by the increasing tendency to treat poetry as a social document and to forget that it is an art. The most widespread error in contemporary criticism is to neglect form and to concern itself entirely with content." The second edition concluded with a discussion of the plays and the *Four Quartets*; the third edition includes a final chapter by C.L. Barber on Eliot's work after the *Four Quartets*.

TSE 14: Gardner, Helen Louise
THE ART OF T.S. ELIOT (London: Cresset Press,
1949; New York: E.P. Dutton, 1959) (1980)

Still one of the best studies of Eliot, particularly of his
metrics and imagery, which concentrates upon the *Four
Quartets*, but examines earlier poetry and earlier plays in
so far as they point forward to the themes and style of the
later poems. Particularly good on the analysis of Eliot's
musical structure in *Four Quartets*.

TSE 15: Robbins, Rossell Hope
THE T.S. ELIOT MYTH (New York: H. Schuman,
1951)

Attacks Eliot as a poet and thinker because he lacks faith
in man.

TSE 16: Maxwell, Desmond E.S.
THE POETRY OF T.S. ELIOT (London: Routledge &
Kegan Paul, 1952; New York: Hillary House, 1959) (1970)

A fine and comprehensive discussion of the poetic and
critical context of Eliot's poetry, showing his debt to
French Symbolism, his relation to Georgian poetry, and
defining the nature of his classicism and humanism.

TSE 17: Kenner, Hugh
THE INVISIBLE POET: T.S. ELIOT (New York:
McDowell Obolensky, 1959; London: W.H. Allen, 1960)
(1965)

Still the best critical biography of Eliot, providing an
excellent account of his life, his intellectual and poetic
development, with subtle and intelligent close reading of
his poetry. Excellent on his debt to Jules Laforgue, his
debt to F.H. Bradley, and his theory of poetry.

TSE 18: Lucy, Séan
T.S. ELIOT AND THE IDEA OF TRADITION
(New York: Barnes & Noble, 1960; London: Cohen and
West, 1960)

Eliot's theory of tradition argued for the "cultural unity of Europe." The study discusses the influence of this theory upon Eliot's criticism, poetry and drama.

TSE 19: George, Arapura Ghevarghese
T.S. ELIOT: HIS MIND AND ART (Bombay and New York: Asia Publishing House, 1962)

An attempt to argue that there is an underlying unity to Eliot's work. "My own view is that what relates Eliot to the existential tradition is his effort to grasp the nature of man in terms of the concept of 'crisis'." George discusses the poetry, drama, criticism and social theory.

TSE 20: Jones, Genesius
APPROACH TO THE PURPOSE: A STUDY OF THE POETRY OF T.S. ELIOT (London: Hodder and Stoughton, 1964; New York: Barnes & Noble, 1964) (1980)

A difficult but rewarding study of Eliot's poetic self-questioning. "A symbolic form is a way in which the human mind operates in order to 'create' the world of its experience. The mind knows the phenomenal world only as the forms shape it; and the forms are called symbolic precisely because their functioning produces the symbols whereby the phenomenal is apprehended. There are six symbolic forms — myth, religion, language, history, art and science — and each shares this general 'creative' function." Each has its own morphology, which Eliot's poetry explores.

TSE 21: Unger, Leonard
T.S. ELIOT: MOMENTS AND PATTERNS (Minneapolis: University of Minnesota Press, 1966; London: Oxford University Press, 1966)

A collection of essays, written at various times, which present a scrupulous and illuminating close reading of Eliot's poetry and plays, concentrating upon their images, symbols and themes.

TSE 22:     Montgomery, Marion
            T.S. ELIOT: AN ESSAY ON THE AMERICAN
            MAGUS (Athens: University of Georgia Press, 1969)

            An exploratory essay which discusses "Eliot's commit-
            ment to Christianity as reflected in his poetry". Mont-
            gomery analyses "the realisation in the poems themselves
            of the incompleteness of both emotional and intellectual
            response to the world, whose point of coincidence with
            the mind is the image." Eliot's poetry "comes to insist
            upon an enlargement of awareness by grace, even as
            Dante's emotional and intellectual awareness comes to be
            enlarged at a point of ascent in his poetry by the mystery of
            Beatrice, the God-bearing image." A subtle and convinc-
            ing account of the nature of Eliot's Romanticism; of his
            relation to the Imagism of T.E. Hulme; of his transcen-
            dental sense of the image. One of the finest studies of
            Eliot.

TSE 23:     Kirk, Russell
            ELIOT AND HIS AGE (New York: Random House,
            1971)

            The best defence of the "conservative" Eliot, who
            opposed the movement of his age toward politics instead
            of moral effort. He was "the principal champion of the
            moral imagination in the 20th century."

TSE 24:     Patterson, Gertrude
            T.S. ELIOT: POEMS IN THE MAKING
            (Manchester: Manchester University Press, 1971; New
            York: Barnes & Noble, 1971)

            "The purpose of this book [is] to offer a redefinition of the
            principles underlying Eliot's early method and to examine
            them in relation to the background roots of the modernist
            movement in general." Discusses in particular the
            relation with Imagism, Symbolism, Ezra Pound and the
            Cubists. Concentrates on the early poetry and *The Waste
            Land*. One of the most important and helpful recent
            studies of Eliot.

TSE 25:     Bergonzi, Bernard

T.S. ELIOT (New York and London: Macmillan, 1972)
(1978)

Sympathetic biographical and critical study of Eliot's life
and career, with a short appendix on the full manuscript of
*The Waste Land*. A fine synoptic account of Eliot's work
and ideas.

TSE 26:    Chiari, Joseph
           T.S. ELIOT: POET AND DRAMATIST (London:
           Vision Press, 1972; New York: Barnes & Noble, 1973)
           (1979)

           Somewhat rhetorical defence of Eliot's view of tradition.
           "He is among those artists and thinkers whose names
           cannot be dissociated from that of Europe, and the
           survival of our civilization depends on our will to keep
           alive the values and the works which have truly
           contributed to the growth of man."

TSE 27:    Ward, David
           BETWEEN TWO WORLDS: A READING OF T.S.
           ELIOT'S POETRY AND PLAYS (London and Boston:
           Routledge & Kegan Paul, 1973)

           Analyses the poet's intellectual development and its
           relationship to his poetry and drama. Particularly valuable
           for its account of Eliot's early philosophical work on
           F.H. Bradley.

TSE 28:    Schneider, Elisabeth
           T.S. ELIOT: THE PATTERN IN THE CARPET
           (Berkeley, Los Angeles and London: University of
           California Press, 1975)

           "Considered together, the writings of Eliot give evidence
           of a deliberate intention to unify the whole body of his
           poetry and plays quite as he saw Shakespeare's and
           Dante's work unified and marked by a single 'developing
           personality'."

TSE 29:    Rajan, Balachandra

THE OVERWHELMING QUESTION: A STUDY
OF THE POETRY OF T.S. ELIOT (Toronto and
Buffalo: University of Toronto Press, 1976)

The unity of Eliot's *oeuvre* comes, in part, from the fact
that his poetry records and grows out of a spiritual quest,
in part, from Eliot's acceptance that he must make the
journey by means of words, images and symbols which are
those of an historical tradition. A difficult but illuminating
"exploration of the pattern of wholeness in Eliot's
writing."

TSE 30:       Traversi, Derek
T.S. ELIOT: THE LONGER POEMS (London:
Bodley Head, 1976; New York: Harcourt Brace, 1976)

A discussion of *The Waste Land, Ash Wednesday* and
*Four Quartets*. Much criticism of Eliot has been
"rendered nugatory" by "religious prejudices" which
have "little or nothing to do with the poetry *qua* poetry.
This applies to those who advance a Christian or religious
view of life, and to those who oppose it." Accordingly, the
poet's "truth to experience and skill in the poet's craft"
has been overlooked.

TSE 31:       Moody, Anthony David
THOMAS STEARNS ELIOT, POET (Cambridge,
London and New York: Cambridge University Press,
1979) (1980)

A profoundly stimulating and intelligent attempt to
provide "a critical study of Eliot's life-work in poetry" by
analysing the changing relationship between Eliot's
sensibility and the poetic forms which embodied it. The
study traces "the main stages of his development: the
early originality; the years of personal crisis which found
its fullest expression, and an initial resolution, in *The
Waste Land*; the fashioning of a transcendent and
increasingly assured poetic self in *The Hollow Men* and
*Ash Wednesday*; the perfection of that self in 'Burnt
Norton', which in 1935 he thought was the end of his
poetry; then, in the wartime *Quartets*, the final expansion
of the poet into the protagonist of an ideal English and
European culture." The study contains a detailed and

extensive account of Eliot's poetics and of his thinking about society, in his drama of the thirties and particularly in "his one effective political work, the three wartime *Quartets*." A short appendix, "The Christian philosopher and politics" provides one of the most balanced accounts of Eliot's political thought and its relation to his whole work.

The problems raised by Eliot's life found their resolution in the ascetic tradition of Christianity. But, for Moody, these problems were themselves the expressions of a neurosis endemic to that idealising, Christian culture: "It is probably this more than anything else that gives him his common ground with his readers. Moreover, it is what makes him a classic, a true type of the mind of Europe." One of the most important recent studies of Eliot, particularly good on the *Four Quartets* and on Eliot's social and political writings.

# Articles and Chapters from Books on T.S. Eliot's Work and Career

TSE 32:     Winters, Yvor
"T.S. Eliot or The Illusion of Reaction," THE ANATOMY OF NONSENSE (Norfolk, Conn.: New Directions, 1943), pp. 120-67

The classic argument against Eliot's influence on modern letters: "the theory and influence of Eliot, with which I am at present dealing, seem to me the most dangerous and least defensible of our time."

TSE 33:     Schwartz, Delmore
"T.S. Eliot as the International Hero," *Partisan Review*, 12:2 (Spring 1945), 199-206

One of the best single articles on Eliot. "Eliot's work is important in relationship to the fact that experience has become international. We have become an international people, and hence an international hero is possible." This, however, also involves a sense of deracination: "We are all the bankrupt heirs of the ages, and the moments of the crisis expressed in Eliot's work are a prophecy of the crises of our own future.''

TSE 34:     Kenner, Hugh
"Eliot's Moral Dialectic,'' *Hudson Review*, 2:3 (Autumn 1949), 421-48

An important and influential analysis of the relations between Eliot's moral and religious views and the dramatic manner in which they were expressed. The principle of dramatic organisation which governed each poem also governed the *oeuvre*. There was no essential division in Eliot's work into early and late periods.

TSE 35:     Shapiro, Karl
"T.S. Eliot: The Death of Literary Judgement,'' IN DEFENSE OF IGNORANCE (New York: Random House, 1960), pp. 35-60

The case put against Eliot with gusto: "Eliot is a poet of religion, hence a poet of the second or third rank; he is a thoroughgoing anachronism in the modern world, a poet of genius crippled by lack of faith and want of joy.''

TSE 36:     Wasserstrom, William
"T.S. Eliot and *The Dial*,'' *Sewanee Review*, 70:1 (Winter 1962), 81-92

Wasserstrom argues that *The Waste Land* epitomised the ideal of *The Dial* to publish the writings of those, in America and in Europe, who participated in "the Western-civilized-Christian-European-American tradition.''

TSE 37:     Brooks, Cleanth
"T.S. Eliot: Discourse to the Gentiles,'' THE HIDDEN GOD: STUDIES IN HEMINGWAY, FAULKNER, YEATS, ELIOT AND WARREN (New Haven: Yale University Press, 1963), pp. 68-97

Explains Eliot's use of analogy and indirection in writing of Christianity.

TSE 38:    De Laura, David J.
"The Place of the Classics in T.S. Eliot's Christian
Humanism," HEREDITAS: SOME ESSAYS IN THE
MODERN EXPERIENCE OF THE CLASSICAL,
ed. Frederic Will (Austin: University of Texas Press,
1964), pp. 153-97

An intelligent essay on Eliot's humanism, religious views,
and approach to the classics.

TSE 39:    Stead, Christian Karlson
THE NEW POETIC: YEATS TO ELIOT (London:
Hutchinson, 1964) (1979)

Presents an important revision of views of Eliot. (See
MOD 127).

TSE 40:    Watson, George
"The Triumph of T.S. Eliot," *Critical Quarterly*, 7:4
(Winter 1965), 328-37

Eliot's success "was total and instantaneous within the
terms it had set itself — the capture of young intellectuals
of creative energy in England and the United States in the
1920s."

TSE 41:    Speaight, Robert
"Music and Meaning in T.S. Eliot," STUDIES IN THE
ARTS, ed. Francis Warner (Oxford: Basil Blackwell,
1968), pp. 41-61

On the musical organisation of Eliot's poetry.

TSE 42:    Kermode, Frank
"The Classic," *University of Denver Quarterly*, 9:1
(Spring 1974), 1-33

The concept of 'the classic', as discussed by T.S. Eliot and
others, is inextricably related to the concept of Empire —
and to the Holy Roman Empire in particular.

# Anthologies of Articles on T.S.Eliot's Work and Career

TSE 43:    Rajan, Balachandra (ed.)
T.S. ELIOT: A STUDY OF HIS WRITINGS BY
SEVERAL HANDS (London: Dennis Dobson, 1947;
New York: Funk and Wagnalls, 1948) (1967)

A collection of first-rate articles and excerpts from books:
Cleanth Brooks, *"The Waste Land*: An Analysis,"
pp. 7-36. The classic exegesis of the poem.
E.E. Duncan Jones, *"Ash Wednesday,"* pp. 37-56. On
the Dantesque quality of *Ash Wednesday* which "is
religious poetry . . . not didactic in any degree."
Helen Gardner: *"Four Quartets*: A Commentary,"
pp. 57-77. On the musical structure of the poem.
B. Rajan: "The Unity of the Quartets," pp. 78-95. On
the spiritual quest which underlies the poetry.
Philip Wheelwright: "Eliot's Philosophical Themes,"
pp. 96-106. On Eliot's debt to Eastern thought.
Anne Ridler: "A Question of Speech," pp. 107-18. If
his emotion was personal, Eliot taught us that its poetic
expression must be typical.
M.C. Bradbrook: "Eliot's Critical Method," pp.
119-28. On the quest for order (amidst post First World
War chaos) in Eliot's criticism.
Wolf Mankowitz: "Notes on 'Gerontion'," pp. 129-38.
". . . it is the whole nature of contemporary barrenness
which is examined in the course of an old man's reverie."

TSE 44:    Unger, Leonard (ed.)
T.S. ELIOT: A SELECTED CRITIQUE (New York:
Rinehart and Co., 1948)

A comprehensive collection, with a comprehensive
bibliography, of the best early criticism of Eliot,
containing brief extracts from Conrad Aiken, p.3; Richard
Aldington, pp. 4-10; E.M. Forster, pp. 11-17; Ezra
Pound, pp. 18-20; Mark Van Doren, pp. 21-3; Paul Elmer
More, pp. 24-9; Malcolm Cowley, pp. 30-3; Granville
Hicks, pp. 34-5; and Harold Laski, pp. 36-42. These
show the variety of early responses to Eliot in the twenties
and thirties.
There follow untitled articles and fuller extracts from

full-length studies: Delmore Schwartz, pp. 43-50 (on Eliot as an international culture hero, see TSE 33); John Crowe Ransom, pp. 51-74 (on Eliot's criticism, an essay of great significance for New Criticism); Yvor Winters, pp. 75-113 (on Eliot's baleful influence); Van Wyck Brooks, pp. 114-19 (attacks Eliot's critical judgements); Ferner Nuhn, pp. 120-37 (somewhat jumbled observations on Eliot and his poetry); D.S. Savage, pp. 138-57 (Eliot's later views can only inhibit individual creativity); Karl Shapiro, a poem, pp. 158-60; T.H. Thompson, pp. 161-9 (a parody of over-ingenious criticism); Edmund Wilson, pp. 170-94 (a classic appreciation of and criticism of Eliot's poetry); F.R. Leavis, pp. 195-215 (a survey of Eliot's poetry, concentrating on *Ash Wednesday* and explicating the particular modernity of Eliot's poetry); I.A. Richards, pp. 216-20 (*The Waste Land* speaks of "the plight of a generation."); F.O. Matthiessen, pp. 221-35 (on *Triumphal March*); R.P. Blackmur, pp. 236-62 (". . . the modern reader is not fitted to appreciate either a mind or its works conceived in relation to Christianity as a living discipline."); Stephen Spender, pp. 263-86 (expresses doubts about Eliot's poetry and beliefs); W.B. Yeats, pp. 287-8 (Eliot's poetry is cold and dry); Allen Tate, pp. 289-95 (we do not need to share Eliot's religious beliefs to appreciate *Ash Wednesday*); Mario Praz, pp. 296-318 (an excellent account of Eliot's debt to Dante); Cleanth Brooks, pp. 319-48 (reprints his classic exegesis of *The Waste Land*, see TSE 60); Leonard Unger, pp. 349-94 (a scholarly study of the literary sources of *Ash Wednesday*, emphasising St John of the Cross's *Dark Night of the Soul*); James Johnson Sweeney, pp. 395-414 (an excellent study of the sources of "East Coker"); C.L. Barber, pp. 415-43 (*The Family Reunion* is an artistic failure); Louis L. Martz, pp. 444-62 (on the meaning of the "still point" in the poetry and in *Murder in the Cathedral*); bibliography, pp. 463-78.

TSE 45:   Braybrooke, Neville (ed.)
T.S. ELIOT: A SYMPOSIUM FOR HIS
SEVENTIETH BIRTHDAY (London: R. Hart-Davis,
1958; New York: Farrar, Straus and Cudahy, 1958)

A collection of essays and poems on Eliot and his career, some of minor importance. See W.F. Jackson Knight, "T.S. Eliot as a Classical Scholar," pp. 119-28; Vincent

Cronin: "T.S. Eliot as a Translator," pp. 129-37;
J.M. Cameron, "T.S. Eliot as a Political Writer," pp.
138-51 (questions the logic of Eliot's basing his Christian
society on Anglicanism); Iris Murdoch: "T.S. Eliot as a
Moralist," pp. 152-60 (criticises Eliot's rejection of
liberalism in favour of dogma and authority); John
Betjeman: "T.S. Eliot the Londoner," pp. 193-5 ("London percolates most of his poems.")

TSE 46:     Kenner, Hugh (ed.)
T.S. ELIOT: A COLLECTION OF CRITICAL
ESSAYS (Englewood Cliffs, N.J.: Prentice-Hall, 1962)

A collection of essays from the forties and fifties, drawn
largely from the New Critics and from the *Scrutiny* group.
Hugh Kenner: "Introduction," pp. 1-14.
Arthur Mizener: "To Meet Mr. Eliot," pp. 15-27. An
appreciative survey of Eliot's career.
Wyndham Lewis: "Early London Environment," pp.
28-35. Reminiscences.
Hugh Kenner: "Bradley," pp. 37-57. Excellent essay
on Eliot's debt as thinker and poet to Bradley's
metaphysics.
R.P. Blackmur: "Irregular Metaphysics," pp. 58-64.
Difficult essay on analogy in Eliot's poetry.
Elizabeth Sewell: "Lewis Carroll and T.S. Eliot as
Nonsense Poets," pp. 65-72.
S. Musgrove: "Eliot and Tennyson," pp. 73-85. On
the echoes of Tennyson in Eliot's poetry.
George L.K. Morris: "Marie, Marie, Hold on Tight,"
pp. 86-8. On Eliot's use of Countess Marie Larisch's *My
Past* in *The Waste Land*.
F.R. Leavis: "*The Waste Land*," pp. 89-103. A classic
appreciation of the poem, stressing its significance as
"modern" poetry.
D.W. Harding: "T.S. Eliot, 1925-1935," pp. 104-09.
Discusses Eliot's changing attitude to suffering.
F.R. Leavis: "T.S. Eliot's Later Poetry," pp. 110-24.
Eliot presents Christian views without "invoking Christian dogma."
D.W. Harding: "*Little Gidding*," pp. 125-8. A fine,
early appreciation of the poem.
Allen Tate: "On *Ash Wednesday*," pp. 129-35. We do
not need to share Eliot's religious beliefs to appreciate the
poem.

R.P. Blackmur: "In the Hope of Straightening Things Out," pp. 136-48. Eliot's personality gives unity to his criticism.

William Empson: "The Style of the Master," pp. 152-4. Anecdotes about Eliot's conversations.

John Peter: "*Murder in the Cathedral*," pp. 155-72. The play has a unity which the later plays do not.

Denis Donoghue: "*The Cocktail Party*," pp. 173-86. "*The Cocktail Party* is a more ample play because it at least gives serious representation . . . to a way of life other than that which issues in beatitude or martyrdom."

Hugh Kenner: "For Other Voices," pp. 187-91. Defends *The Elder Statesman* as drama.

Donald Davie: "T.S. Eliot: The End of an Era," pp. 192-205. "The Dry Salvages" must be seen as a parody of Walt Whitman.

TSE 47:    Tate, Allen (ed.)
T.S. ELIOT: THE MAN AND HIS WORK (New York: Delacorte Press, 1966; London: Chatto and Windus, 1967)

An uneven collection of memoirs and articles on Eliot. The first seven pieces provide reminiscences of Eliot: Herbert Read, "T.S.E. — A Memoir," pp. 11-37; Stephen Spender, "Remembering T.S. Eliot," pp. 38-64; Bonamy Dobrée, "T.S. Eliot. A Personal Reminiscence," pp. 65-88; Ezra Pound, "For T.S.E.," p. 89; Frank Morley, "A Few Recollections of Eliot," pp. 90-113; C. Day Lewis, "At East Coker," (a poem), pp. 114-5; E. Martin Browne, "T.S. Eliot in the Theatre: the Director's Memories," pp. 116-32. There follow nineteen articles on the various stages of Eliot's career:

John Crowe Ransom: "*Gerontion*," pp. 133-58. A brilliant analysis of the language and rhythm of the poem.

Helen Gardner: "The Comedies of T.S. Eliot," pp. 159-81. On *The Cocktail Party, The Confidential Clerk* and *The Elder Statesman*.

Robert Speaight: "With Becket in *Murder in the Cathedral*," pp. 182-93. Reminiscences of the first actor to play Becket.

Conrad Aiken: "An Anatomy of Melancholy," pp. 194-202. *The Waste Land* succeeds "by virtue of its incoherence."

Leonard Unger: "T.S. Eliot's Images of Awareness,"

pp. 203-30. A wide-ranging discussion of Eliot's imagery.

Frank Kermode: "A Babylonish Dialect," pp. 231-42. "*The Waste Land* is in one light an imperial epic."

Robert Richman: "The Day of Five Signs," (a poem), p. 244.

G. Wilson Knight: "T.S. Eliot: Some Literary Impressions," pp. 245-61. One of the most illuminating memoirs of Eliot, throwing light upon the nature of his religious conversion.

Mario Praz: "T.S. Eliot as a Critic," pp. 262-77. On the "empirical" and personal nature of his criticism.

Austin Warren: "Eliot's Literary Criticism," pp. 278-98. On Eliot's quest for order.

Wallace Fowlie: "Baudelaire and Eliot: Interpreters of their Age," pp. 299-315. On Eliot's debts to Charles Baudelaire — not least to his preoccupation with time and memory. A fine essay.

Cleanth Brooks: "T.S. Eliot: The Writer and Artist," pp. 316-32. On Eliot as a poet of urban reality who sought harmony through his art in a time of disharmony.

Janet Adam Smith: "T.S. Eliot and 'The Listener'," pp. 333-6. On Eliot's advice on modern poetry for publication.

Robert Giroux: "A Personal Memoir," pp. 337-44.

Francis Noel Lees: "Mr. Eliot's Sunday Morning Satura: Petronius and *The Waste Land*," pp. 345-54. On the influence of *The Satyricon*.

H.S. Davies: "Mistah Kurtz: He Dead," pp. 355-63. Personal reminiscences.

B. Rajan: "The Overwhelming Question," pp. 364-81. The unity of Eliot's poetry comes from the spiritual quest which inspires it.

Neville Braybrooke: "T.S. Eliot in the South Seas," pp. 383-8.

Allen Tate: "Postscript of the Guest Editor," pp. 389-93.

TSE 48:    Martin, Graham (ed.)
ELIOT IN PERSPECTIVE: A SYMPOSIUM
(London: Macmillan, 1970; New York: Humanities Press, 1970)

Perhaps the best single collection of essays to date on Eliot's career and achievement, which points to the conclusion that "Eliot's place in our own poetic and cultural tradition" cannot be really understood "without a fuller understanding of his American inheritance."

Graham Martin: "Introduction," pp. 11-28.

F.W. Bateson: "The Poetry of Learning," pp. 31-44. Explains Eliot's learning as "an aspect of his Americanism": often superficial and inaccurate, akin to the enjoyment "that every pilgrim of our cathedrals, galleries and museums experiences." While used with comic effect in the early verse, "learned allusions tend to persist only as a matter of literary habit."

Francis Scarfe: "Eliot and Nineteenth-century French Poetry," pp. 45-61. "Eliot's 'debt' to French poetry was mainly to what he had read at an early, impressionable age . . . and his subjection to this was by no means total."

Donald Davie: "Pound and Eliot: a distinction," pp. 62-82. ". . . as I read Eliot he is the one poet writing in English who is centrally in the *symboliste* tradition. What Eliot puts into his poems is determined preponderantly by his being an American; how he structures his poems is determined preponderantly by his sitting at the feet of the French."

Gabriel Pearson: "Eliot: an American use of symbolism," pp. 83-101. "Eliot was an American who was not so much an exile . . . as one who voluntarily excluded himself from a whole phase of civilisation. In departing from America, he departed out of the twentieth century." One of the best discussions of Eliot's American background, and of the effects upon his poetry of his withdrawal from American life.

Ian Hamilton: "*The Waste Land*," pp. 102-11. In Eliot's poem, the past acts as a barrier not as an aid to a fuller understanding of the present.

Graham Martin: "Language and Belief in Eliot's Poetry," pp. 112-31. Discusses the changes in Eliot's poetic idiom as he accepts Christianity.

Harold F. Brooks: "*Four Quartets*: the structure in relation to the themes," pp. 132-47. The poem, exploring spiritual experience, affirming the continual presence and accessibility of timeless values, speaks to many (like the author) who are not Christians.

Katharine Worth: "Eliot and the Living Theatre," pp. 148-66. ". . . Eliot's plays must be seen in the context of the living theatre, not as an extension of the poetry and the dramatic theory, nor as a special kind of activity called 'religious drama'." Eliot's themes of lost identity and metaphysical despair combine with his linguistic and

theatrical inventiveness to anticipate much recent drama.
Richard Wollheim: "Eliot and F.H. Bradley: an account," pp. 169-93. An outstanding discussion of Eliot's doctoral thesis on F.H. Bradley and of his debt, as a poet and as a critic, to Bradley's idealism.

John Chalker: "Authority and Personality in Eliot's Criticism," pp. 194-210. On the Arnoldian tone of Eliot's criticism. Its permanent value lies less in the separate usefulness of its main ideas than in the interplay between them and the new poetry they defended.

Adrian Cunningham: "Continuity and Coherence in Eliot's Religious Thought," pp. 211-31. Discusses briefly Eliot's debts to F.H. Bradley, T.E. Hulme and Charles Maurras. There is a continuity in Eliot's view of tradition which is unchanged by his conversion to Christianity. Before that conversion, Eliot had been encouraged by his reading of Maurras to think of the Church as an essential social and political structure. The Papal condemnation of Maurras isolated Eliot from other European Catholic thinkers and led to the pronounced sectarian character of Eliot's writing on religious and theological matters in the thirties. A rich and rewarding essay.

Martin Jarrett-Kerr: " 'Of Clerical Cut': retrospective reflections on Eliot's churchmanship," pp. 232-51. Discusses Eliot's active membership and his revulsion (intensified as an American) from the Puritan tradition in Anglo-Saxon religious history.

John Peter: "Eliot and 'The Criterion'," pp. 252-66. First-rate account of the history of the *Criterion* and of Eliot's editorship. The crises of the thirties made it impossible for him to maintain the aloofness of the twenties from social and political problems.

Ian Gregor: "Eliot and Matthew Arnold," pp. 267-78. "For both men poetry becomes the perception and the creation of order, with a final distinction that, whereas for Arnold it always remains an interpretation of reality, the poet speaking to others, for Eliot it is a revelation, the poet speaking primarily to himself."

Terry Eagleton: "Eliot and a Common Culture," pp. 279-95. Criticises Eliot's "elitist" idea of culture from the viewpoint of Raymond Williams's "radical case for a common culture."

TSE 49:   Sullivan, Sheila (ed.)
CRITICS ON T.S. ELIOT (London: George Allen and Unwin, 1973)

A stimulating collection of articles, distinguished by their close attention to Eliot's texts. Particularly good in its treatment of Eliot's drama.

Elizabeth Drew: "Belief and Achievement," pp. 1-5. On the quest for integration in his poetry and thought.

D.S. Savage: "A Decline in Quality," pp. 6-10. On the poetic decline which begins with the religious poems.

D.E.S. Maxwell: "The Early Poems," pp. 11-20. A detailed reading of the early poems, emphasising the influence of French and Jacobean poets.

Keith Wright: "Word Repetition in the Early Verse," pp. 21-5.

John B. Vickery: "*Gerontion*," pp. 26-31. One of the best explications of the multiple levels of the poem: individual life, religion, nature and history.

George Williamson: "The Structure of *The Waste Land*," pp. 32-43. Examines the materials out of which the poem is structured and assesses the success of their organisation.

Audrey F. Cahill: "*The Hollow Men*," pp. 44-9. "The tragedy of the hollow men is intensified because it is presented within the context of possible ultimate meaning."

E.E. Duncan Jones: "*Ash Wednesday*," pp. 50-62. On the Dantesque quality of the poem.

Grover Smith: "The *Ariel* Poems," pp. 63-71. On their sources and possible meaning.

Frank Wilson: "The Musical Structure of the *Four Quartets*," pp. 72-8.

John F. Danby: "Language and Manner in the *Four Quartets*," pp. 79-85. On the use (and questioning of) language in the poem.

John Peter: "*Murder in the Cathedral*," pp. 86-92. On the unity of the play.

Carol H. Smith: "*The Family Reunion*," pp. 93-8. On the use of mythical sources.

Walter Stein: "After the Cocktails," pp. 99-105. *The Cocktail Party* is a failure because its author, losing faith in Christianity, turns to Manicheanism.

Robert A. Colby: "*The Confidential Clerk*," pp. 106-13. Eliot explores man's contemporary anxieties: loneliness in crowds and insecurity amidst prosperity.

Peter Milward: "*The Elder Statesman* and *The Waste Land*," pp. 114-20. In his final plays, Eliot presents us with his solution to the problem of *The Waste Land*.

# Articles and Anthologies of Articles on the Early and the Shorter Poems: 'Prufrock,' 'Gerontion' and *Ash Wednesday*

TSE 50:    Halverson, John
"Prufrock, Freud, and Others," *Sewanee Review*, 76:4
(Autumn 1968), 571-88
Freudian interpretations of "Prufrock" and "Gerontion"
stand on feeble foundations. The poems are concerned
essentially with religious failure.

TSE 51:    Gardner, Helen
"The Landscapes of Eliot's Poetry," *Critical Quarterly*,
10:4 (Winter 1968), 313-30

Visits to St Louis and the New England sea-coast make
clear that Eliot is a "poet of places."

TSE 52:    Cox, C.B.
"T.S. Eliot at the Cross-Roads," *Critical Quarterly*, 12:4
(Winter 1970), 307-20

Gives reasons for the uncertainties and contradictions in
Eliot's pre-conversion poetry.

TSE 53:    Hargrove, Nancy D.
"Symbolism in T.S. Eliot's 'Landscapes'," *Southern
Humanities Review*, 6:3 (Summer 1972), 273-82

Excellent discussion of "New Hampshire," "Virginia,"
"Usk," "Rannoch, by Glencoe," and "Cape Ann,"
which, for the author, anticipate *Four Quartets*.

TSE 54:    Schneider, Elisabeth
"Prufrock and After: The Theme of Change," *PMLA*,
87:5 (October 1972), 1103-18

Eliot's poems explore the difficult process of inner
change.

TSE 55:   Kinnamon, Rebeccah A.
"Eliot's *Ash Wednesday* and Maritain's Ideal for
Poetry," *Georgia Review*, 27:2 (Summer 1973), 156-65

Jacques Maritain's *Poetry and Religion* provided Eliot
with the means to reconcile art and religion.


TSE 56:   Rodgers, Audrey T.
"Dance Imagery in the Poetry of T.S. Eliot," *Criticism*,
16:1 (Winter 1974), 23-38

Images of the dance in Eliot's poetry suggest, at different
times, futility and cosmic unity. Contains a fine analysis of
"Prufrock."


TSE 57:   Scofield, Martin
" 'A gesture and a pose': T.S. Eliot's Images of Love,"
*Critical Quarterly*, 18:3 (Autumn 1976), 5-26

Detailed discussion of the changes in Eliot's style from the
vividly visual early poems to the discursive, symbolic
later poems.


TSE 58:   Arrowsmith, William
"Daedal Harmonies: A Dialogue on Eliot and the
Classics," *Southern Review*, 13:1 (January 1977), 1-47

An analysis of "Dans le Restaurant," which leads to a
subtle exploration of Eliot's assimilative method.


TSE 59:   Southam, Brian Charles (ed.)
T.S. ELIOT: *PRUFROCK, GERONTION, ASH
WEDNESDAY*, AND OTHER SHORTER POEMS
(London: Macmillan, 1978)

A first-rate collection of excerpts from full-length studies
and of articles on the shorter poems, with an introduction
by the editor which describes the critical reception of
Eliot's poetry, pp. 13-24; nine selections from Eliot's own
writing on poetry, pp. 27-51; comments on Eliot's shorter
poetry by critics from 1917 to 1966: Ezra Pound,
"Confound it, the fellow can write," pp. 55-60 (Pound

compares Eliot to French writers, praising his intelligence and emotion); Edgell Rickword, "The Modern Poet," pp. 61-5 (on Eliot's excellent sense of rhythm and his deficient verbal imagination); I.A. Richards, "A Music of Ideas," pp. 66-70 (Eliot's doubts express those of a generation); M.D. Zabel, "T.S. Eliot in Mid-Career," pp. 71-6 (Eliot's religious concerns "deprive his art of its once incomparable distinction and tone"); F.O. Matthiessen, "The Sense of His Own Age," pp. 77-80 (relates the changes in the poetry to external circumstances, which the poet could not resist, but identifies a pattern of recurrent imagery linking the early and the later poetry); D.W. Harding, "The Submission of Maturity," pp. 81-4 (the rebel poet has become "more personal and mature"); W.B. Yeats, "Alexander Pope," pp. 85-6 (Eliot is a cold and dry satirist); Allen Tate, "Logical Versus Psychological Unity," pp. 87-91 (an analysis of "Rhapsody on a Windy Night," and a defence of Eliot's poetry against the charge of obscurity); George Orwell, "Escape from the Consciousness of Futility," pp. 92-6 (Eliot's *Quartets* are the symptom of severe decline); Helen Gardner, "Auditory Imagination," pp. 97-102 (the *Quartets* represent an advance, the achievement of a personal poetic voice); Hugh Kenner, "Eliot's Moral Dialectic," pp. 103-10 (rejects the division of Eliot's poetry into an early and a late stage: "the principles of dramatic organisation that govern each poem also govern the *oeuvre*"); B. Rajan, "The Unity of the *Oeuvre*," pp. 111-15 (on the organic unity of the *oeuvre*).

There follow three separate sections:

(1) "Prufrock" to "Gerontion": Ezra Pound, " 'Prufrock'," p. 119; F.R. Leavis, " 'Prufrock,' 'Portrait of a Lady,' 'Gerontion'," pp. 119-27 (explains why these are the poems of modern sensibility); Hugh Kenner, " 'Prufrock'," pp. 127-35 (on the linguistic strategies of the poem); Wallace Fowlie, " 'Prufrock,' 'Gerontion' and Baudelaire," pp. 136-8; J. Grover Smith, " 'Preludes,' 'Rhapsody' and Bergson," pp. 139-42 (on the philosophic bases of the poems); Gertrude Patterson, " 'Preludes' and 'Rhapsody'," pp. 143-51 (the characterisation of the poems follows from Eliot's metaphysical interests); C.K. Stead, " 'Gerontion'," pp. 152-4 (the poem concerns sexual experience); John Crowe Ransom, " 'Gerontion'," pp. 155-76 (an extended explication of the poem's technique and meaning, on the grounds that it is one of Eliot's major works).

(2) The Quatrain Poems: Robert Graves and Laura Riding, " 'Burbank'," pp. 177-81 (the anti-Semitism of the poem is irresponsible); F.W. Bateson, " 'Burbank'," pp. 182-6 (a semi-comic satire, whose learning is used playfully); Ernest Schanzer, "Mr Eliot's Sunday Morning Service," pp. 186-91 (questions the principles of coherence in Eliot's poem); David Ward, "Mr Eliot's Sunday Morning Service," pp. 191-5 (distinguishes between the "anxiety" of Eliot's metaphysical mode, with its roots in his life, and that of the Metaphysical poets, to whom Eliot felt drawn); Hugh Kenner, " 'Whispers of Immortality'," pp. 195-8 (Eliot turns the traditional mock-heroic convention into a "convention of mock-casualness"); P.G. Mudford, " 'Sweeney among the Nightingales'," pp. 198-204 (we need to attend to the "different levels of intensity that the verse achieves").

(3) 'The Hollow Men,' *Ash Wednesday* and The Aerial Poems: Allen Tate, "*Ash Wednesday*," pp. 205-11 (we can appreciate the poem without sharing Eliot's beliefs); F.R. Leavis, "*Ash Wednesday* and *Marina*," pp. 212-22 (Eliot's religious poetry deals with direct experience as did his earlier work); F.R. Leavis, "*Marina*," pp. 223-5; Helen Gardner, "*Ash Wednesday*," pp. 226-30 (the "intensity of apprehension" of the earlier poetry becomes "an intensity of meditation" after Eliot's conversion); Northrop Frye, "*Ash Wednesday*," pp. 230-4 (traces the purgatorial vision in *Ash Wednesday* into the later poems and plays); B. Rajan: "*Ash Wednesday*," pp. 235-6 ("the story of a quest"); Herbert Read, " 'The Hollow Men'," pp. 237-9 (this is the last example of Eliot's pure poetry, before a decline into moralistic poetry); David Ward: "The Ariel Poems," pp. 240-7 (the emotional appeal to the reader is hindered by the intellectual content).

# Full-length Studies and Articles on *The Waste Land*

TSE 60: Brooks, Cleanth
"The Waste Land: Critique of the Myth," MODERN POETRY AND THE TRADITION (Chapel Hill: University of North Carolina Press, 1939), pp. 136-72

A defence of the integrity of the poem and of its method. The best expository essay on *The Waste Land*.

TSE 61:     Korg, Jacob
"Modern Art Techniques in *The Waste Land*," *Journal of Aesthetics and Art Criticism*, 18:4 (June 1960), 456-63

"Critics seeking illuminating analogies have turned most often to music. The sensibility displayed by *The Waste Land*'s innovations resembles that which animated the technical experiments of the Cubists, Futurists, Dadaists and Surrealists." Korg compares the techniques of the poem with Analytic Cubism, collage, Surrealism.

TSE 62:     Craig, David
"The Defeatism of *The Waste Land*," *Critical Quarterly*, 2:3 (Autumn 1960), 241-52

The best sustained case against *The Waste Land*. "*The Waste Land* seems to me to work essentially against life, for the range of opinions it mobilises, that come welling up in response to it, are all negative... . Eliot's poem, we need only recall, was being written when the civilised armies of Britain, America, France and Japan were invading Russia on twenty-three fronts."

TSE 63:     Kermode, Frank
"A Babylonish Dialect," T.S. ELIOT: THE MAN AND HIS WORK, ed. Allen Tate (New York: Delacorte Press, 1966; London: Chatto and Windus, 1967), pp. 231-42

"*The Waste Land* is in one light an imperial epic." (See TSE 47).

TSE 64:     Sutton, Walter
"*Mauberley, The Waste Land*, and the Problem of Unified Form," *Contemporary Literature*, 9:1 (Winter 1968), 15-35

On the similarities and dissimilarities of these two "modern cultural epics."

TSE 65:     Williams, Helen
T.S. ELIOT: *THE WASTE LAND* (London: Edward

Arnold, 1968; New York: Barron's Educational Series, 1968)

". . . it is with the form and patterning of material in *The Waste Land* that I want to deal rather than with the nature of the material itself or the significance of the emotion generated."

TSE 66:   Lucas, John and Meyers, William
*"The Waste Land* Today," *Essays in Criticism*, 19:2 (April 1969), 193-209

On the failure of Tiresias as a narrator who is not able to establish a relationship between the poem and reader.

TSE 67:   Pritchard, William H.
"Reading *The Waste Land* Today," *Essays in Criticism*, 19:2 (April 1969), 176-92

On Eliot's brilliant art of satirical showmanship.

TSE 68:   Everett, Barbara
"Eliot In and Out of *The Waste Land*," *Critical Quarterly*, 17:1 (Spring 1975), 7-30

An important critique of those who approach the poem through musical analogies.

# Anthologies of Articles on *The Waste Land*

TSE 69:   Martin, Jay (ed.)
TWENTIETH CENTURY INTERPRETATIONS OF *THE WASTE LAND* (Englewood Cliffs, N.J.: Prentice-Hall, 1958)
Disappointing collection, useful only for its reprint of Jacob Korg's "Modern Art Techniques in *The Waste Land*." (See TSE 61).

TSE 70:   Knoll, Robert E. (ed.)

STORM OVER *THE WASTE LAND* (Fair Lawn, N.J.:
Scott, Foresman, 1964)

By far the best anthology of criticism of the poem.
Hugh Kenner: "How the Poem Was Constructed,"
pp. 2-7. "Since 'the form in which it appears in print' . . .
remained for many years the most sensational aspect of
*The Waste Land*, this transaction requires looking into."
D.E.S. Maxwell: "How the Poem Was Received and
Its Critical Issues Defined," pp. 8-12. On the poem's
method and purposes: "a poetic treatment of certain
aspects of a civilisation, placing them in the perspective of
time."
William Wasserstrom: "How the Poem Appeared in
America," pp. 13-22. On the role of *The Dial* in
promoting the poem.
F.R. Leavis: "The Poem's Unity," pp. 24-38. "The
rich disorganisation of the poem attempts to focus an
inclusive human consciousness." Such organisation may,
by analogy, be called musical.
F.O. Matthiessen: "The System of Allusion," pp.
39-57. Eliot's reminiscences point to "the similarity that
often lies beneath contrasting appearances, and can thus
stress the essential equivalence of seemingly different
experiences."
Cleanth Brooks, "The Beliefs Embodied in the Work,"
pp. 58-87. "Life devoid of meaning is death; sacrifice,
even the sacrificial death, may be life-giving, an awaken-
ing to life."
Delmore Schwartz: "T.S. Eliot as the International
Hero," pp. 88-95. "Difficulty in love is inseparable from
the deracination and the alienation from which the
international man suffers."
Graham Hough: "Imagism and Its Consequences,"
pp. 98-121. "This is a general description of Imagist
technique; it is . . . the procedure of *The Waste Land*."
We have not faced the "problems raised by its structure."
David Craig: "The Defeatism of *The Waste Land*,"
pp. 122-35. "*The Waste Land* seems to me to work
essentially against life, for the range of opinions it
mobilises . . . are all negative." (See TSE 62).
Karl Shapiro: "The Death of Literary Judgement,"
pp. 136-53. *The Waste Land* "was very shortly made the
sacred cow of modern poetry and the object of more pious
literary nonsense than any modern work save the *Cantos*
of Pound."

TSE 71:     Cox, C.B. and Hinchliffe, Arnold P. (eds.)
T.S. ELIOT: *THE WASTE LAND* (London and New
York: Macmillan, 1968; Nashville: Aurora, 1970)

A fine collection of essays, with an excellent, brief
introduction by the editors, pp. 11-18; letters and comments by Eliot on the poem, pp. 21-6; early reviews,
pp. 27-44; brief comments by George Watson, pp. 47-50,
I.A. Richards, pp. 51-5, William Empson, pp. 56-7,
C. Day Lewis, pp. 58-9, Yvor Winters, pp. 60-1, Karl
Shapiro, pp. 62-3, Graham Hough, pp. 64-7; and longer
studies of the poem, from its publication to 1968:
     Daniel H. Woodward: "Notes on the Publishing
History and Text of *The Waste Land*," pp. 71-90.
     Conrad Aiken: "An Anatomy of Melancholy," pp.
91-9. The poem succeeds by virtue of its incoherence.
     Edmund Wilson: "The Puritan Turned Artist," pp.
100-7. Explains why the poem "enchanted and devast-
ated a whole generation."
     F.O. Matthiessen: "The Achievement of T.S. Eliot,"
pp. 108-27. Useful comparison with Joyce's *Ulysses*.
     Cleanth Brooks: "*The Waste Land*: Critique of the
Myth," pp. 128-61. The classic exposition of the poem as
a unified whole.
     George Williamson: "*The Waste Land* and '*Dans Le
Restaurant*'," pp. 162-4. The later poem concludes the
earlier poem.
     George L.K. Morris: "Marie, Marie, Hold On Tight,"
pp. 165-7. On the sources of the opening lines of the poem.
     Hugh Kenner: "The Invisible Poet," pp. 168-99.
Places the poem in its literary context and argues that the
fragments of the poem are held together in "a zone of
consciousness."
     David Craig: "The Defeatism of *The Waste Land*,"
pp. 200-15. The poem "seems to me to work essentially
against life, for the range of opinions it mobilises . . . are
all negative."
     C.K. Stead: "The Poem and Its Substitutes," pp.
216-23. The experience of Eliot's poetry should be above
all an emotional, not an intellectual one.
     Frank Kermode: "A Babylonish Dialect," pp. 224-35.
The poem embodies an imperial myth.

TSE 72:     Gunter, Bradley (ed.)
STUDIES IN *THE WASTE LAND* (Columbus, Ohio:
Merrill, 1971)

The first section contains important contemporary reviews of the poem: Burton Roscoe, "Review," pp. 3-4; Gilbert Seldes, "T.S. Eliot," pp. 5-12; Conrad Aiken, "An Anatomy of Melancholy," pp. 13-18; Harriet Monroe, "A Contrast," pp. 19-22; from the *Times Literary Supplement*, "A Fragmentary Poem," pp. 23-5; William Rose Benet, "Among the New Books," pp. 26-7; F.L. Lucas, "The Waste Land," pp. 28-33.

The second section reprints two classic accounts of the poem, with three further extracts from well-known critics:

Cleanth Brooks: "The Waste Land: Critique of the Myth," pp. 37-66. The most important single explication of the poem.

Helen Gardner: "The Dry Season: *The Waste Land*," pp. 67-78. The poem's "true subject is ageless; it discovers a radical defect in human life and makes clear the 'insufficiency of human enjoyments'."

M.L. Rosenthal: "T.S. Eliot and the Displaced Sensibility: *The Waste Land*," pp. 79-85. Suggests links with the writing of other modernists — Joseph Conrad, Ezra Pound and W.B. Yeats.

Roy Harvey Pearce: "The Poetics of Myth: *The Waste Land*," pp. 86-90. Places the poem in the tradition of American poetry.

Philip Wheelwright: "Pilgrim in the Wasteland," pp. 91-116. Discusses Eliot's consciousness of "the symbolic possibilities of language."

TSE 73:     Litz, Arthur Walton (ed.)
ELIOT IN HIS TIME: ESSAYS ON THE OCCASION OF THE FIFTIETH ANNIVERSARY OF *THE WASTE LAND* (Princeton, N.J.: Princeton University Press, 1973; London: Oxford University Press, 1973)

Contains a number of outstanding essays, which deal with *The Waste Land* in the light of the publication of the facsimile of the full version of the poem.

A. Walton Litz: "*The Waste Land*: Fifty Years After," pp. 3-22. Discusses Eliot's "Jamesian consciousness."

Hugh Kenner: "The Urban Apocalypse," pp. 23-49. Discusses the influence of John Dryden on the poem as it was first written: ". . . an urban poem, traceable to the decorums of urban satire." Considers its metamorphosis under Ezra Pound's influence into a Symbolist poem. A brilliant and important essay.

Richard Ellmann: "The First *Waste Land*," pp. 51-66. Provides biographical background to the writing of the poem.

Helen Gardner: "*The Waste Land*: Paris 1922," pp. 67-94. Discusses the intentions of the first *Waste Land*; its debt to James Joyce's *Ulysses*; the value of Ezra Pound's deletions.

Robert Langbaum: "New Modes of Characterization in *The Waste Land*," pp. 95-128. "... the poem is organized around new concepts of identity and new modes of characterization."

Robert M. Adams: "Precipitating Eliot," pp. 129-53. "Eliot imposed himself on the literary conscience of my generation in a way and to a degree that is only becoming clear."

Michael Goldman: "Fear in the Way: The Design of Eliot's Drama," pp. 155-80. "I turn to the matter of ghosts to stress Eliot's art as a dramatist."

Donald Davie: "Anglican Eliot," pp. 181-96. On Eliot's place in, and relation to, English culture.

TSE 74:  Moody, Anthony David (ed.)
*THE WASTE LAND* IN DIFFERENT VOICES
(London: Edward Arnold, 1974; New York: St. Martin's, 1975)

"Our occasion was the fiftieth year of *The Waste Land*. It was time for a new look at that poem: time to see it as no longer 'modern' but established; to see it as no isolated monument but as an integral part of a life's work; and to see it as the product of a past era, one which ended with the death in 1972 of Ezra Pound. It is time to ask, what does Eliot's work mean to us, now, in the next age?"

B. Rajan: "The Dialect of the Tribe," pp. 1-14. On the unity of Eliot's work.

D.W. Harding: "What the Thunder Said," pp. 15-28. Discusses the autobiographical elements of the poem.

Richard Drain: "*The Waste Land*: The Prison and the Key," pp. 29-45. "Eliot walks into the prison of Culture, where his poem lives after him, illustrious and trapped."

A.D. Moody: " 'To fill all the desert with inviolable voice'," pp. 47-66. The poem "is an expression of intense personal feeling, but only in impersonal form."

J.S. Cunningham: "Pope, Eliot and 'The Mind of

Europe'," pp. 67-85. Compares *The Dunciad* and *The Waste Land*. Each poem brings "special kinds of remembering to bear upon a culture that has lost its memory or suffered its memory to grow random and chaotic." In each poem, "the redeeming creative act occurs, within the zone of what excites it, resists it, or is fundamentally hostile to it." Exemplary.

Nicole Ward: " 'Fourmillante Cité: Baudelaire and *The Waste Land*," pp. 87-104. Unlike Charles Baude-lairs, Eliot failed "to make a song out of his own exploration."

Bernard Harris: " 'This music crept by me': Shake-speare and Wagner," pp. 105-16. "Shakespeare and Wagner provide the musical means by which the poem achieves its ends. . . . We need to recover that sense of the possibilities of the transforming power of art which was so readily available to Shakespeare's world and was revived in Wagner's art."

A.C. Charity: "T.S. Eliot: The Dantean Recogni-tions," pp. 117-62. ". . . the crucial difference between the poets . . . lies in their very different engagements with the idea or the experience of love."

J. Dixon Hunt: " 'Broken Images'; T.S. Eliot and Modern Painting," pp. 163-84. Discusses the similarities between Eliot, the Cubists and the Surrealists. Modern poetry and modern painting locate "the organising, creative process in the mind rather than the senses." Rewarding.

Denis Donoghue: " 'The Word Within a Word'," pp. 185-201. *The Waste Land* is "a distinctly American work" which places "inordinate demands upon language and the poetic imagination."

Kathleen Knott: "Ideology and Poetry," pp. 203-20. Analysis of Eliot's critical language. Eliot's criticism was committed to "*Propaganda Fide*, propaganda of the faith."

Donald Davie: "Eliot in One Poet's Life," pp. 221-37.

# Autobiography and Libel: The Controversy over *The Waste Land*

TSE 75:     Peter, John
"A New Interpretation of *The Waste Land*," *Essays in Criticism*, 2:3 (July 1952), 242-66

A celebrated essay, which argues that *The Waste Land* was an imaginary dramatic monologue of a speaker who had been "irretrievably" in love with a young man, subsequently drowned. It was, on its original publication, suppressed by Eliot on the threat of a prosecution for libel.

TSE 76:    Peter, John
*Essays in Criticism*, 19:2 (April 1969), 140-75

The original essay above (TSE 75) is reprinted, with minor corrections and a postscript discussing Eliot's reaction and its possible biographical origins in his friendship with Jean Verdenal.

TSE 77:    Watson, George
"Quest for a Frenchman," *Sewanee Review*, 84:3 (Summer 1976), 466-75

Presents a portrait of Jean Verdenal through French military records and conversations with a younger brother, Pierre Verdenal, and a surviving friend, Dr. André Schlemmer. "I believe Eliot's debt to Verdenal was in the conversation he gave and the literary acquaintance he offered."

TSE 78:    Miller, James E.
T.S. ELIOT'S PERSONAL WASTE LAND: EXORCISM OF THE DEMONS (University Park and London: Pennsylvania State University Press, 1977)

Miller discusses the validity of the biographical approach to Eliot's *The Waste Land*, concentrating in particular upon an article by John Peter (TSE 75) which Eliot had himself suppressed through law. He argues, accepting Peter's thesis, that *The Waste Land* was "a personal poem written out of pressures and intensities which the poet himself did not fully understand or try fully to comprehend." The poem expressed the deep psychic wound caused by the death of Eliot's male friend, Jean Verdenal. Causing sexual impotence, this "plunged him into an anguish and despair which caused him to see a waste land all about him, modern London converted into Dante's hell, sexual depravity everywhere he looked."

*The Waste Land* referred throughout, in a private, cryptic way, to the intense spiritual (and possibly sexual) relationship with Verdenal, killed at Gallipoli and to Eliot's fear and hatred of women, intensified after his marriage to Vivienne Haigh-Wood in 1915. "All the details of the poem may be interpreted in the biographical context which we have constructed for Eliot, his devastating loss of Jean Verdenal, his precipitous marriage to Vivienne Haigh-Wood, and his life in agony torn between revulsion toward the present and memory of and desire for the past." Contains a chapter on the *Four Quartets*, which, Miller argues, also draw upon the repressed memories of the past.

The reader of such speculation would do well to recall "The Dry Salvages":

To explore the womb, or tomb, or dreams; all these are usual
Pastimes and drugs, and features of the press:
And always will be, some of them especially
When there is distress of nations and perplexity

# Full-length Studies, Articles and Anthologies on *Four Quartets*

TSE 79:     Preston, Raymond
*FOUR QUARTETS* REHEARSED (London and New York: Sheed and Ward, 1946)

"A commentary on T.S. Eliot's cycle of Poems" which provides valuable suggestions for understanding the religious aspects of the poems.

TSE 80:     Bodelsen, Carl
T.S. ELIOT'S *FOUR QUARTETS*: A COMMENTARY (Copenhagen: Rosenkilde & Bagger, 1958)

An excellent introduction: "its object is to help the ordinary reader or student to an understanding [of the poem] by trying to explain, passage by passage, what are the poet's thoughts and arguments, and what are the references of the symbols by which he expresses them."

TSE 81:     Bergonzi, Bernard (ed.)
T.S. ELIOT: *FOUR QUARTETS* (London: Macmillan, 1969; Nashville: Aurora, 1970)

The most complete collection of essays on the poem, with an excellent introduction by the editor, pp. 11-20, and two statements by T.S. Eliot on "The Genesis of *Four Quartets*," p. 23, and "Dante and 'Little Gidding'," pp. 24-5. The volume presents the criticism of the poem chronologically:

D.W. Harding: "A Newly Created Concept," pp. 29-31. Discusses the techniques of "Burnt Norton".

*Times Literary Supplement*: "Mr. T.S. Eliot's Confession," pp. 32-5. "East Coker" is "the confession of a lost heart and a lost art."

James Johnson Sweeney: " 'East Coker': A Reading," pp. 36-56. The poem is a wartime elegy for the secular and progressive attitudes which arose with the Renaissance. Identifies for the first time many of the key allusions of the poem.

Curtis Bradford: "Footnotes to 'East Coker'," pp. 57-63. Enlarges on Sweeney above, and stresses parallels with "Burnt Norton."

" 'Little Gidding': A Disagreement in Scrutiny," pp. 64-80. Presents the laudatory review of D.W. Harding; R.N. Higginbotham's objections; and F.R. Leavis's vehement defence of the *Quartets*.

George Orwell: "T.S. Eliot," p. 81-7. The deterioration in Eliot's later poetry comes from the need to give assent to "doctrines which no one seriously believes in."

F.O. Matthiessen: "*The Quartets*," pp. 88-104. Argues that the poems are intellectually and poetically unified and stresses the importance of the doctrine of the Incarnation in the poems as a whole.

F.W. Flint: "The *Four Quartets* Reconsidered," pp. 107-18. "I hope . . . to clarify . . . Eliot's position in the religious and philosophical controversies which have become more real to us since the *Quartets* first appeared."

Helen Gardner: "The Music of *Four Quartets*," pp. 119-37. A classic discussion of the work's musical organisation.

Morris Weitz: "T.S. Eliot: Time as a Mode of Salvation," pp. 138-52. Eliot's sense of time is not Heraclitean but derived from Christian Neo-Platonism.

Donald Davie: "T.S. Eliot: The End of an Era,"

pp. 153-67. "The Dry Salvages" is, on the face of it, a thoroughly bad poem. Its badness must be deliberate. Davie considers the quartet a parody, representing "the end of an era" of neo-Symbolist complexity and indirection.

Hugh Kenner: "Into Our First World," pp. 168-96. In the first two Quartets, Eliot advanced opposing elements which are falsely reconciled in "The Dry Salvages" (in a parody of the collective voice of the late nineteenth century), then truly reconciled by Love at the end of "Little Gidding." Widely regarded as one of the outstanding essays on the poem.

C.K. Stead: "The Imposed Structure of the *Four Quartets*," pp. 197-211. Rigorous analysis of the repeated fivefold structure of the *Quartets*. The poem is an uneasy compromise between the language of discourse and the "music of images."

Denis Donoghue: "T.S. Eliot's Quartets: A New Reading," pp. 212-36. Sympathetic and detailed analysis of the recurring five-movement structure of the poem. "The strategy . . . is to set up several voices, each charged with the evacuation of one area, until nothing is left but 'prayer, observance, discipline, thought and action'." The poem "is offered as a stay for our vanity; this is the condition of its being." As a Christian, Donoghue approves of Eliot's purposes in the poem, only wishing he showed "a warmer sense of human value in all its limitation."

Marshall McLuhan: "Symbolic Landscape," pp. 239-40. The poem contains no personal speaker: "it is the places and things which utter themselves."

A. Alvarez: "A Meditative Poet," pp. 240-4. Eliot belongs to "a tradition of what might be called Puritan art . . . aiming always at a sort of superhuman perfection."

Karl Shapiro: "Poetic Bankruptcy," pp. 245-7. "*Four Quartets* . . . a deliberately bad book."

William F. Lynch, S.J.: "Dissociation in Time," pp. 247-53. Discusses the conflict between flux and stasis in Eliot's poem.

David Perkins: "Rose-Garden to Midwinter Spring: Achieved Faith in the *Four Quartets*," pp. 254-9. Contrasts the moment in the rose-garden of "Burnt Norton" and the midwinter scene of "Little Gidding" to show the Christian resolution of the poem.

TSE 82:     Blamires, Harry
            WORD UNHEARD: A GUIDE THROUGH
            ELIOT'S *FOUR QUARTETS* (London: Methuen,
            1969; New York: Barnes & Noble, 1969)

            Not only a superb, interpretative guide to *Four Quartets*,
            this study also provides illuminating insights into the
            nature of poetic Modernism. (See TSE 8).

TSE 83:     Patrides, Constantinos A.
            "The Renascence of the Renaissance: T.S. Eliot and the
            Pattern of Time," *Michigan Quarterly Review*, 12:2
            (Spring 1973), 172-96

            An outstanding essay on views of time in Eliot, arguing
            that in his poetry Eliot revives the Christian notion of time
            presented by St Augustine.

TSE 84:     Jones, Grania
            "Eliot and History," *Critical Quarterly*, 18:3 (Autumn
            1976), 31-48

            On the way in which Eliot redeems history in *Four
            Quartets* by denying its temporal aspects.

TSE 85:     Alldritt, Keith
            ELIOT'S *FOUR QUARTETS*: POETRY AS
            CHAMBER MUSIC (London: Woburn Press, 1978)

            "The theoretical metaphor of music is but a perspective,
            a device for talking very particularly about certain
            qualities of words and of methods of employing them. The
            words of the poem are my chief concern . . . *Four
            Quartets* is a poem that struggles to employ the fullest
            powers of the medium of English as they were available
            during the thirties and forties of this century."

TSE 86:     Gardner, Helen Louise
            THE COMPOSITION OF *FOUR QUARTETS*
            (London: Faber and Faber, 1978; New York: Oxford
            University Press, 1978)

An account of the composition of the poem by the leading authority on *Four Quartets*. In the first part Gardner presents chapters on the growth of *Four Quartets* and on its sources, using letters and manuscript drafts. In the second part she discusses the composition of each Quartet by examining the typescript drafts of the poem. Immensely valuable for all students of the poem.

# Full-length Studies, Articles and Anthologies on the Plays of T.S. Eliot

TSE 87:     Williams, Raymond
"T.S. Eliot," DRAMA FROM IBSEN TO ELIOT
(London: Chatto and Windus, 1952; New York: Oxford University Press, 1953), pp. 223-46

An excellent discussion of Eliot's plays. *Murder in the Cathedral* is "the best example in the years I have been considering of the discovery of an adequate form for serious drama." (See MOD 166).

TSE 88:     Peter, John
"*Murder in the Cathedral*," *Sewanee Review*, 61:3 (Summer 1953), 362-83

". . . the play is lucid and integral in a way which the later plays are not."

TSE 89:     Donogue, Denis
THE THIRD VOICE: MODERN BRITISH AND AMERICAN VERSE DRAMA (Princeton, N.J.: Princeton University Press, 1959; London: Oxford University Press, 1959), pp. 76-179

Contains six separate chapters, one each on *Murder in the Cathedral, The Family Reunion, The Cocktail Party, The Confidential Clerk* and *The Elder Statesman*, with one on Eliot's verse line. Robust criticism, finding structural flaws and an evasion of the problems of dramatic verse in Eliot's work.

TSE 90: Jones, David E.
THE PLAYS OF T.S. ELIOT (Toronto: University of
Toronto Press, 1960; London: Routledge & Kegan Paul,
1960)

Perhaps the best single study of Eliot's whole dramatic
output. Excellent both on Eliot's contribution to drama, to
"poetry in the theatre" and on the intellectual and
spiritual significance of his plays.

TSE 91: Smith, Carol H.
T.S. ELIOT'S DRAMATIC THEORY AND
PRACTICE FROM *SWEENEY AGONISTES* TO
*THE ELDER STATESMAN* (Princeton, N.J.:
Princeton University Press, 1963)

Discusses the fusion of theme and technique in the plays.
"The origin of [Eliot's] attempt to develop a new theatre is
to be seen in his view that, just as man's nature needs to be
guided by discipline and order, so dramatic art needs to be
given a form which can draw a circle of abstraction around
experience in order to make drama conform to the
standard of all art — the ordered relationship of the parts
to the whole. Believing that of all literary forms drama has
the greatest capacity for recreating a complete and
ordered world, Eliot developed a dramatic structure
which was intended to lead the audience to a sense of
religious awareness by demonstrating the presence of the
supernatural order in the natural world." A comprehensive and rewarding study.

TSE 92: Williams, Raymond
"Tragic Resignation and Sacrifice," *Critical Quarterly*,
5:1 (Spring 1963), 5-19

Subtle and detailed examination of the meaning of
*sacrifice* in *Murder in the Cathedral* and *The Cocktail
Party*.

TSE 93: Browne, Elliott Martin
THE MAKING OF T.S. ELIOT'S PLAYS
(Cambridge and New York: Cambridge University Press,
1969)

The study "is a record of the way in which T.S. Eliot's plays came to be written and of their first appearance on stage," written by the man who first staged Eliot's plays. "Much of its contents are from Eliot's pen. . . . The unique advantage which I enjoy is that I worked with Eliot from 1933 to 1958, directing the first production of all the plays written during that time, and acting as consultant in their making." Discusses *The Rock, Murder in the Cathedral, The Family Reunion, The Cocktail Party, The Confidential Clerk*, and *The Elder Statesman*.

TSE 94:     Clark, David R. (ed.)
TWENTIETH-CENTURY INTERPRETATIONS
OF *MURDER IN THE CATHEDRAL* (Englewood
Cliffs, N.J.: Prentice-Hall, 1971)

A comprehensive collection of essays and extracts from full-length studies, with an excellent introduction by the editor, pp. 1-13.
Louis L. Martz: "T.S. Eliot: The Wheel and the Point," pp. 15-26. On the meaning of the "still point" in the play.
Francis Fergusson: "*Murder in the Cathedral*: The Theological Scene," pp. 27-37. On the unusual structure of the play.
Grover Smith: "Action and Suffering: *Murder in the Cathedral*," pp. 38-53. On the polarity of action and suffering in the play.
William V. Spanos: "*Murder in the Cathedral*: The *Figura* as Mimetic Principle," pp. 54-72. Using a figural aesthetic, Eliot "transcends the univocal realism of naturalistic drama without resorting to the strategy that altogether by-passes or dissolves concrete reality."
Patricia M. Adair: "In the Cathedral," pp. 73-4. Stresses the importance of the setting (and the production) of the play at Canterbury.
J.T. Boulton: "Sources," pp. 74-9. On Eliot's use of original sources "to realise his central theme: the conflict between the values . . . of religion and those of 'Secularism'."
David E. Jones: "The Chorus," pp. 79-81. "Eliot has not just copied Aeschylus: he has given the chorus a new significance in the light of the Christian dispensation."
E. Martin Browne: "The Priests," pp. 81-2. On the subtle nature of Eliot's characterisation.

Carol H. Smith: "Blessed Thomas," pp. 82-6. On the ritual at the heart of the play.

Robert N. Shorter: "Becket as Job," pp. 86-93. In the first part of the play, Becket is presented as a Job-figure.

H.Z. Maccoby: "Thomas's Temptation," pp. 93-6. On the Fourth Tempter as the servant of God.

David E. Jones: "The Temptation of the Audience," pp. 96-7. On the audience's implication in the death and sacrifice of Thomas.

Kristian Smidt: "A Shaft of Sunlight," pp. 97-8. Eliot's plays await "moments of illumination."

E. Martin Browne: "The Variations in the Text," pp. 99-106.

TSE 95:    Mudford, P.G.
"T.S. Eliot's Plays and the Tradition of 'High Comedy'," *Critical Quarterly*, 16:2 (Summer 1974), 127-40

The revelation of human folly depends upon shared moral and metaphysical belief. Despite the absence of this in the present century, *The Cocktail Party* does succeed as high comedy.

# Full-length Studies, Articles and Anthologies on Eliot's Criticism

TSE 96:    Kermode, (John) Frank
ROMANTIC IMAGE (London: Routledge & Kegan Paul, 1957; New York: Macmillan, 1958)

Presents a profoundly important re-evaluation of T.S. Eliot's critical principles. (See MOD 7).

TSE 97:    Buckley, Vincent
POETRY AND MORALITY: STUDIES ON THE CRITICISM OF MATTHEW ARNOLD, T.S. ELIOT AND F.R. LEAVIS (London: Chatto and Windus, 1959)

Contains two excellent chapters, "T.S. Eliot: Impersonal Order," pp. 87-128, which discusses Eliot's relations to

Matthew Arnold, to Romanticism, and his debt to
T.E. Hulme; and "T.S. Eliot: The Question of
Orthodoxy," pp. 129-57, on Eliot's Christianity.

TSE 98:    Lu, Fei-Pai
T.S. ELIOT: THE DIALECTICAL STRUCTURE
OF HIS THEORY OF POETRY (Chicago and London:
University of Chicago Press, 1966)

A systematic (and often abstruse) analysis of T.S. Eliot's
criticism. Seldom did Eliot's critics realise that his
inconsistencies issued from philosophical roots and could
never be explained fully on historical grounds alone.
Explicates the dialectical method of Eliot's criticism.
Contains a full bibliography of writing on Eliot's criticism.

TSE 99:    Austin, Allen
T.S. ELIOT: THE LITERARY AND SOCIAL
CRITICISM (Bloomington and London: Indiana
University Press, 1971)

Austin analyses Eliot's literary and social criticism,
closely defining his key terms, and places it in its historical
and literary-historical context. A detailed and judicious
account. Contains a useful annotated bibliography of
Eliot's literary and social criticism.

TSE 100:    Newton-de Molina, David (ed.)
THE LITERARY CRITICISM OF T.S. ELIOT
(London: Athlone Press, 1977; Atlantic Highlands, N.J.:
Humanities Press, 1977)

A series of new essays which consider "the question of
T.S. Eliot's all-pervasive recent *influence* in literary
criticism in English, and the question of his true or
distinctive *greatness* as a literary critic."
    F.W. Bateson: "Criticism's Lost Leader," pp. 1-19.
Contrasts the early and late criticism (drawing an analogy
with Wordsworth); regrets the change from the freshness
and sceptical tone of the early poetry and criticism;
notices the strain of snobbery in the writing. "Eliot had
signed up with the Establishment."
    Denis Donoghue: "Eliot and *The Criterion*," pp.20-41.

The failure of *The Criterion* is "immediate and personal," arising from Eliot's consistent evasiveness and ultimate depression in the face of politics and of contemporary history. A subtle analysis of the contradictions of Eliot's post-war career and the best short account of the history of *The Criterion*.

Graham Hough: "The Poet as Critic," pp. 42-63. Eliot's career as a critic was throughout inspired by the needs of his poetry and changed as they changed.

Samuel Hynes: "The Trials of a Christian Critic," pp. 64-88. Discusses the changes in his criticism necessitated by Eliot's conversion to Christianity. "Eliot would have succeeded as a Christian critic if he had made his Christianity invisible; but he made it visible, and so made his religion seem a way of being reactionary, ungenerous and cold."

R. Peacock: "Eliot's contribution to Criticism of Drama," pp. 89-110. ". . . Eliot worked out in his drama criticism some valuable central principles of the poetic form he most admired."

William Righter: "The 'Philosophical' Critic," pp. 111-38. "The movement of Eliot's mind . . . is more that of the careful sifting of alternatives than a dialectical path to an ultimate fusion." For "Eliot was caught between two languages and two traditions," (the continental and the Anglo-Saxon).

W.W. Robson: "A Poet's Notebook: *The Use of Poetry and the Use of Criticism*," pp. 139-59. Sympathetic and comprehensive discussion of *The Use of Poetry*, applauding its "good sense which we honour with the name of wisdom."

Roger Sharrock: "Eliot's 'Tone'," pp. 160-83. "The . . . extraordinary thing about the success of Eliot's literary essays is that their appeal depends so much on a marked personal tone, and yet their plea for impersonal, objective methods in literary study effected a critical revolution."

C.K. Stead: "Eliot, Arnold, and the English Poetic Tradition," pp. 184-206. Eliot's criticism effected a complete revaluation of the English poetic tradition. Discusses the nature, the strengths and the limitations of Eliot's revaluation. An important and stimulating discussion.

TSE 101:    Lee, Brian

THEORY AND PERSONALITY: THE
SIGNIFICANCE OF T.S. ELIOT'S CRITICISM
(London: Athlone Press, 1979; Atlantic Highlands, N.J.:
Humanities Press, 1979)

A lively discussion (and rejection) of Eliot's theory of
impersonality.

TSE 102:    Lobb, Edward
            T.S. ELIOT AND THE ROMANTIC CRITICAL
            TRADITION (London and Boston: Routledge & Kegan
            Paul, 1981)

Places Eliot's criticism firmly within the Romantic
tradition. The study presents a detailed account of Eliot's
unpublished Clark Lectures of 1926: "The view of literary
history which the Clark Lectures set forth has roots in the
European Romantic tradition...; the aesthetic embodied
in Eliot's historiography owes much, ironically, to the
English Romantics, especially Keats." An important and
convincing account.

# Full-length Studies and Articles Placing Eliot in his Intellectual Context

TSE 103:    Hoffman, Frederick John
            THE TWENTIES: AMERICAN WRITING IN THE
            POST-WAR DECADE (New York: Viking Press,
            1955), pp. 291-303

*The Waste Land* exemplifies the doubts and anxieties of
the post-war generation. (See MOD 140).

TSE 104:    May, Henry F.
            THE END OF AMERICAN INNOCENCE: A
            STUDY OF THE FIRST YEARS OF OUR OWN
            TIME 1912-1917 (New York: Alfred A. Knopf, 1959)

The major history of the new generation of American
intellectuals of which Eliot, who is mentioned throughout,
was a part.

TSE 105:    Smidt, Kristian
            POETRY AND BELIEF IN THE WORK OF
            T.S. ELIOT (London: Routledge & Kegan Paul, 1961;
            New York: Humanities Press, 1961) (1976)

            A comprehensive study which examines the influence of
            F.H. Bradley, Henri Bergson, Oriental philosophy,
            modern anthropology and religious thought. Not only
            does Smidt trace the diverse and complex sources of
            Eliot's ideas, he also shows how Eliot synthesises these
            into his poetic writing and criticism. Still a formidable and
            illuminating study.

TSE 106:    Freed, Louis
            T.S. ELIOT: AESTHETICS AND HISTORY (La
            Salle, Ill.: Open Court, 1962) (1977)

            Demanding but rewarding discussion of Aristotle, Kant
            and F.H. Bradley as figures essential for an understand-
            ing of Eliot's views on criticism, metaphysics and religion.

TSE 107:    Thompson, Eric
            T.S. ELIOT: THE METAPHYSICAL
            PERSPECTIVE (Carbondale and Edwardsville:
            Southern Illinois University Press, 1963; London and
            Amsterdam: Feffer and Simons, 1963)

            Eliot is "a *philosophical* poet; but he is also a
            philosophical *poet*. He requires a double vision."
            Discusses Eliot's thesis on F.H. Bradley, relating it to his
            criticism and to "Burnt Norton."

TSE 108:    Howarth, Herbert
            NOTES ON SOME FIGURES BEHIND T.S. ELIOT
            (Boston: Houghton Mifflin, 1964; London: Chatto and
            Windus, 1965)

            An excellent account of Eliot's family, teachers and
            friends which provides an indispensable guide to the
            intellectual background of his work.

TSE 109:    Holder, Alan
            THREE VOYAGERS IN SEARCH OF EUROPE: A

STUDY OF HENRY JAMES, EZRA POUND AND
T.S. ELIOT (Philadelphia: University of Pennsylvania
Press, 1966)

An excellent discussion of the theme of expatriation in
Henry James, T.S. Eliot and Ezra Pound; with useful
analysis of the debts of Eliot and Pound to James; of the
similarities and dissimilarities of James, Eliot and Pound.
Concentrates on the quarrel of James, Eliot and Pound
with America; considers their relation to cosmopolitan-
ism; their views of history; and of their final sense of the
"failure of Europe." A detailed and rewarding study.

TSE 110:    Lynen, John F.
"Selfhood and the Reality of Time: T.S. Eliot," THE
DESIGN OF THE PRESENT: ESSAYS ON TIME
AND FORM IN AMERICAN LITERATURE (New
Haven and London: Yale University Press, 1969),
pp. 341-441

An outstanding essay which presents Eliot's poetry in the
light of traditional American literary, philosophical and
religious preoccupations. One of the most complete and
significant essays on Eliot's poetry.

TSE 111:    Margolis, John D.
T.S. ELIOT'S INTELLECTUAL DEVELOPMENT
1922-1939 (Chicago and London: University of Chicago
Press, 1972)

An elegant, detailed and important account of Eliot's
literary, religious, political and social ideas. "The year
1922 is a convenient one at which to begin: it was the year
in which his early career was crowned with the publication
of *The Waste Land* and in which his middle phase — the
period that Eliot spoke of as 'middle age' — began with his
editorship of *The Criterion*. . . . During the following
several years he experienced the most important (and
perhaps the least understood) of his conversions, that to
Anglo-Catholicism . . . I am anxious to insist that the
conversion to Anglo-Catholicism was not so much an
arrival at a resting-place as an event from which other
important conversions radiated." Certainly the best
discussion of Eliot's editorship of *The Criterion* and of the
unity of his inter-war criticism.

TSE 112:  Schuchard, Ronald
"Eliot and Hulme in 1916: Toward a Revaluation of
Eliot's Critical and Spiritual Development," *PMLA*, 88:5
(October 1973), 1083-94

Argues that Eliot's classicism had been developed by 1916
under the influence of T.E. Hulme.

TSE 113:  Torrens, James
"Charles Maurras and Eliot's 'New Life'," *PMLA*, 89:2
(March 1974), 312-22

Discusses Maurras' influence on Eliot, an influence
which has been insufficiently examined.

TSE 114:  Scott, Stanley J.
"Beyond Modern Subjectivism: T.S. Eliot and American
Philosophy," *Thought*, 51:203 (December 1976), 409-27

On Eliot's changing view of selfhood throughout his
career.

# Full-length Studies, Articles and Chapters from Books on Eliot's Political and Social Thought

TSE 115:  Williams, Raymond
"T.S. Eliot," CULTURE AND SOCIETY 1780-1950
(London: Chatto and Windus, 1958; New York:
Columbia University Press, 1958), pp. 227-43

"If Eliot, when read attentively, has the effect of checking
the complacency of liberalism, he has also, when read
critically, the effect of making complacent conservatism
impossible."

TSE 116:  Harrison, John Raymond
"T.S. Eliot," THE REACTIONARIES: A STUDY
OF THE ANTI-DEMOCRATIC INTELLIGENTSIA
(London: V. Gollancz, 1966; New York: Schocken,
1966), pp. 145-60

"Although he was strongly anti-democratic and often expressed a preference for some kind of strict, authoritarian rule, Eliot did not openly sympathise with fascism. . . . This was simply because he adhered to the principle of non-action." Discusses Eliot's "misunderstanding" of the English and of English traditions. (See MOD 54).

TSE 117:     Kojecky, Roger
T.S. ELIOT'S SOCIAL CRITICISM (London: Faber and Faber, 1971; New York: Farrar, Straus and Giroux, 1972)

Kojecky's well-researched and original account is rightly regarded as the most authoritative and judicious account of Eliot's social criticism. "Eliot's reputation as a critic of society has been worse than his record. The number of those who have been shocked or repelled by his irreverent attitude towards ideals such as liberalism and democracy is greater than the number who have set themselves to discover what, possibly, Eliot did believe. . . . My aim is to trace the course of Eliot's social ideals, to see his outlook as far as possible from the inside, and to take account of its relation to the public world in which he lived. The approach is expository and biographical."
     Eliot was neither an aesthete who ignored public themes, nor a fascist and anti-Semite. After his conversion to Christianity, "he was not a member of that part of the Church which considered the socio-economic situation with complacency." Kojecky concentrates on Eliot's participation in the Moot, an informal discussion group which met from 1938 to 1947, and in various Christian bodies in the thirties. For Eliot, the idea of a Christian world order provided "a way between the extremes of Communism and Fascism."

TSE 118:     Chace, William
THE POLITICAL IDENTITIES OF EZRA POUND AND T.S. ELIOT (Stanford: Stanford University Press, 1973)

"This study of Ezra Pound and T.S. Eliot confronts the fact that two of the most artistically influential writers of our time were reactionaries." Yet we must also confront the fact "that Pound and Eliot were also radicals." Chace argues that both writers sought in the objective world the embodiment of their subjective dreams and ideals — their partisan activities involved "an awkward emergence from the Symbolist quarantine." But their dreams could not comprehend social and human diversity or complexity. "Because they had proceeded so far with ways of thinking that repudiated conflict, Pound and Eliot could do little more than practice the exclusiveness, and the cruel reductive mastery, that alone could produce the kind of wholeness they wanted." Contains a detailed discussion of Eliot's criticism, particularly *Notes towards the Definition of Culture*. Perhaps the study discusses more successfully the discomfiture felt by liberals in the face of Pound and Eliot than the actual content of their illiberal positions.

TSE 119:     Maccoby, Hyam
"The Anti-Semitism of T.S. Eliot," *Midstream*, 19:5 (May 1973), 68-79

Anti-Semitism was a major thematic and intellectual element in Eliot's poetry.

TSE 120:     Panichas, George A.
"T.S. Eliot and the Critique of Liberalism," *Modern Age*, 18:2 (Spring 1974), 145-62

A detailed and convincing explication of Eliot's anti-liberalism.

# Full-length Studies and Articles on Eliot's Literary Influences

TSE 121:     Praz, Mario
"T.S. Eliot and Dante," *Southern Review*, 2:3 (Winter 1937), 525-48

The best essay on the relationship between Eliot and Dante. "Eliot's indebtedness to Dante ranges from quotation and the adaptation of single lines or passages to

the deeper influence in concrete presentation and
symbolism." Reprinted in Leonard Unger (ed.) (TSE 44).

TSE 122:    Musgrove, Sydney
            T.S. ELIOT AND WALT WHITMAN (Wellington:
            University of New Zealand Press, 1952; New York:
            Gordon Press, 1952)

            The poetry of Whitman and of Eliot belongs to the same
            native background, the northern seaboard of Massa-
            chusetts. "It would be therefore in no way extraordinary
            to find memories of him embedded deep in Eliot's
            poetry." While "much of Eliot's poetry, considered as the
            work of an American, can be readily understood as a
            recoil from Whitman's too loud and too easy optimism,"
            the similarities, in style, theme and intention, are
            profound. Both are the heirs of Romanticism. "To
            understand Eliot's poetical descent from Whitman helps
            in the attainment of a true poetical perspective, for it
            reveals him as the last (or perhaps the penultimate)
            romantic musing amidst the shattered gothic fragments of
            the collapsed paternal 'gashouse'. Once again, the term is
            American, and not English." An important (and unduly
            neglected) study.

TSE 123:    Holder, Alan
            "T.S. Eliot on Henry James," *PMLA*, 79:4 (September
            1964), 490-7

            Discusses Eliot's relation, as writer and critic, to Henry
            James.

TSE 124:    Weinberg, Kerry
            T.S. ELIOT AND CHARLES BAUDELAIRE (The
            Hague and Paris: Mouton, 1969)

            Eliot drew more from Charles Baudelaire "than is
            commonly acknowledged and he himself realised." The
            later Anglican Eliot saw Baudelaire "differently from the
            way he saw him before."

TSE 125:  Donker, Marjorie
"*The Waste Land* and the *Aeneid*," *PMLA*, 89:1 (January 1974), 164-73

On the links between the two poems.

TSE 126:  Hough, Graham
"Dante and Eliot," *Critical Quarterly*, 16:4 (Winter 1974), 293-305

Hough discusses both the influence of Dante on Eliot, who saw him as the central poetic expression of Christianity, and the limitations of Eliot's view of Dante, arising from his Puritan background.

TSE 127:  Storey, Robert F.
"Pierrot Ephèbe: T.S. Eliot and Wallace Stevens," PIERROT: A CRITICAL HISTORY OF A MASK (Princeton, N.J.: Princeton University Press, 1978), pp. 156-93

Traces the theme of the pierrot in French literature and, via Jules Laforgue, in the work of T.S. Eliot and Wallace Stevens.

TSE 128:  Perloff, Marjorie
THE POETICS OF INDETERMINACY: RIMBAUD TO CAGE (Princeton, N.J.: Princeton University Press, 1981)

Argues that "what we loosely call 'Modernism' in Anglo-American poetry is really made up of two separate though often interwoven strands": the Symbolist mode that Robert Lowell inherited from T.S. Eliot and Charles Baudelaire and, beyond them, from the great Romantic poets, and "the 'anti-Symbolist' mode of indeterminacy or 'undecidability,' of literalness and free play, whose first real exemplar was the Rimbaud of the *Illuminations*." Eliot's work brilliantly and suggestively placed in the context of modern European and Anglo-American letters.

# Index of Subjects

## *Modernism*

Adam, Villiers de l'Isle: MOD 1
Adams, Henry: MOD 72
*Adelphi*: MOD 107
Adorno, W.T.: MOD 195
Alberti, Rafael: MOD 85
Aldington, Richard: MOD 75,
    MOD 131
American Modernism: MOD 106,
    MOD 116, MOD 121, MOD 124,
    MOD 128, MOD 132, MOD 134,
    MOD 136, MOD 137-49, MOD 167,
    MOD 169, MOD 172, MOD 188,
    MOD 199
Anderson, Sherwood: MOD 92
anti-Semitism: MOD 56
Apollinaire, Guillaume: MOD 85
Auden, W.H.: MOD 4, MOD 6,
    MOD 8, MOD 44, MOD 61,
    MOD 97, MOD 112, MOD 115,
    MOD 118, MOD 119, MOD 121,
    MOD 129, MOD 182, MOD 196,
    MOD 202, MOD 208, MOD 210,
    MOD 212
avant-garde: MOD 18, MOD 25,
    MOD 75-84, MOD 177

Bacon, Francis: MOD 216
Barthelme, Donald: MOD 34
Barthes, Roland: MOD 161
Bartók, Béla: MOD 216
Baudelaire, Charles: MOD 31,
    MOD 95, MOD 128, MOD 202
Bayley, John: MOD 8
Beckett, Samuel: MOD 27, MOD 64,
    MOD 108, MOD 154, MOD 168,
    MOD 181, MOD 185, MOD 216
Bellow, Saul: MOD 24, MOD 30,
    MOD 175
Benjamin, Walter: MOD 30, MOD 195
Bennett, Arnold: MOD 12, MOD 151,
    MOD 212
Bergson, Henri: MOD 156, MOD 165
*Between the Acts*: MOD 32
*Blast*: MOD 107
Bloch, Ernst: MOD 195
Brecht-Lukacs debate: MOD 185
*The Bridge*: MOD 108

Bridges, Robert: MOD 119
Bronte, Emily: MOD 92
Brooks, Cleanth: MOD 190
Browning, Robert: MOD 68, MOD 71,
    MOD 97
Byron, Lord: MOD 173

Camus, Albert: MOD 40
Coleridge, Samuel Taylor: MOD 31,
    MOD 37
Compton-Burnett, Ivy: MOD 34,
    MOD 210
Conrad, Joseph: MOD 41, MOD 73,
    MOD 87, MOD 104, MOD 150,
    MOD 151, MOD 155, MOD 160,
    MOD 161, MOD 173, MOD 182,
    MOD 183, MOD 205, MOD 210
Crane, Hart: MOD 108, MOD 118,
    MOD 120, MOD 121, MOD 136,
    MOD 140, MOD 142, MOD 144,
    MOD 201
*The Criterion*: MOD 107, MOD 109
Cummings, E.E.: MOD 8, MOD 52,
    MOD 142

Dante, Alighieri: MOD 39
Davidson, Donald: MOD 192
Davidson, John: MOD 43, MOD 45
*The Dial*: MOD 106
Doolittle, Hilda: MOD 75
Dos Passos, John: MOD 112
Dreiser, Theodore: MOD 45
Duncan, Robert: MOD 142

Eliot, George: MOD 92
Eliot, Thomas Stearns: American
    Modernism, MOD 137-140,
    MOD 141, MOD 142, MOD 144,
    MOD 145, MOD 147, MOD 148,
    MOD 149; anti-Semitism, MOD 56;
    critique of, MOD 172, MOD 178,
    MOD 179, MOD 182, MOD 186,
    MOD 196, MOD 199; fascism,
    MOD 54, MOD 57; First World War,
    MOD 47; free verse, MOD 97; *The
    Golden Bough*, MOD 46; language,
    MOD 49, MOD 52; and modern

241

# William Butler Yeats

## Percy Wyndham Lewis

# David Herbert Lawrence

## Thomas Stearns Eliot

# Index of Contributors

## *Modernism*

# *William Butler Yeats*

## *Percy Wyndham Lewis*

## *David Herbert Lawrence*

# Thomas Stearns Eliot